A History of the
Baseball Fan

ALSO BY FRED STEIN
AND FROM McFARLAND

*And the Skipper Bats Cleanup : A History of the
Baseball Player-Manager, with 42 Biographies
of Men Who Filled the Dual Role* (2002)

Mel Ott : The Little Giant of Baseball (1999)

A History of the Baseball Fan

FRED STEIN

McFarland & Company, Inc., Publishers
Jefferson, North Carolina, and London

LIBRARY OF CONGRESS CATALOGUING-IN-PUBLICATION DATA

Stein, Fred.
    A history of the baseball fan / Fred Stein.
        p.   cm.
    Includes bibliographical references and index.

    ISBN-13: 978-0-7864-2148-0 ∞
    softcover : 50# alkaline paper

    1. Baseball fans—United States—History. 2. Baseball—
Social aspects—United States—History. I. Title.
GV863.A1S84   2005
796.357—dc22   2005012771

British Library cataloguing data are available

©2005 Fred Stein. All rights reserved

No part of this book may be reproduced or transmitted in any form or by any means, electronic or mechanical, including photocopying or recording, or by any information storage and retrieval system, without permission in writing from the publisher.

Cover illustrations ©2005 Wood River Gallery.

Manufactured in the United States of America

McFarland & Company, Inc., Publishers
  Box 611, Jefferson, North Carolina 28640
    www.mcfarlandpub.com

For Helen, a close friend as a fellow student
at Penn State in 1948-49 and, after a
fifty year separation, an even closer friend

Contents

Introduction   1

1. The Early Years   15
2. Coming of Age   26
3. Boom, Depression, War   40
4. Post–World War II Expansion   59
5. Since Then   73
6. The Writers   84
7. Radio   101
8. Television   114
9. Player Popularity   127
10. Gambling   141
11. Attendance   152
12. Famous and Infamous Fans   164
13. Fans' Impact on Games   180
14. The Fan as a Participant   192
15. Summing Up   202

Chapter Notes   207
Bibliography   217
Index   221

Introduction

The baseball fan is the least publicized or recognized figure in baseball. Baseball essentially is about the player, the individual who captivates with his performance on and sometimes off the field, or the manager who directs the game and controls it by his strategic handling of players and game situations. The game secondarily is about such off-field figures as club owners and front-office officials who secure and sign players, who operate the ball club off the field, and who are continually subject to praise or criticism for their success or failure. The media is another highly-visible element as it reports the games and club operations in newspapers and on radio and television. And player agents have become increasingly influential in their impact on the game. But the baseball fan gets little attention. This, even though the fan keeps baseball in operation by attending games and patronizing companies paying to have games on radio or television or that market merchandise or memorabilia.

This is the story of the unsung baseball fan, beginning in the 1860s, when few people followed the game except for those interested only because their social clubs were involved. The story continues through the following 140 years, during which time baseball became a flourishing commercial enterprise played by highly paid professionals and witnessed by on-scene fans. The advent of greater newspaper coverage and eventually radio and television permitted a growing number of fans to follow the fortunes of players and teams without attending games. And the computer has increased the ways in which the baseball follower can involve himself in the game in a virtually participatory role. This is the story of the evolution of the baseball fan, of the especially colorful ones, and of the ways in which fans have contributed to baseball without stepping onto the playing field.

A typical scene as a father and son watch a Grapefruit League game in Clearwater, Florida, in 2004. The author is on the right with son Bill.

A dictionary definition of a fan (the word derived from "fanatic") is "an enthusiastic devotee or admirer of a sport, pastime, [or] celebrity." In the case of a baseball fan, this definition needs to be expanded to include a baseball enthusiast who is a devotee of the game, whether or not he has a monetary or other material interest in a game or a player. Such a fan often goes into a state of euphoria when his favorites win or a deep depression when they lose. By contrast, a mere spectator at a game requires little or no effort to shake any emotional reaction to the result of a game in which he has little more than a passing interest.

In baseball's early days, enthusiasts were called "kranks." St. Louis Browns manager Ted Sullivan claimed to have invented the word "fan" in the early 1880s to describe the more rabid baseball buffs. About the same time, Thomas Lawson wrote an informal publication about the krank. The book described the characters who hung around the Boston ballpark. Lawson wrote that the krank's main characteristic was his deep curiosity about every baseball aspect—players, umpires, writers, and other kranks. During the winter off-season, kranks lived for the usual hot stove league information regarding player deals and discussed this information with anyone who would listen and probably bored others who were not interested. Lawson wrote that kranks haunted the ballparks in search of inside information, becoming nuisances to players, reporters, and other onlookers. He also wrote of the tactics kranks employed to enter ballparks without paying, mentioning a Boston gang who fooled turnstile employees until it was discovered that their secret entrance was a large drainpipe.

Albert G. Spalding described the truly devoted 1911 baseball fan in his classic *America's National Game*:

> In every town, village and city is the local wag.... He knows every player in the League by sight and name. He is a veritable encyclopaedia [sic] of information on the origin, evolution and history of the game.... He never misses a game.... His words of encouragement to the home team, his shouts of derision to the opposing players, find sympathetic responses in the hearts of all present.... His sole object in life for two mortal hours is to gain victory for the home team.... And so it comes to pass that at every important game there is an exhibition in progress ... that is quite as interesting ... as is the contest on the field, and ... is sometimes a factor nearly as potent as are the efforts of the contesting players.... As [fans become familiar with the rules] their enjoyment has immeasurably increased; because just in so far [sic] as those in attendance understand the features presented in every play, so far are they able to become participators in the game itself.

Baseball fans differ widely in many ways, including financial status, educational level, age, sex, and geographical area. The relationship has not been established between degree of baseball fanaticism and financial status or educational level. But with the increased popularity of other sports since World War II, it is logical to assume that baseball fans tend to be older than devotees of other sports. Women's interest in baseball has increased over the years but male baseball fans undoubtedly remain in the majority just as they do for most other sports.

Geographic location is a more difficult factor to pinpoint. Conventional wisdom (pure speculation) places baseball interest highest in the Northeast and Midwest simply because these are the areas in which major league baseball originally took root. Every city, whether it has a major or minor league ballpark, has a coterie of hardcore fans who live for the game and who follow and support it regardless of such provocations as baseball strikes and inept league and team operation. But there is another even larger group of less-dedicated fans who are more casual about the game but whose patronage is vital to the local team's financial welfare.

Some baseball fans attend many games while others are satisfied seeing their favorites infrequently or exclusively on television. Other fans are continually on the move at a ballgame, walking, cheering constantly in response to redundant urging from public address announcements while others sitting quietly are no less involved in the game. Many women are equal to men in their knowledge and enthusiasm for baseball. But this was not the case in the early days of the game when women's attendance at games was encouraged in the questionable belief that their presence would discourage undesirable conduct by male fans.

In 1950 the Chicago Cubs were seeking women not so much as moderating influences but as paying customers when they talked down to female radio listeners with the following sweet-talking radio advertisement:

> [Wrigley Field is] like an afternoon vacation in the country and there's nothing more relaxing. Gee, you can sit in the sun if you want—or relax in the shade…. And what a wonderful way to forget about washing, ironing, cooking. It's a fun place made for comfortable clothes and just relaxing. Get away from it all and have fun at … Wrigley Field.

The "slowness" of baseball is a familiar complaint. This view has some validity given the increase in game slowdowns during the last 30 years. Some of today's hitters step out of the batters box after every pitch, unlike great hitters in the past who rarely stepped out. Also, few pitchers remain on the mound between deliveries, and that consumes considerable extra time. And managers make more pitching changes than in the past. The net result has been extended games which Major League Baseball has unsuccessfully sought to shorten.

William Freedman discussed the slower pace of baseball relative to other games. He wrote: "Between its periodic explosions of speed and power, baseball moves slowly. It is a long time … between pitches, a longer time between batters, a still longer time between innings. [Its] slow deliberateness distinguishes baseball from other sports in much the same way that bridge distinguishes itself from blackjack." Freedman went on to point out that the baseball fan has the opportunity to contemplate and savor a significant play rather than having his attention diverted immediately to rapid-fire action, the usual case with faster sports such as football, basketball, and hockey.

Actually, baseball only appears to be a slow game, as political columnist and baseball fanatic George Will has written: "The reality of baseball is that the action involves blazing speeds and fractions of seconds. Furthermore, baseball is as much a mental contest as a physical one. The pace of the action is relentless. There is barely enough time between pitches for all the thinking that is required, and that the best players do."

Television may in time reduce the number of deep-thinking baseball fans, the fans who appreciate the subtleties of the game. Leonard Koppett expressed a concern about a slackening in this appreciation:

> Television is conditioning everyone, especially children, to short-attention-span, quick-action, let's-get-on-to-the-next-thing viscerally visual responses—not just to sports, but to everything. The coming generation's interest in baseball *results* will certainly continue to grow as more games—and highlights—are delivered by television.... Will this audience, however, ever develop a taste for the ball game itself? For the three-hour, slow-paced ... rhythm of a ball game in the flesh?

Baseball is an easy game to learn to play but a difficult game to play well, especially at the professional level. It has been said that most sufficiently large, husky, young men can be placed at a defensive lineman's position on a football team and, ineffective as they may be, can contribute something to the team's success by impeding a runner's progress so that other defensive players can bring the runner down. But this cannot be done in the case of a shortstop who, without any supporting assistance, has about 3.2 seconds from the time a ground ball reaches him until the first baseman receives his throw. The fastest that a player has been clocked from home plate to first base is about 3.4 seconds. He will be out by at least a step if the play is made properly. A contribution also may come from an outfielder who runs down a long drive and, with no wasted motion, throws accurately to the plate from some 350 feet to cut down a runner.

Baseball fans appreciate the fact that their game ends after a given number of innings have been played and the winner decided, rather than have the game played within a given time period with the clock deciding when the game is over. No matter how desperate the situation late in the game may be, frequently there is a chance for the losing team to pull out a victory. When the home team is four runs behind with two out and the bases empty in the bottom of the ninth, the crowd starts heading for the exits. Yet most of the spectators do not actually leave until they have seen the final out. And if the batter beats out an infield hit, and the next hitter draws a walk, the game becomes exciting again. The people preparing to leave find a place to sit, or jam the front of the exit ramps, refusing to move. They are rooting for a miracle finish, and sometimes they get it.

There are many reasons for baseball's place as the most important American game over the last century and a half despite some feeling that the game's popularity has been supplanted by other "faster" sports. Baseball's special appeal has been attributed to a number of factors. It is a game spanning the generations; it grew up in the 1800s with America. And it has been the one sport a child can play in some manner with a parent or even a grandparent. A familiar family picture could include a youngster playing catch or hitting a baseball with his father and even his grandfather.

This close tie between the American people and the "national pastime" is the basis for historian Jacques Barzun's well-worn pronouncement, "Whoever wants to know the heart and mind of America, had better learn baseball, the rules and realities of the game." Poet Robert Frost agreed, saying that he never felt more at home in the United States than when he was at a ballgame because baseball, like America, combined physical prowess, courage, and (he thought) justice. And Walt Whitman wrote of baseball in 1888, "We are in some ways a dyspeptic, nervous set: anything which will repair such losses may be regarded as a blessing to the race."

Writer Lev Grossman pondered an interesting question:

> What draws intellectual types to [baseball]? There's something about the mere act of punishing a ball with a stick that brings about a truce in the eternal struggle between jock and nerd, and lures such luminaries as John Updike ... George Plimpton and the late [eminent evolutionary biologist] Stephen Jay Gould to take their cuts. Are they slumming?... The lure of the game, what draws the Nobelists and the laureate, may be the elusive but ever present possibility: the no-hitter, the flawless diamond of a double play....

Because baseball has been an integral part of our society for so long, many older fans can recall earlier experiences in their lives by relating them to a baseball event. People often are asked where they were when they learned about Pearl Harbor, the John F. Kennedy assassination, or the horrific events of September 11, 2001. A truly dedicated baseball fan can recall where he was and what he was doing when Bobby Thomson's last-ditch home run pulled out the 1951 pennant for the New York Giants. Looking back over the years, baseball fans often realize belatedly that the game meant much more to them when they were young than they had thought.

Growing up as a New York Giants fan, I took Giants defeats hard. In my case, I recognized how much the game meant to me before I was a teenager. My 15-year-old brother died because of a faulty appendicitis diagnosis in 1935, and my mother died at 49 of cancer the following year. I have always felt that my deep involvement as a baseball fan began in those years when I desperately needed to find an emotional lift for my terrible losses, and baseball provided it. I can identify with TV journalist Ken Burns, whose mother died when he was 11. Burns's brother Ric has suggested that Ken's documentaries on the Civil War and on baseball, which were obsessed with the themes of unity, family, and home, were a reaction to the trauma of losing his mother when he was so young.

I was a fanatical Giants fan, and right fielder Mel Ott was my special hero. In 1942, Ott's first year as a player-manager, my father gave me a shiny birthday present — a bicycle with a new feature for the time, a second gear. I rode my new bike happily one morning before taking a trolley to the Polo Grounds for a Giants game against the rival Brooklyn Dodgers. The Giants needed a spark to have any chance to finish in the first division, and player-manager Ott struggled to provide one. He started his slumping Giants off with a home run in the first inning but my real thrill came in the third inning. With runners on second and third, Ott was walked intentionally to set up a double play. Johnny Mize bounced a hard ground ball to Dodgers first baseman Dolph Camilli and a double play seemed inevitable. Camilli threw to shortstop Pee Wee Reese to force Ott but, Reese, streaking across second base, presented a perfect target. In a rough but clean play, Ott knifed into Reese as he crossed the base, bowling the shortstop over. As a result, Reese's relay was wild, and two Giants runs scored.

I was completely thrilled by the normally easygoing, gentlemanly Ott's aggressive leadership and the Giants resulting win. I didn't realize how thrilled I was until I returned home to discover that my bike had been stolen. I accepted the loss with surprising equanimity. The Giants win and Ott's inspired play were enough to help me overcome the loss of my treasured bicycle. That was the event that confirmed my love for the game. I proved to myself that I was a truly dedicated baseball fan.

My youthful recognition of my addiction to baseball is typical of most avid baseball fans. As it developed, I was in good company. *The New Yorker's* gifted Roger Angell felt baseball's irresistible pull as a young teenager growing up in the heady baseball scene in New York City in the 1930s. Sportswriter Red Smith was bitten by the baseball bug before he was nine, growing up in Green Bay, Wisconsin. Historian Doris Kearns Goodwin gave her heart to the Brooklyn Dodgers as a six-year-old growing up in Rockville Centre, Long Island. Sportswriter Roy Blount Jr. discovered baseball when he was 11 in Decatur, Georgia. Fanatic George Will has written:

> I am sometimes asked when I first came upon that stream [baseball] which irrigates my life. I answer that I do not know, because I have no memory of life before baseball. My mother recalled that at age six, after listening to a broadcast of a 1947 World Series game that the Yankees lost, I asked her if the Yankees' mothers would be sad.... Out in central Illinois, at age seven, I made a mad, fatal blunder. I fell ... in love with the Cubs.... All I remember about my wedding day in 1967 is that the Cubs dropped a doubleheader.

I spent much of my misspent youth in the right field bleachers of the Polo Grounds and there I became the disciple of a most unforgettable baseball fan. He was a round, swarthy man named Louie whose voluminous knowledge of the game and seniority as a bleacher resident made him master of all he surveyed. Louie (we did not know his last name) impressed us mightily. He came to the ballpark two hours before the game and occupied himself by reading Shakespeare and other classics not normally considered pregame entertainment in a ballpark. Moreover, the players recognized him and acknowledged his presence during their strolls to and from the Giants' dugout and the center field clubhouse. The bleacher occupants expected to be ignored by the players when we shouted to them. But we were deeply impressed by the responses Louie received—"Howdy" from bouncy. shortstop Dick Bartell, a friendly nod from catcher Harry Danning, or a warm smile from Mel Ott. As a group we gloried in the players' recognition of Louie, which we took as an indirect recognition of all of us in those 55-cent bleacher seats.

There is a postscript to the Louie story. Many years after Louie had disappeared from the bleacher scene, in one of the years when Bowie Kuhn was the baseball commissioner, *The Sporting News* carried the following squib: "Who says there's no sentiment in baseball? Commissioner Bowie Kuhn's office received a letter from a tuberculosis hospital in Phoenix. The letter was from a patient who wrote the Commissioner that he was a longtime Giant fan and asked whether, in view of the writer's long involvement as a baseball fan in New York, the Commissioner could use his influence in convincing the New York baseball clubs to subsidize a trip for him to the World Series. The Commissioner wrote back that he would help all he could. The patient's name is Louis Kloppett." After all those years, I finally learned Louie's last name and whereabouts, although I never learned whether he made it to that World Series.

Baseball is a highly unpredictable game. This fact is the basis for the bromide, "The game is never over until the last man is out." It can be predicted that a major league team will win one-third of its games and lose another third of its games. But it cannot be predicted how well the team will perform in the other third, and that's where playoff berths are won or lost.

Unlike other sporting locales, the baseball stadium has always been a special place for its occupants. There is something beautiful and comforting about a baseball field with its carefully laid-out diamond and lovingly manicured green outfield. Older baseball stadiums evoke precious memories of historic and other meaningful games. The baseball devotee's attachment to ballparks was illustrated when Chicago Cubs fans campaigned strenuously, although unsuccessfully, against equipping the well-loved park with lights for night games. Boston fans exhibited an equally strong reaction to suggestions that Fenway Park be remodeled or, even worse, be replaced by a more modern ballpark. Few things bring out deeper regret, and lyrical expression, than a closed ballpark. The demolition of the New York Giants' historic Polo Grounds in 1964 brought out these recollections from Roger Angell:

> The things I liked best about the Polo Grounds were sights and emotions so inconsequential that they will surely slide out of my recollection. A flight of pigeons flashing out of the upper stands, wheeling past the right-field foul pole, and disappearing.... The steepness of the ramp descending [to the ballpark] toward the upper-stand gates, which pushed your toes into your shoe tips.... The "Plock!" of a line drive hitting the green wooden barrier above the stands in deep left field.... As our surroundings become more undistinguished and undistinguishable, we sense that we may not ... remember who we are and what we have seen and loved.

Baseball can be understood and enjoyed on a number of levels. The basic elements are easily understood: The batter hitting the ball and then running around the bases with the goal of scoring a run. The pitcher throwing to the hitter to either strike him out or force him to hit a ball which can result in his failure to reach base. The fielders trying to retire the batter by catching a fly ball, etc.—all with the goal of scoring more runs than the opposition. But the bona fide baseball fan is concerned with more complicated considerations—should a pitcher be removed; how shall the defense position itself for a given hitter; should a hitter be allowed to swing at, or take a pitch, in a given situation, and other involved strategic questions.

In some respects, playing major league baseball has been considered one of the most difficult skills demanded of an athlete. Hitting a 98-mile pitch with a round bat with any consistency takes remarkable hand-eye coordination and strength, not to mention the courage to stand in against a streaking, hardball that can hurt or damage. Relatively few sports observers recognize the degree of physical coordination required of a major league hitter. Almost every experienced fan can remember an outstanding high school or college player he has seen, one whose skills so far exceeded those of the players around him that he seemed to be playing a different game. Yet he never came close to making it in the big leagues. Once you have watched the failure of such a player, you realize just how much talent is required to play in the major leagues, let alone become a star.

Baseball generates mountains of statistics assembled in a meaningful and usable form. There have always been players who, without compiling eye-catching numbers, had a flair for doing the right thing when it was needed most, and they have been popular with fans and relatively well paid. But game statistics also paint a picture of the game. A fan can look at a box score in the morning newspaper and visualize what the previous day's game was like. The significant columns for a hitter traditionally have been batting average, runs batted in, and home runs. Doubles, triples, and runs scored are good indicators of a hitter's contribution, but BA, RBI, and HR are the columns the fans look at first, and therefore the ones that encourage fan attendance. (As we will see in Chapter 14, baseball fans with a statistical bent have developed other, more sophisticated, measures of offensive ability.) Similarly, the key numbers for a pitcher are games won and earned run average. Knowledgeable fans pay more attention to the ERA figure than the won-lost record because a pitcher's goal is to keep his team in the game and a low ERA tells how well he has accomplished that goal. Stolen base statistics indicate a runner's speed and ability to read the pitcher's motion to first base.

Statistics do not reflect the most exciting baseball skill — the ability to continually pull off astonishing fielding plays a la Ozzie Smith or Omar Vizquel. Fielding averages, meticulously compiled for hundreds of plays by individual players in each season, do not give a true picture of the comparative fielding merits of players. And in the case of breathtaking plays, except for illustrative anecdotes, there is no way of conveying the impact the play has made on a game.

Baseball fans love numbers, even recalling statistics dating to the late 1800s. The universe of data on every aspect of the game has made today's fan something of a participant in the game. With the computer capabilities available, baseball fans with sabremetric (again, see Chapter 14) skills have been able to manipulate statistics to gain analytical insights not possible just a few years ago.

Unlike any other sport, baseball has been a sport of year-round interest to its fans. The constant off-season speculation as to possible baseball trades — the so-called hot stove league — always kept baseball interest high even when leaves and snow were falling. But baseball news during the off-season has changed over the years. Very little of it has to do with trade and playing prospects. It has largely related to such off-field matters as negotiations between players' agents and club officials, to club attempts to gain public funds for building new stadiums, or to possible transfers of franchises.

But these factors do not completely explain why baseball has had such a hold on so many fans. One explanation is that the game also provides an emotional release. There is a theory that many fans live out their dreams, and possibly their frustrations, through the players. That could explain why a fan can be so happy when his favorite player or team has a good day and so sad after a poor day on the field. This identification makes the fan feel vicariously like a winner or loser depending upon results. It also explains why fans can become overzealous in reacting to a game in which they have no material stake but a powerful emotional one. A ballpark is a great place for the leather-lunged fan to release his aggressions, but in many cases the fan doesn't mean it when he verbally abuses a player. He may actually be a fan of the player, and this is a way of insulating himself against failure.

For all of the seriousness with which baseball fans approach baseball, in the final analysis, it still is a fun game. As esteemed writer Thomas Boswell put it: "Baseball ... is meant to be irresponsible, anti-adult, silly ... and generally disreputable. The ballpark is the place you go to play hooky ... peanut shells on the floor, as much noise as you can make.... They call baseball the summer game, which, to a child, means vacation and laziness."

Fans have reacted negatively to some features of today's game, most notably the exorbitant salaries paid players, the frequent strikes and threats of strikes by players, and games lengthened by unnecessary delays. The late Ed "Dutch" Doyle, a respected veteran Philadelphia fan, expressed his unhappiness with today's players in *More Than a Pastime*. He told author William Freedman (somewhat unrealistically):

> A ball team used to be a family, but it isn't anymore. Money killed it. I just can't stand the fact that there's not one guy playing who's willing to come along and say, "Listen, you write my contract and I'll sign it." Or that the players' union can't finally say, "Well, we're making enough. We're not gonna ask for an increase if you'll lower the ticket prices for the fans." Same with the owners. If you're making so much money that you can pay [players] 30 million dollars for four of five seasons that means you can lower the ticket prices so other people can come to the games. But it's not gonna happen. It can't be a family. It just can't.

Franchise shifts have disenchanted many fans. A number of Brooklyn Dodgers fans were disillusioned by the movement of the Dodgers from Brooklyn to Los Angeles after the 1957 season. The loss of the Dodgers was more than just the loss of a team to Brooklyn fans to whom baseball was virtually a religion. It disrupted the borough's social pattern. Conversations were muted and listless on street corners and in bars. A Brooklyn fan recalled in Peter Golenbock's *Bums*: "It wasn't just a franchise shift. It was the total destruction of a culture."

Most major league players are not natives of the city or area represented by their teams. Nevertheless, the fan looks upon the local team's players as representatives of his area. And many players have adopted as their permanent home the city for which they played and became well known. This became the natural choice of many retired players either because they developed or became affiliated with local businesses or because they married local women and stayed in the area to raise their families.

The elimination of the reserve clause has benefited players, but it has been a disconcerting development to many fans just as interested in the careers of individual players as in their teams. The shifting of an eligible player from team to team has shortened the length of his stay with his original team. Many fans bemoaned the "premature" loss of their favorites because of this change. Of course, after a decent interval, a new favorite usually emerges to take the place of the departed hero.

In addition to the effects of the reserve clause change, fans have seen other profound changes over the last few decades in the way baseball is managed and played. Major league baseball has always suffered from some competitive imbalance, but the situation has remained a problem despite attempts to transfer revenues from wealthier teams to financially weaker teams. These revenue differences largely reflect differences in the teams' broadcasting revenues. In 2002, the Yankees' broadcasting revenues came to $62 million, more than the total broadcasting revenues of seven other small-city teams. The effect of these income disparities tends to be apparent in team performance over the years.

Between 1995 and 2001, of 224 postseason games played, 219 were won by teams in the top two payroll quartiles. New York–area teams have had an overwhelming financial advantage over their rivals. For example, in a May 2002 game against the Tampa Bay Devil Rays, the Yankees fielded a team with a $135 million payroll, dwarfing the $38 million Devil Rays payroll. In the same month, the New York Mets had a starting lineup with a $63 million payroll against the San Diego Padres and their $4 million lineup.

Baseball management has truly become big business in other ways as well. There have been big increases in club revenues from increased attendance, player salaries, and increased pressure from clubs on local governments (at the threat to move teams elsewhere) to obtain public funds to support new stadium construction. Most team operators' machinations have been largely ignored by baseball fans except where higher admission fees or possible franchise movements have been threatened. However, fans resent exorbitant salaries, not only at the Alex Rodriguez level, but, as one fan put it, "by utility players who hit in the low .200s." The continuing threat of player strikes is the most bothersome concern baseball fans have faced in recent years. And fans, deeply concerned about the integrity of baseball records, look askance at the record-breaking home run displays of the last several seasons because of the suspicion they may have been drug-enhanced.

Roger Angell has expressed the disillusionment many fans feel today over the changes in baseball over the years:

> We know everything about [baseball today], thanks to instant replay and computerized stats.... Thanks to television and sports journalism, we also know everything about the skills and financial worth and private lives of the enormous young men we have hired to play baseball for us, but we don't seem to know how to keep their salaries or their personalities within human proportions. We don't like them as much as we once did, and we don't like ourselves as much, either.... We fans must make prodigious efforts to ... allow our old pleasures to reach us.

Art Hill wrote of his difficulty in explaining his love for baseball: "I wish I could explain my lifelong obsession with baseball. But it is like trying to explain sex to a precocious six-year-old. Not that I have ever done this, but I assume the child would say something like 'Okay, I understand the procedure. But *why*?' There is no answer for that. You have to be there. With baseball, too, you have to be there. But once you have been there ... you are likely to be hooked for the rest of your life."

Sportswriter Red Smith was a great fan as well as a magnificent journalist. He praised Alexander Joy Cartwright who, in 1845, is said to have stepped off 30 paces in laying out the first diamond in Manhattan. Smith considered the selection of 90 feet between bases as man's closest approach to an absolute truth. The world's fastest man cannot run to first ahead of a sharply hit ball that is cleanly handled. He reasoned that 90 feet provides a perfect measure of the accuracy of infielder placement, or the cunning, speed and finesse of the base stealer against the velocity of a thrown ball. Smith was convinced that that single dimension alone makes baseball a fine art.

Smith quoted a devoted Philadelphia fan who expressed the baseball fan's credo perfectly. Smith wrote: "I had a bartender friend who told me, and he said this with tears in his eyes, that the most beautiful thing in the world, more beautiful than any blond [sic] ... was bases filled, two out, three and two on the batter, and everybody moving on the pitch."

1

The Early Years

The primitive version of baseball played in the early 1800s was not a spectator sport. These unorganized games were a common sight on village greens and college campuses in the New York and New England areas. And the games were rarely covered by the press. The first organized baseball team was the Knickerbocker Base Ball Club of New York City in 1842. The 40-man Knickerbockers were an upper-crust social club whose games were attended by very few people who were not club members.

The game spread rapidly in the New York area, usually played on vacant lots. By 1856, games were played before nonpaying, but enthusiastic, spectators. In late November of that year, several hundred spectators, including a few women, shivered through a freezing game between two Brooklyn teams, the Excelsiors and the Atlantics. Two years later, in July 1858, all-star teams representing Brooklyn and New York played on the Fashion Race Course on Long Island before an estimated 1,500 fans, with the Brooklyn team winning 29–8. Fifty cents admission was charged to cover the cost of putting the grounds in shape for the game, the first time onlookers were reported to have paid to see a ballgame. The proceeds of the game were donated to a local firemen's fund for widows and orphans. Women were in attendance as reported in Harold Seymour's *Baseball—The Early Years*. Apparently infatuated with his own words, a reporter wrote, "A galaxy of youth and beauty in female form who, smiling on the scene, nerved the players to their task, and urged them … to do their devoirs [duty] before their 'ladyes fair.'"

The New York team evened the series in August with a win and the New Yorkers won the rubber game 29–18 in September before several thousand spectators, the largest crowd to see a game up to that time. Despite the high scores, only one home run was hit in the three games. Pioneer sportswriter Henry Chadwick described how two fans had bet $100 on whether player John Holden would hit a home run. Chadwick reported that the fan who had bet on a Holden home run had told Holden he would give the player $25 if he delivered the homer and Holden had come through, hitting a drive over right fielder Harry Wright's head. In his *America's Natonal Game*, Albert G. Spalding noted forebodingly, "This tale is interesting as showing that already, almost at the inception of playing of match games between organized teams in rival cities, betting on the result, which was to make so much … mischief in the future, was beginning to be in evidence."

In the 1850s, there were those who were not convinced that baseball was a game for all Americans, questioning whether the game was only a city-slicker's pastime, and not a favorite pastime for those who lived in rural areas. And there were few indications that the game had caught on with rural people. But it clearly was catching on in several cities. Although New York remained the primary city for baseball activity in the late 1850s, teams were organized and fan interest grew throughout New York state, especially in Albany, Syracuse, and Buffalo, as well as in smaller towns and cities in the state. At the same time, interest in the game grew in other areas of the growing country, from New England, to the midwestern cities of Cleveland, Chicago, and Minneapolis, and out to the West Coast.

By 1860 baseball games were an important source of entertainment in the New York area. But sometimes the spectators got out of hand. Rooting at games had become noisier and occasionally downright rowdy. One reporter complained that paying fans acted as though they were doing the players a favor by attending games. Gambling on games had increased and even women attendees were making small wagers on games.

The popularity of the game in the pre–Civil War years was attributable to the openness of the game; the result of each play was readily apparent to fans whose familiarity with the game and the players increased rapidly. Moreover, the games were played between highly competitive teams from rival areas. And the games were played through without time constraints and under constantly modified rules aimed at making the game more understandable to the onlookers.

"Base ball," as it was referred to in its earlier days, had no serious competition from other sports competing for the time and interest of those with leisure time. Horse racing was a sport for the elite and, additionally, the puritanism of the time discouraged betting. Football, as we know it today, had not been standardized and "refined" (assuming that the roughness and frequent injuries of today's football can be considered "refined"). Basketball would not be invented for many years. And boxing was illegal with matches held surreptitiously before relatively small numbers of people.

Some other factors at the time increased interest in baseball for those persons watching it. Most adults knew about the game because they had played it as youngsters. Then, too, as we grow older, we tend to remember our younger days nostalgically, and baseball was part of most adults' growing-up. The increased coverage of games by the press whipped up interest in the game and increased the public's knowledge of it, and a mutually beneficial relationship developed. Newspaper publishers realized that baseball news sold papers and sports fans discovered their enjoyment of baseball was enhanced by reading about it. At first newspaper accounts of games were one or two paragraphs long, accompanied by a primitive box score. But by 1860, with the recognition of the game's growing popularity newspapers published longer, more descriptive, coverage of games and inning-by-inning accounts. Newspapers also began printing letters from fans on many technical and organizational aspects of baseball.

Baseball of that era was a crude but a recognizable version of the game the fan sees today. There were no grandstands and fans traveling to games by carriage sat in their carriages while they watched games. Male fans without carriages stood along the sidelines or, if accompanied by women, stood under tents or pavilions provided in deference to "the weaker sex." There were no base paths or player benches so players sprawled in the grass outside the unmarked base paths. Unless the game was being played before a particularly raucous or rowdy crowd, most fans did not boo or complain loudly on a close play. Usually, a fan would have to wait until the following day to read a short summary of the game, and he could obtain a more complete account of the game a few days later in one of many sporting weeklies.

The hardships of the Civil War reduced the number of teams playing baseball but interest in the game remained high before and during the war. During the war, Union troops played baseball. David Q. Voigt wrote: "In relieving the monotony of camp life, the game early demonstrated an ability to attract hordes of spectators. Perhaps the largest crowd of the nineteenth century was the throng of forty thousand Union soldiers who watched a Christmas Day game in 1862 between two picked teams of their comrades. And in southern prison camps, northern prisoners found the game useful as a tension-reliever.... It is not surprising then that the stimulating influence of the Civil War triggered a veritable 'mania' in eastern cities during the late 1860's."

Before the war southerners were subscribing to the New York *Clipper,* which featured baseball news, and were writing letters to the editor about the game. And when the war started, the *Clipper* boasted that even though South Carolina had seceded, its readers had no intention of giving up their subscriptions. Red-hot fans were certainly not limited to the Northeast.

The game continued to grow in popularity at an even faster pace after the Civil War. Record attendance and a 10-fold increase in baseball clubs made the 1866 season the most successful yet. By 1868, a total of about 200,000 people saw the leading games and in the larger cities crowds of 10,000 were common. An estimated 40,000 people saw the Brooklyn Atlantics play the Philadelphia Athletics in 1866 in a wild game which ended unceremoniously when the crowds poured uncontrollably onto the field.

The National Association of Base Ball Players, a group of amateur New York–area ball clubs formed in 1858, had mushroomed into a 202-club, 17-state organization by 1866. The large increase in the number of ball clubs, and increasing numbers of fans, changed the game from an amateur pastime played by a privileged minority and watched by nonpaying onlookers to a game performed by professionals before fans who paid to attend games.

After the Civil War, "gifts" were offered to competent players to play for the local team. Outstanding players were given jobs and paid salaries by companies ostensibly for their work but actually to play baseball. Professionalism took on another aspect in 1864 when highly regarded New York and Brooklyn teams played for a share of the gate receipts derived from a 10-cent admission charge. (Some clubs charged as much as 25 cents a head.) To justify the admission charge, ballparks were enclosed and wooden benches and seats were provided to paying spectators. Before long, games were played primarily for gate receipts.

Increasing numbers of people showed their willingness to pay admission to a ballgame. By 1868, the eight best teams in the New York area split about $100,000 in gate receipts. At this level, baseball had become a business with players and other team employees deriving their summertime incomes from their teams' revenues. Professionalism had some undesirable effects for the fan in addition to the financial burden of buying tickets. Harold Seymour described a practice in which ball clubs arranged unofficial games (which did not count in the standings) and played ineligible players or amateurs without informing paying fans that such a game was unofficial and therefore amounted to an exhibition game. Spectators at these games were disappointed and disgusted to learn later that, without their knowledge, they had paid to see a game with no bearing upon the championship. Gambling was another negative factor. The higher level of professional play increased gambling at games and the possibility that game results might be fixed. Newspapers questioned whether public interest would continue after spectators became aware that players were primarily concerned with helping gamblers win their bets rather than in winning games fairly.

By 1868, many teams comprised a mix of paid professional players and unpaid amateurs. The opening game that season between picked teams from New York and Brooklyn was considered something of a test as to how fans felt about professional players because it was known that the majority of the players on the two teams were professionals. A thousand people paid 25 cents apiece to see the game, a further indication that fans would pay to see professional players perform.

The influence of professionalism changed the way the game was played. Rule changes were made which had the effect of increasing attendance because they made baseball a faster and more exciting game to watch. Playing for money brought about better playing and stiffer competition on the field. Only the most skillful players made the grade as big leaguers and, unlike earlier players who played all positions as needed, they tended to gravitate to the playing positions at which they were most proficient.

Paying for admission not only attracted spectators who liked to watch skillful play, but also those who took partisan delight in their local team's ability to defeat teams representing rival communities. Such local rivalries explain much of the excitement generated by these games, as well as the tendency of fans to express dissatisfaction with umpires, opposing teams, and supporters of opposing teams. Occasionally, these partisan feelings were so strong that opposing teams would refuse to play teams supported by vulgar fans. Sometimes fan devotion during that era took on a more beneficent tone as they honored their heroes with watches, jewelry, and other gifts.

The Cincinnati Red Stockings of 1869 became a legend as the first professional team although this was not necessarily the case. There were a number of other teams who also may have been paying all of their players. Henry Chadwick, one of baseball's most important figures before 1900 and certainly most significant writer and off-field critic, listed a number of other commercial teams as the 1869 season opened. He mentioned the Brooklyn Atlantics, the New York Mutuals, the Troy (New York) Haymakers, the Philadelphia Athletics, and the Chicago White Stockings among others.

But the Red Stockings were immortalized because of an impressive string of victories (56 plus one tie game) in 1869 and their extremely able player-manager, Harry Wright. The Red Stockings were formed in 1867 and four of their players were paid professionals in 1868. Baseball fans in Cincinnati had been paying 10 cents to attend home games and 25 cents for away games. Their rabid interest in supporting their team financially led the operators of the Red Stockings to hire English-born Harry Wright to run and play for the Red Stockings. Wright played both baseball and cricket as well as serving as an instructor for a cricket club. The result was the formation of a team of skilled professional players under Wright's competent direction. The Red Stockings steamrollered all competition, including teams composed of only amateurs and other clubs comprising a mixture of professionals and amateurs.

The Cincinnati fans were crazy about their all-conquering club — so enamored that a local newspaper admitted that Cincinnati fans "get so excited that they ... cheer and applaud before either player or spectator knows what decision the umpire has to give." After completing a triumphant eastern tour, the Red Stockings arrived back in Cincinnati a day before they were expected. A local newspaper reported that they were greeted at their train by small boys and shortly after by a much larger number of fans with "dignified citizens and solid businessmen mingled with the throng." The team was carried by carriage through streets filled with cheering rooters. Professional baseball had become a fact of baseball life from then on, with the financial engine provided by baseball fans.

The National Association of Professional Base Ball Players, the game's de facto ruling body, attempted to establish a 50-cent admission charge, one-third of which would go to the visiting team. Harry Wright, one of the strongest advocates of this admission charge, stated:

> It is well worth 50 cts to see a good game of base ball, and when the public refuse to pay that, then good bye base ball. They do not object to paying 75 cts to $1.50 to go to the theatre, and numbers prefer base ball to theatricals. We must make the games worth witnessing and there will be no fault found with the price of admission. A good game is worth 50 cts, a poor one is dear at 25 cts.

Baseball fans have been fickle as many players and general managers can attest. Cincinnati's domination of the baseball world did not last for long. The 1870 season started well but the Red Stockings' undefeated streak ended when the Brooklyn Atlantics beat them in 11 innings. Suddenly Wright's club was just another good team, one that was no longer invincible. The Cincinnati fans lost their enthusiasm for the club and the team barely broke even. The club threatened to reorganize the roster by eliminating "growlers and shirkers" and other players who would "not contract to abstain from the use of intoxicating beverages at all times unless prescribed by a physician in good standing."

The team operators read the handwriting on the wall and moved the team to Boston. The club was extremely successful in Boston, winning four straight pennants, but it was unable to appeal to the Boston fans as it had its Cincinnati rooters in the magical 1869 season. As the game became more commercial, the atmosphere both on and off the field changed. The gentlemanly Wright found himself in continuing disputes with leaders of other teams. Some of these interclub tensions spilled onto the playing field and there were bitter fights between players on opposing teams and between players and spectators. In Philadelphia crowds entered on the field, physically hampering Wright's players. Fan conduct in Boston was equally obnoxious. Eventually, team directors restored order but these were years when many fans were out of control. And increasing gambling activities made the games even more contentious.

By 1875 the reeling National Association of Professional Base Ball Players found itself completely unable to deal with problems resulting from out-of-control gambling, outright fixing and throwing of games, and "revolving" of players; that is, players jumping one team for another in complete disregard of their contractural obligations. The better players gravitated to the few strong clubs reducing competition between clubs, a situation still afflicting baseball. Many baseball followers lost faith in the game, gate receipts fell, and a number of franchises folded.

In response to these abuses a new league, the National League, was formed in 1876. The league came into being largely through the planning and organizational efforts of Chicago White Stockings director William A. Hulbert and Harry Wright's former Boston pitching star and ultimate rugged individualist, Albert G. Spalding. In 1875, Spalding had jumped Wright's Boston team to join Hulbert's club, taking with him three of Wright's other stars.

The eight-club National League began operations in 1876, with franchises representing Boston, Chicago, Cincinnati, Hartford, Louisville, Philadelphia, New York, and St. Louis. The new league experienced considerable trial and error. For example, the New York Mutuals and the Philadelphia Athletics clubs were expelled for failing to complete their 1876 season schedules and only six teams were in the league in 1877. During that season, the St. Louis, Hartford, and Louisville franchises failed financially and were replaced by teams representing Indianapolis, Milwaukee, and Providence.

There were other serious problems in addition to financial ones, most notably the scourge of dishonest players throwing games. The questions of playing games on Sunday or selling alcoholic beverages at ballparks were addressed. Feeling it would draw more fans, the league sought to present a dignified, moral image. Sunday games and sales of alcoholic beverages were forbidden along with prohibitions on betting at ballparks. Police protection was required at the ballparks. Players were barred from fraternizing with fans, and umpires were instructed to eject rowdy fans from the scene.

Also of special concern to fans was the old question of admission prices. By 1880, the National League constitution included a 50-cent admission price. Two clubs, Buffalo and Syracuse, had serious problems with the 50-cent requirement and the public and press also protested the high cost. Even with women let in to the game free on Ladies Day, a New York City working man taking his wife and daughter to a game in Brooklyn still would incur a $2.50 cost ($1.25 for taking half a day off without pay, plus carfare charges to Brooklyn, plus his 50-cent ticket). This was a price most fans could not afford. But the league held that many fans were willing to pay 50 cents to see games "of the high grade of skill offered by League nines, especially in light of the higher cost of other entertainment." Another rationale for the 50-cent charge was that reducing admissions would mean reducing player salaries, thereby increasing the attractiveness of bribes to players from gamblers.

Syracuse newspapers implied that some local fans were not exactly sterling citizens. Harold Seymour wrote:

> [The Syracuse papers] advocated charging different rates on the basis of class, because a single admission charge would "throw the entire assemblage into promiscuous [sic] relations"—something intolerable to the "higher social classes." Reminding their readers of the "drunken rowdies, unwashed loafers, and arrant blacklegs" who went to the ball games, they decried any policy which prevented "the wealthy and respected gentleman" from getting a seat apart from "his social inferior" by paying a higher price.

At the time, fans knew players only distantly as field performers. The redoubtable Henry Chadwick did his best to introduce professional players to the public. In 1872 he published a complete list of major league players with their names, height and weight statistics, hometown and team affiliation. A few years later, firms published guidebooks on players and teams as an advertising tool. These publications enabled fans to become acquainted with frequent rule changes, franchise changes, and team schedules. This information enabled fans to keep current on game statistics and the activities and exploits of their favorite players.

Fed by expanded information on individual players, the fans of the 1880s focused on the achievements of their favorites. Adrian "Cap" Anson was the first player whose personal career was followed as closely as were the doings of his club, the Chicago White Stockings, for whom Anson played for 22 seasons. Anson was a highly skilled hitter, winning four hitting titles and hitting .333 over his long career. A rough, tough, outspoken man who was recognized as an important strategist and innovator, he bullied his players into five pennant wins in his 20 years as the White Stockings' player-manager.

As a first baseman-manager, Anson was one of the first popular fan favorites. A formidable figure, the fans around the National League idolized the 6'2", 220-pounder for his colorful antics and his hitting skill. Anson was something of an early-day Dizzy Dean in that he often backed up his outrageous boasts by carrying them out on the field. But against a background of his tomfoolery, bravado, and playing achievements, the fans loved him and seemed to find escape from their humdrum lives in the always-entertaining Anson.

There were a number of other fan favorites in the National League during the 1880s. Outfielder-catcher Mike "King" Kelly played part of the decade with the White Stockings. The handsome Kelly was a much-adored player, the fans loving his flashy play, outgoing personality, handsome dark hair, luxuriant mustache, and flashing smile. David Voigt wrote: "In making him [Kelly] their superhero, many fans probably found in his antics a vicarious freedom which was otherwise attainable only in their dreams." First baseman Dan Brouthers was the Mickey Mantle of his day, noted for his massive home runs and his .519 lifetime slugging average, the highest attained by any 19th-century player. Right-hander Charles "Ol' Hoss" Radbourn won a remarkable 59 of the 75 games in which he pitched to carry Providence to the 1884 pennant.

The newly named New York Giants had several colorful, popular players as they won their first pennant in 1888. The Giants appeared to be nothing more than an average club until July 1888. But the faith their rooters had in them (more than 13,000 fans showed up at the Polo Grounds on Memorial Day) inspired the club. A *New York Times* reporter wrote of the enthusiasm of the fans who "jumped about like colts, stamped their feet, clapped their hands, threw their hats in the air, slapped their companions on the back, [and] winked knowingly." Field leader and shortstop John Montgomery Ward was a brilliant player who was idolized by the fans, if not the club owners who he would bedevil in future years with his leadership of the players against the owners. First baseman Roger Connor was a powerful fan favorite who held the career home run record broken by

Babe Ruth in 1921. Catcher Buck Ewing was an accomplished catcher and versatile player who later experts rank among the greatest catchers ever. And right-handers Mickey Welch and Tim Keefe were a well-liked, highly successful pitching duo. It was the same story in 1889 as the Giants won the pennant again—a popular, exciting team which seemed to feed its fans' enthusiasm.

The development of the American Association of Base Ball Clubs in 1881 was another source of baseball fan interest in the 1880s. It was in large part the handiwork of beer producers who saw an opportunity to build a rival league similar to the National League but a league, in contrast to the National League, which would permit the sale of beer and one with a lower admission charge of 25 cents. The American Association began operating in 1882 with six teams—in Baltimore, Cincinnati, Louisville, Philadelphia, Pittsburgh, and St. Louis. It expanded to eight teams the following year with additional teams in New York and Columbus, and to 14 teams in 1884.

The St. Louis Browns were the most successful American Association team in the 1880s. The club was owned by beer garden owner Christopher Von der Ahe, a promoter with a heavy German accent referred to by baseball historians as "half-genius and half-buffoon." Von der Ahe compensated for his ignorance of baseball with unstoppable chutzpah and the wit to hire a bright, aggressive baseball man to run his club. That man was first baseman-manager Charles Comiskey, who led the Browns to four straight pennant wins beginning in 1885.

The successful Browns gained considerable fan support while dominating the new league and winning an upset postseason series win against Cap Anson's Chicago White Stockings. Comiskey, nicknamed the "Old Roman" because of his handsome profile and wavy hair, was a mere .264 lifetime hitter. But he was an intimidating force on the field, enlisting the violent support of Browns fans in his vicious tirades against umpires. A *Sporting Life* writer found Comiskey's club "vile of speech, insolent in bearing [and] ... exciting the wrath of the spectators." After the Browns' dramatic post season win in 1886, the hero-worshipping St. Louis fans carried the Browns' players, manager, and portly owner off the field in a highly emotional parade.

Fans in the rough-and-ready 1880s found it appealing to observe their home teams' verbal "jockeying" of opposing team players. During this period, captains and managers moved up and down the first- and third-base lines directing a continuing stream of taunts and invective at the opposition trying to distract them. Because fans enjoyed the practice, it was not banned but in 1887 rule makers established fixed coaches boxes outside of first and third bases within which coaches were to remain. Another innovation for the benefit of fans was the sale of tickets at various places in the city to avoid long pregame ticket lines. Fan interest in the 1880s increased throughout the decade. As it ended, none of the fans could visualize the traumatic baseball era which followed.

2

Coming of Age

During the late 1880s, the players had become increasingly resentful of the policies of the team owners as reflected in the reserve clause and its abuses and salary limitations. And there were other provocations, among them arbitrary fines, blacklisting of players, and the lack of any mechanism for players to deal with their grievances. As a result, in October 1885 nine members of the New York Giants formed a local chapter of the Brotherhood of Professional Base Ball Players to protect themselves collectively and individually against these objectionable owner practices. Such Giants favorites as chapter leader John Montgomery Ward, Roger Connor, Buck Ewing, and Tim Keefe were active in the effort in 1888 and 1889, at the time that the Giants were thrilling their rooters with pennant wins. Following Ward's leadership (he was a natural leader and a lawyer), the Brotherhood players pressed their case against the National League clubs.

Concerned about fan opinion, the league did all it could to impress the fans as to the rightness of the clubs' positions. The fans, who ultimately would determine the outcome, were told that all player demands had been met. They also were told that the salary matter was a dead issue, and that players about to be sold would be consulted.

After unproductive legal maneuvers, the National Brotherhood set up teams in eight cities, seven of them in direct competition with National League teams in the same city. The only exception was the Brotherhood team in Buffalo, a city without a National League franchise. In addition to the National League and the Players League, the American Association fielded nine teams as it had in 1889. The plethora of teams in the three leagues provided fans in a given city more than one team to choose to patronize. As an example, a New York City-area fan had a total of five local teams (including two teams in Brooklyn) to root for.

Fans tended to relate more to the players than to the owners. In explaining the Brotherhood position, David Voigt wrote:

> As onetime rulers of major league baseball, the players were no ordinary intruders, and they deserved special consideration. Indeed, not only did players predate administrators, but the first commercial major league was a players league, and in the eyes of fans who worshipped them, they were first in importance.

Inasmuch as the leagues were competing for the same fans on the same playing dates, the financial struggle almost overshadowed the action on the playing field. (As a matter of interest, the New York teams representing the National League and the Players League played in adjoining ballparks.) With both leagues fighting for fan support, major league tickets were easy to obtain in 1890. However, late in the season the National League's advantage in financial and diplomatic firepower began to tell and indications of weakening loyalty to the Players League by some of its players and financial backers came to light. Faced with weakening support from the backers of its teams, the Players League members realized that they could not continue to operate. And so the new league folded at the end of its first season and most of the players returned to their last National League clubs.

Baseball fans reacted with relative indifference to the players' struggles, to their establishment of the Players League, and to the hasty dissolution of the new league. Fans have historically shown little interest in the off-field financial and institutional struggles between baseball teams and franchises except where there is a threat to the team's continuing existence within the fan's city. But after the 1890 season, fans were tired of the instability of franchises and leagues.

The instability of the game continued throughout the 1890s, a decade in which attendance dwindled because of an economic recession and serious instability in the game's structure. In 1892, the American Association also had folded and joined the National League. This created a poorly balanced 12-team National League with the weaker teams finishing more than 50 games out of first place. Eventually, this imbalance led to the corrupt practice of syndicate ownership in which one person or group owned stock in more than one National League team. This permitted the obviously unacceptable results of transferring without restriction players from a weaker team to another team owned by the same group. In 1898, a prominent baseball writer wrote that a disgusted public was boycotting major league baseball and he blamed the team owners for mismanaging the game.

As it has always been, the primary focus of fans in the 1890s was on the playing field. The 1890s was marked by extreme turmoil on the field. It was an era of dirty baseball, epitomized by the play of the Baltimore Orioles of John McGraw. McGraw complemented his crafty, heads-up third-base play with outrageous tactics. These included tripping base runners or slowing them up by grabbing them by their belts, slapping the ball out of infielders' hands, and substituting new baseballs to shorten the time needed by outfielders to field drives hit deep into the outfield. And a prime tactic was inciting drunken fans to threaten the opposing team. It has never been clear whether the fans of that time enjoyed, or were offended by, such practices, although unquestionably they approved of the success of the Orioles teams.

But there is little doubt that many fans of that time approved of the mistreatment of umpires. Albert Spalding took the questionable view that, in vilifying umpires, fans were merely exercising their democratic right to protest against tyranny. And in the 1890s, prominent baseball figures like Orioles manager Ned Hanlon and third baseman McGraw argued that fans favored their club's rowdy, umpire-baiting style. Hanlon justified this view with the thought, "Patrons like to see a little scrappiness in the game."

Before the 1890s, managers like Cap Anson and Charles Comiskey had enlisted the active support of the home fans in abusing umpires. But the fans of the 1890s needed little help in making life a living hell for umpires. The *New York Clipper* wrote that the umpire was the "mortal enemy" of players and fans, and *The Washington Post* reported a game during which women spectators pursued an umpire and struck him with their parasols. Umpires were cursed by fans and bombarded with beer bottles and rotten eggs. Bill James commented:

> It was hell to be an umpire in the 1890s; it's a wonder anyone would do it.... As nearly as I can figure out, the fans never killed an umpire. They tried. Umpires required police protection countless times, and there was an incident in Minnesota in 1906 in which a crowd got hold of an umpire with apparent intent to do bodily harm, but was dissuaded by a local athlete.... But if they [the fans] didn't kill [an umpire deliberately] in the 1890s, then it just wasn't destined to happen, because they sure tried. The mess was preserved by a persistent myth that the fans liked this kind of thing. Many owners believed this [including St. Louis Browns owner Chris Von der Ahe] ... who deliberately encouraged rowdyism. But there were cooler, fairer men in the game. Washington manager Gus Schmelz felt that fans of the 1890s wanted "quick and vigorous action" but with a minimum of on-field fisticuffs.

During the 1890s, umpires were indeed an endangered species. Abuse from fans occasionally turned violent and umpires were cursed loudly by fans and bombarded with beer bottles and rotten eggs, and even subjected to beatings dealt out by unrestrained fans.

Of course, umpires were an endangered species well before the 1890s. In 1884, for example, the Baltimore club felt it necessary to install a barbed wire fence around its playing field to protect umpires from being mobbed by aggrieved spectators. In that same year, angry fans assaulted league umpire Tom Gunning after he called a game because of darkness, and a Philadelphia crowd turned on umpire Billy McLean, formerly a professional boxer. McLean retaliated by throwing a bat into a group of fans. He had to be rescued and escorted off the field by police. A year later the pugnacious McLean needed another police escort after being threatened by enraged fans.

Opposing teams' players also were fair game for many rough-hewn fans. Jack Kavanagh and Norman Macht wrote of the season-ending series in 1895 between the rough Cleveland Spiders and the even-rougher Baltimore Orioles:

> It is difficult to say whether the Orioles reflected or incited the citizenry of Baltimore.... When the Spiders arrived in Baltimore... a fired-up band of fans greeted them. Players in those days dressed in their hotels and rode in open horse-drawn carriages or omnibuses to the ballpark and returned the same way. Those rides often resembled running a gauntlet. The unprotected, slow-moving vehicles left their occupants vulnerable to rocks and brickbats mixed with defunct vegetables and rotten eggs.

Fans of the Boston Beaneaters, Baltimore Orioles, and Brooklyn Dodgers were able to see more home games than fans of some of the weaker teams. Weaker teams drawing fewer fans shifted home games to other teams because they grossed more money as a visiting team than by playing poorly attended games at home. In 1899, for example, the Cleveland Spiders gave up all of their scheduled home games for the last two months of the season because short-term economics favored playing road games and taking their visitors' cut of the gate. That year the last-place Spiders had an incredible .130 (20–134) season with an inglorious 1–34 record after September 1 on the road. David Voigt wrote:

> Cleveland attendance fell off so sharply that [owner Stanley Robison] stupidly sought to "punish" local fans by [having his club] play its late-season games on the road.... In the face of such arrogance, it was a tribute to the American character that Cleveland fans ... staged a genuine boycott, which ultimately killed Cleveland as a National League franchise.

This was a period of severe racial intolerance within American society. Most fans considered black players to be curiosities to be harassed with vicious remarks from the stands. Led by the violently anti–Negro attitudes of Cap Anson and other important major league figures, players thought to be Negroes were hounded out of the league.

The 1890s witnessed one favorable development, the scorecard, which proved to be a boon to the baseball fan in identifying the players and in systematically keeping track of a game. By 1900, the enterprising Harry M. Stevens owned the scorecard concession at most major league parks. The practice of placing numbers on the backs of player uniforms followed, although some major league teams did not adopt this practice for many years.

In that era before radio, most fans not attending a game usually had to wait until the day after the game to learn how their favorites fared. In addition to newspaper reports, theaters erected large electric boards inside and outside of the theater depicting play-by-play game activities. Hall of Fame writer Fred Lieb described another way in which fans learned the game score sooner after its completion. Growing up in South Philadelphia in the 1890s, Lieb wrote of the "scoreboard boys." They were delivery boys who brought paying clients large cards on which were printed the day's scores and the updated league standings. In Lieb's neighborhood, cards were delivered to a tobacco shop near his home or to a nearby saloon. As a seven-year-old fan, Lieb and his friends made a game of dashing into the saloon, taking a quick look at the ball scores, and darting back through the swinging doors before the barkeeper could swat them with his broom.

Baseball clubs had sought the patronage of women as early as the 1870s in an effort to calm down the more exuberant or rowdy male fans, as well as to increase game attendance. So it is interesting that Ladies Days were curtailed in 1900 by Brooklyn owner Charles Ebbets. It seems that dedicated Brooklyn fans (presumably males) had complained that women attending games were using Ladies Days for "outdoor conversation bees." Apparently some of the women had brought along their children who treated the ballpark as a playground while their mothers talked.

Even less dedicated baseball fans take a much greater interest in the game when the regular season ends and the post-season championship games begin. After the Players League folded following the 1890 season and the National League crushed the American Association in the 1892 World's Series, there was a decrease in fan interest (at least among the more casual baseball rooters) because the National League had no other league to compete against. Without interleague competition and with the resulting diminished fan interest, baseball profits and player salaries slumped. And fans were alienated by the pompous attitude of baseball team owners who fancied themselves as magnates in the manner of the captains of American industry who emerged in the 1800s.

And so baseball remained in the doldrums until 1903 with the emergence of the newly formed American League. The new league was created largely through the efforts of former sportswriter Byron Bancroft Johnson, a dynamic, larger-than-life man who had been president of the Western League since 1893 but who had long shown interest in developing a league to compete with the National League. He accomplished this by bringing together a collection of wealthy men to bankroll new clubs, and arranging for the recruitment of established National League players to staff these clubs. Johnson felt strongly that baseball needed to be made a cleaner game with less rowdiness on the field and in the stands, and less harassment of umpires by players and fans. Eventually, the National League followed Johnson's lead and cleaned up its act.

The new league rekindled fan interest in the game as the American League fought for recognition as the equal of the entrenched National League. The two leagues signed a peace pact in 1901 and the American League began operations in 1903. The first "modern" World's Series was played that year between the pennant winners of each league. Unlike a few of the intransigent National League club owners, fans generally accepted the American League as the equal of the National League after the Boston Puritans defeated the Pittsburgh Pirates in the first series. The classic was not played in 1904 because of the stubborn refusal of a few National Leaguers to accept the new league. But the fans wanted interleague competition and the World's Series became an annual fixture in 1905.

Pittsburgh Pirates infielder Tommy Leach credited the Boston fans — a group of loyal fans called the Boston Royal Rooters, led by John F. Kennedy's grandfather John "Honey" Fitzgerald — with playing an important part in the Pirates' loss to the Puritans in 1903. Leach was quoted by Lawrence S. Ritter to that effect:

> That was probably the wildest World Series ever played. Arguing all the time between the teams, between the players and the umpires, and especially between the players and the fans.... The fans were *part* of the game in those days. They'd pour right out onto the field and argue with the players and the umpires.... I think those Boston fans actually won the Series for the Red Sox. We beat them three out of the first four games, and then they started singing that damn *Tessie* song, the Red Sox fans did. They called themselves the Royal Rooters and their leader was some Boston character named Mike McGreevey. He was known as "Nuf Sed" McGreevey, because any time there was an argument about anything to do with baseball he was

the ultimate authority. Once McGreevey gave his opinion that ended the argument: nuf sed!

There was a violent scene before the deciding seventh game when Royal Rooters, who assumed mistakenly that their customary pavilion seats were being held for them, discovered that the seats were occupied by other fans who had bought them on a first-come, first-serve basis. Some 500 Royal Rooters stormed the stands and blocked the aisles, delaying the start of the game for half an hour until they were forced away by mounted police.

Major league baseball became a truly integral part of American life with the two major leagues firmly established in the early 1900s. Harold Seymour described poet Carl Sandburg's recollection of his being a quintessentially American boy and fan:

> [I remember] ... times when my head seemed empty of everything but baseball names and figures. I could name the leading teams and the tail enders in the National League and the American Association. I could name the players who led in batting and fielding and the pitchers who had won the most games. And I had my opinions about who was better than anybody else in the national game.

Fans watch a 1905 World's Series game from Coogan's Bluff, overlooking the Polo Grounds. From this view outside of the ballpark behind the home plate area, fans could view only a portion of the second base area and the entire outfield. But from this free vantage point, fans could determine much of the game action by the visible players' moves and the crowd noises (Transcendental Graphics, Boulder, CO).

And who were these baseball fans anyhow? Harold Seymour wrote of the feeling among the wealthy and middle classes (and also among team owners and even sportswriters) of the early 1900s that baseball and baseball players were lowbrow. The baseball establishment reacted by assuring fans (who very likely were either unaware or completely unconcerned about this impression) that their numbers included not only laborers but also merchants, learned professionals, and certified members of the intelligentsia. New York Giants owner John T. Brush noted with pride that owners of seasons tickets to Giants games were members of the same social set who purchased boxes at the Metropolitan Opera House.

Women were introduced to the game through various marketing schemes, most importantly Ladies Days. And there were black fans although their numbers were small as the major influx of blacks into baseball cities had yet to occur. But women and minorities comprised a small percentage of the baseball fans of the early 1900s. And, unprotected from the elements in the lowest-priced seats, bleacher fans were considered the most devoted rooters largely by virtue of their willingness to brave the elements in support of their heroes and teams. Then as now devoted baseball fans have always included people from all walks of life, income levels, and social strata.

The first years of the new century were exciting times for baseball fans. There were exciting pennant races, rivalries, and players to follow. From 1901 through 1910, National League fans were treated to exciting pennant races between three dominant teams—Frank Chance's Cubs, Fred Clarke's Pirates, and John McGraw's Giants. Chance and Clarke were aggressive, gifted leaders but neither could match the impact that McGraw had on the game and its fans during that decade. Sportswriter Grantland Rice summed up McGraw's effect on the fans: "His very walk across the field in a hostile town is a challenge to the multitude."

The Giants often were referred to as "the McGraws." They were described as a team imbued with their energetic leader's resourcefulness, gameness and aggressiveness. The Giants were heartily despised in all opponent cities, a target of eggs (both fresh and rotten), all manner of produce, rocks, and bricks. In Philadelphia McGraw's warriors carried rocks in their carriages to throw back at tormenting fans. The weapon of choice in Brooklyn was spears fashioned from umbrella tips and hurled at Giants players. And the fiery McGraw was pleased; he knew the fans who loathed him had paid good money for the privilege of abusing him and his players. He normally remained indifferent to written slurs so long as they were not overly personal and he refused to take umbrage at a writer who wrote of him, "McGraw is a rough, unruly man, who is constantly playing dirty ball…. He adopts every low and contemptible method that his erratic brain can conceive to win a play by a dirty trick."

In the American League, the most important managers were Boston's Jimmy Collins, Philadelphia's Connie Mack, Chicago's Fielder Jones, and Detroit's Hughie Jennings. But much of the fans' attentions were focused on well-publicized star players in both leagues, of which Ty Cobb, Honus Wagner, Napoleon Lajoie, and Christy Mathewson were only a few. David Voigt indicated that there was a prominent baseball player to suit the varying personal tastes of fans. He wrote that for the rural-minded fans there were strong farm-boy types like Sam Crawford or Wagner; and for the romantics seeking a dashing French musketeer there was the flashy, handsome Lajoie. Ed Delahanty was just the player for those who craved grace and power in their heroes. Over his playing artistry, the Philadelphia Athletics' Eddie Collins, like Mathewson, personified the college-educated sophisticate, a status to which the average baseball fan of that era could only aspire. The versatility of Olympic hero and all-around athlete Jim Thorpe had wide fan appeal (which would have been even greater had he mastered the art of hitting curve balls). And then there was illiterate slugger Joe Jackson whose wondrous hitting style could not overcome the consequences of his involvement in the Black Sox disaster of 1919.

A number of larger, permanent stadiums were constructed in the early 1900s. Fans responded handsomely to these attractive playing sites as attendance increased almost every year between 1900 and 1910, more than doubling over the decade. By 1910, popular interest in major league baseball was so high that the National League sought unsuccessfully to extend the regular season from 154 to 168 games.

Fans played a decisive role in the highly competitive 1908 pennant race best remembered as the "Merkle Boner" game of September 23. The Giants' Christy Mathewson and the Cubs' Mordecai "Three Finger" Brown were the pitchers at the Polo Grounds in a crucial game, tied 1–1 with two out in the bottom of the ninth. The Giants' Harry McCormick was the runner at third and young Fred Merkle the runner at first. Giants shortstop Al Bridwell singled cleanly and the Giants apparently were 2–1 winners. But Merkle stopped halfway to second base before heading joyously for the clubhouse. Cubs shortstop Johnny Evers alertly secured a ball from somewhere and touched second base, claiming that he had called for and received the game ball from the outfield, a claim which could neither be proved or disproved. (Giants pitcher Joe McGinnity later claimed that Evers did not have the ball used in the game because he (McGinnity) had thrown the game ball into the stands.) After much deliberation, the umpires ruled that Merkle was forced at second, nullifying the apparent winning run. The tied game had to be called because of "darkness" but the truth was that thousands of fans had descended upon the field, making further play impossible. The regular season ended with the clubs dead even and the Cubs won a playoff game and won the pennant. The Giants and their fans claimed for years later that the pennant had been stolen from them.

Although fans were more mellow in the 1900s than in earlier years, rowdies still roamed major league parks. One violent bottle-throwing episode occurred on July 8, 1907. Cubs first baseman-manager Frank Chance reacted to being bombarded by pop bottles during a game in Brooklyn by tossing a bottle back into the stands, cutting a youngster's leg. Chance had to leave the park in an armored car with a police escort.

Ty Cobb was involved in one of the more celebrated brawls between players and fans before World War I. In May 1912, the Detroit Tigers played the New York Highlanders in New York. A fan in the stands behind third base rode Cobb in crude terms from the start of the game. As Cobb described it:

> By the sixth inning, he was cursing me and reflecting on my mother's color and morals.... [I warned Highlanders management to no avail] There's going to be trouble if this fellow isn't stopped.... As the sixth frame ended...Wahoo Sam Crawford and Jim Delahanty of our team said to me, "If you don't do something about that, you're a gutless no-good."
>
> I don't know *how* I got up there [into the left field stands] but I scaled the barrier and reached him. The next thing, I remember, they were pulling me off him. I didn't slap him around. The statement given by the fan: "He hit me in the face with his fist, knocked me down, jumped on me, kicked me, spiked me and booted me behind the ear."
>
> Reading that in an old scrapbook, I'm pleased to note that I didn't overlook any important punitive measures.

Writer Fred Lieb claimed that Cobb was not guiltless and that he had shouted insultingly at the fan, "I was out with your sister last night." Lieb reported that Cobb had stopped swinging at the fan only when he noticed the little man was handicapped. As a result, Cobb was suspended indefinitely. The Tigers refused to play their next scheduled game in protest of the fiery Cobb's suspension and the Tigers picked up an assortment of semipros and college students who lost their next game convincingly. At Cobb's urging, the Tigers returned to the field for the next game. But the unacceptability of players attacking fans, regardless of the provocation, was reaffirmed as Cobb was suspended for 10 days and fined $50.

Players and managers develop verbal tools for dealing with fans without using their fists. In his *McGraw of the Giants*, Frank Graham described techniques used by John McGraw:

> The Giants were being beaten by the Chattanooga club [in a preseason game]. McGraw was in a vile mood. To make matters worse, the crowd was ridiculing him and his players. He made up his mind to stop that by directing his fire at ... a police captain in uniform, seated in a box just back of the Giants' dugout.
> Coming back from the coaching lines at the end of an inning, McGraw leaned his elbows on the roof of the dugout and said to the officer:
> "You're a fine spectacle."
> The officer's face flushed.
> "Who? Me?" he demanded.
> "Yes," McGraw said. "You. A fine spectacle.... You're a credit to the community, you are. A police captain in uniform sitting up there abusing ball players."
> [The crowd moved closer as McGraw said everything he could think of, and all of it was profane.] And now, suddenly, the crowd was on his [McGraw's] side, because it isn't often a cop — and a captain of cops, at that — is bawled out in public. The crowd loved it.... [It] ended with the captain, his face as red as a four-alarm fire, beating a retreat ... and McGraw felt better.

The interest fans had for their favorites carried over to players' off-field romances. Similar to John Montgomery Ward's marriage to prominent Broadway stage star Helen Dauvray in the 1890s, fans were intrigued by Giants outfielder "Turkey Mike" Donlin's marriage to Mabel Hite, a popular Broadway actress of the day. Fans shared vicariously in Donlin's romantic triumph although their joy was short-lived as the idyllic coupling ended sadly when Donlin fell victim to alcoholic excesses and Hite died of tuberculosis. Similarly, the fans were titillated by Giants lefthander Rube Marquard's marriage to actress-singer Blossom Seeley in 1913. After they were married Marquard appeared with his wife in a vaudeville dance routine.

The Federal League, operating during the 1914 and 1915 seasons, intrigued baseball fans early in its existence. During the first few weeks of the 1914 season, some Federal League games outdrew National or American League games played in the same city. There was a natural curiosity on the part of fans as the new eight-team league had signed a number of major league players and fans were curious as to how favorite players from the established leagues would fare in the new league. But few fans felt that the caliber of Federal League play equaled that of the two established leagues and attendance in Federal League cities dropped after the novelty of the new league wore off. By midseason of 1914, the Federal League clubs had dropped admission prices from 50 cents to 25 cents and, in some cities, to 10 cents. By the end of the 1914 season, Federal League losses were estimated at $176,000 compared with modest profits of the National and American Leagues. The fans had voted with their patronage, and the Federal League was on the ropes although most owners of teams in the Federal League were not yet ready to admit defeat. Fan interest continued as rumors of Federal League raids on major league clubs continued after the 1914 season. After a continuing series of legal skirmishes in 1915, several Federal League owners signaled their desire to terminate the new league after the 1915 season. Baseball fans were free to follow the two major leagues without the distraction of the Federal League in 1916.

Major league teams prospered from 1903 to 1920 even with the increased competition reflected by the emergence of the Federal League. The profitability was due in part to aggressive marketing efforts. Ladies Days, which dated to the 1880s, involved free admission for women escorted by a paying male companion. Although some clubs, feeling that the programs were disadvantageous, had dropped them in the early 1900s, the programs were reestablished during World War I in Cincinnati, Chicago, and St. Louis.

The Cardinals inaugurated their well-received "knothole gang" program in 1917. Originally designed to bail out the financially stressed Cardinals, the plan included a public offering of Cardinals stock by which the purchaser of two shares of club stock, at $25 apiece, entitled the buyer to a season pass for a local youngster. The Cardinals provided the available free tickets to local religious and secular organizations which apportioned them to deserving youngsters.

Providing free tickets to baseball fans has always presented a problem to clubs. Many people who can afford to buy tickets, then as now, sought to obtain complimentary tickets for the privilege of displaying them. Privileged private and public figures often are provided free tickets to important games at the expense of many genuine fans willing to pay for tickets. One of the best-represented groups among the "deadheads" was the clergy. Owners believed that the presence of men of the cloth gave tangible evidence of the respectability and honesty of the game. Some ministers were accused of joining the deadheads on Saturday, preaching against Sunday ball the next day, and then showing up at the park for another free show the following day. Teams began cutting down on their free lists and, likely at the owners' behest, the National League adopted a rule limiting the total number of passes to be dispensed.

Many fans, especially younger ones, have a vital interest in obtaining free baseballs at games. Until the late 1900s, fans were not permitted to keep baseballs hit into the stands. Ballpark employees raced into groups of fans to recover such baseballs to the detriment of relations between the ball club and its patrons. Local politicians (especially those who were not interested in obtaining free passes) introduced legislation to prevent clubs from recovering loose baseballs obtained by fans. In 1916, the Chicago Cubs decided to permit fans to keep baseballs hit into the stands but it was not until many years later that all clubs had adopted this policy. As late as 1937, a fan at Yankee Stadium was severely beaten for appropriating a baseball lodged in the screen behind home plate. Happily, the fan won a $7,500 judgment against the company the Yankees hired to maintain their ballpark. In a reverse twist in recent years, Wrigley Field fans have followed the practice of defiantly throwing home run balls hit by Cubs' opponents back onto the field. Since the players' strike of 1994, as a goodwill gesture, outfielders catching fly balls for the third out in an inning often throw the ball into the stands before trotting into the dugout.

Frequent complaints are heard today about the length of games. This is nothing new. Many fans in the early 1900s expressed the view that a baseball game should be completed within two hours and preferably closer to an hour and a half. Similar to today's game, fans were unhappy when players stalled (usually visiting team players), when pitchers took too long between pitches, and when umpires did not hustle the players along. Years ago some fans complained that 2½-hour games taxed the patience of most fans. (Today's fans would gladly settle for a game of that duration). Eighty years ago, as in the present, both major league presidents sought to shorten games and it seems that if games could not be shortened in that long-ago era, they certainly are not likely to be shortened today given the modern game's increased complexity and specialization.

Unlike today, double headers were a common feature of the 1900–1920 era. Two games for one admission price were scheduled every holiday and on a number of Saturdays and Sundays during the season. And clubs frequently arranged synthetic "twin bills" by canceling a weekday game in playable weather in order to schedule a bargain double-header under the theory that more fans would attend a double-header than the total number attending two single games on different days. Of course, the games of that earlier era were so much shorter than they are today that a double-header in the early 1900s would not require much more time than a single game today.

World War I, which began in Europe in 1914, did not have any visible effect upon major league baseball until the end of 1917, about six months after the United States entered the war. At that time players began to feel the effect of the military draft and many players enlisted in the service hoping to play for service teams. Other prominent players—among them Babe Ruth, "Shoeless Joe" Jackson, Rogers Hornsby, and pitcher Jeff Tesreau—took jobs with defense-involved companies. While ostensibly employing these players as ordinary workers, companies assigned the players to play on their company baseball teams. Public resentment against this practice grew and in September 1918 workers in a Philadelphia shipyard struck the company in protest of player-employees who were paid good wages for playing baseball. Presumably, devoted fans were included among those protesting the special treatment accorded these players.

Attendance at major league games rose markedly from 1900 to 1920 as baseball's popularity increased along with the national population. In 1902, 3.2 million fans attended games and, stimulated by the new American League in 1903, the total climbed to 4.5 million. Attendance averaged more than 5 million over the next four years. During 1908–11, an average of more than 6.5 million fans came to the ballparks. The emergence of the Federal League lowered attendance at major league games in 1914, and the impact of World War I was felt in the shortened 1918 season. But war-weary fans returned to the ballparks in droves after the war ended in 1919 and in the following year attendance rose to 9 million. Baseball's prospects were never brighter as the fans looked forward to the 1920s.

3

Boom, Depression, War

Major league baseball was shaken to its roots by the disclosure that the 1919 World's Series between the White Sox and the Reds had been fixed by eight Sox players. The story has been told in many baseball writings, most notably by Eliot Asinof. The disillusion of all baseball fans is exemplified by the probably apocryphal plea of a youngster reported to have called out plaintively to one of the accused fixers, Sox slugger "Shoeless Joe" Jackson, as Jackson emerged from a courtroom: "Say it ain't so, Joe."

Major league baseball attempted to recover its shattered image by appointing U.S. District Court Judge Kenesaw Mountain Landis as the game's commissioner. The stern Landis was given carte blanche to take all steps needed to restore the fans' faith in the game's honesty after the Black Sox scandal. The white-haired Landis was the ultimate crusty curmudgeon, a rumpled, hawk-eyed bantamweight, complete with jutting jaw, perpetual scowl, profane mouth, an unruly shock of white hair, and a commanding presence belying his small size. He had gained national prominence as a strict judge in 1907 when he imposed a $29.2 million fine on Standard Oil of Indiana in an antitrust case. Landis retained that reputation with baseball fans as a strict protector of baseball's good name although few fans were aware that the Standard Oil fine, along with other of his punitive decisions, were later overturned on appeal.

Most fans enjoy offensive play with many base hits and home runs compared with purists who tend to favor scientific play with emphasis on pitching and tight defense. As a result, fans favored the change in the game after World War I from "small ball" baseball to a "long ball" game. Ty Cobb personified the earlier, low-scoring era with his aggressive, scientific approach to offensive play and emphasis on playing for one run at a time. The basic strategy was to get a man on base and move him into scoring

3. Boom, Depression, War

Fans watch the 1919 White Sox players' pregame warmup in Cincinnati. It would be another year before these unsuspecting rooters learned that eight White Sox players were throwing the series (Transcendental Graphics, Boulder, CO).

position by a sacrifice bunt or steal as early as the first inning of a game. By 1920, Babe Ruth's home run power changed the strategy completely. Use of the sacrifice bunt and the stolen base were de-emphasized as managers shifted to a station-to-station strategy in which teams played conservatively to get runners on base to wait to be driven in by one swing of the bat.

Cleveland shortstop Ray Chapman's death after being beaned by Carl Mays in 1920 led to the use of new, unscarred baseballs benefiting hitters. Bill James discussed league directives aiding hitters after 1921. The spitball and the emery ball were banned, and scuffed baseballs were immediately replaced. Pitchers complained that the new glossy baseballs were difficult to grip properly and made it difficult to throw curveballs.

Apparently there has always been a tacit understanding among baseball equipment manufacturers not to reveal changes in the elasticity of updated baseballs, thereby increasing or decreasing the balls' liveliness. The National League investigated this possibility in 1921, predictably concluding that the baseball in use was unchanged from those used in preceding years and that the increase in hit and run production was solely attributable to the banning of the spitball and elimination of freak deliveries. Regardless, it was apparent that the new balls clearly were livelier than the ones they replaced, as evidenced by the offensive surge in the '20s. This trend was accentuated in 1925 with the introduction of a baseball with a new cork center.

Along with the appointment of Landis, the recovery from the Black Sox affair's profound insult to baseball's good name came with the emergence of 25-year-old Babe Ruth, a first-rate left-hand pitcher and slugger par excellence for the Red Sox. Boston club owner Harry Frazee, badly in need of money to shore up slipping show business investments, sold Ruth to the Yankees after the Babe's powerful 1919 season. Ruth's entrance into New York was the prime factor in the overpowering Yankees teams of the 1920s and early 1930s. For many years, Ruth's transfer to the all-winning Yankees was accompanied by disappointing Red Sox clubs. This has led Boston fans, with more emotion than logic, to attribute the club's continuing disappointments since Ruth left for New York to "the Curse of the Bambino."

Since World War I very few teams have successfully parlayed a strong defense into a world championship. Almost without exception in the 1920s, pennants were won by heavy-hitting clubs. In the 1930s, only manager Bill Terry's New York Giants won pennants on the strength of superb pitching, a strong defense, and a barely adequate offense. As an example, Terry's 1933 Worlds Champions lost a 2–1 game to the St. Louis Cardinals. *New York Daily Mirror* writer Ken Smith consoled Terry after the game. "Just another hit there, Bill, and —." Terry cut him short: "Kenny, they shouldn't have scored two runs."

Baseball team owners, pointing to higher gate receipts, agree that most fans want to see "long ball" baseball. In 1919 Babe Ruth hit 29 home runs for the Red Sox to break the then-existing modern home run record of 24 hit by the Phillies Cactus Cravath in 1915. Traded to the Yankees in 1920 with the Polo Grounds his home field, Ruth blasted an unheard-of season total of 54 home runs and the Yankees doubled their 1919 attendance. Whether the new offensive game in following years resulted from a livelier ball or other factors, the theory was indisputable — baseball fans wanted higher-scoring games with baseballs bouncing off, or disappearing over, outfield walls.

A very intense couple watch a World's Series game. The man's concentration on the action is unaffected by the sandwich in his mouth held by his equally focused wife (Steve Milman).

The baseball fans of the 1920s lived in an era of unrestrained optimism and carefree living, reflecting the prosperity of the times. It was a time of easy money and fans flocked to the ballparks in ever-increasing numbers through the '20s until the Great Depression took hold in the early 1930s. Ruth's herculean feats on and off the field thrilled the fans, and the great Yankees clubs on which he played were the big attraction and the talk of baseball fans everywhere. Some fans admired the Yankees for their power and their success but other fans detested them because of their success and the fact that they represented the brassy, overpowering city of New York. And so the fans flocked to the Polo Grounds and after 1922 to the new Yankee Stadium and to other stadiums visited by the Bronx Bombers.

The years between the World Wars saw important changes in the game

The King and Queen of England politely watch the Giants and White Sox in a post–1924 season exhibition game in London (Transcendental Graphics, Boulder, CO).

and the means by which fans followed the game. Very few fans were even aware of the first radio account of a major league game in August 1921. In 1926 the first amplifiers in use were employed at the Polo Grounds. Before that, field announcers using large megaphones announced the names of only the pitchers and catchers. Three years later the Yankees became the first team to have identifying numbers sewn on the backs of players' uniforms. The first night game came in 1935 as Cincinnati gave working fans the opportunity to watch their favorites play in the evening.

Babe Ruth was the most arresting baseball figure of the 1920s, but there were many other brilliant players who also entertained and fascinated fans during that decade. Ty Cobb remained an exciting figure as the Tigers' player-manager, his great natural ability enhanced by his driving, unbalanced personality and his overwhelming desire to intimidate his opponents and dominate a game. His combination of athletic skill and single-minded intensity to win continued undiminished in his six years as the Tigers player-manager in the early '20s. Unlike Ruth, and despite

Young Babe Ruth fans maintain a vigil outside of New York's St. Vincent Hospital in 1925 as the Bambino recuperates from his famous "bellyache heard 'round the world." The ailment was never publicly described but most likely it was a product of Ruth's out-of-control eating and living style. (Transcendental Graphics, Boulder,Co)

Babe Ruth throws samples of his new "Baby Ruth" candy bar to fans before a game at Yankee Stadium in 1926 (Transcendental Graphics, Boulder, CO).

his greatness as a player, Cobb was one of the most disliked figures of his time among baseball fans and players.

Gifted outfielder Tris Speaker, his great playing career closely paralleling Cobb's, had even more success than Cobb as the Indians' player-manager. One of the great hitters and all-around players in the game before 1920, he revolutionized center field play in the deadball era, playing close enough to the infield to be virtually a fifth infielder. After World War I, the graceful Texan continued to hit and field as the Indians' player-manager with the effectiveness he had displayed before the war.

George Sisler was one of the most effective hitters and graceful first basemen of his era. He was especially brilliant in his prime, hitting .400 over 1920–1922 and treating onlookers to unmatched fielding plays. Sisler was a fan favorite, admired as much for his graceful playing style and pleasing persona as for his marvelous play.

Rogers Hornsby averaged .397 in leading the National League in hitting in each year from 1920 through 1925. He hit with power and his .358 career batting average was exceeded only by Cobb's .367. Consequently, many fans considered him to be baseball's greatest right-handed hitter. He also was a decent fielding second basemen, his only weakness a tendency to mishandle pop flies. (A St. Louis writer's tongue-in-cheek explanation: "He was unfamiliar with pop flies because he himself hit so few of them.") But, other than his wonderful playing skills, the completely tactless, hard-bitten Texan was unpopular with anyone in baseball with whom he came in contact.

Frankie Frisch was a sparkling, inspirational infielder through the '20s with a .316 career average. He never played in the minors, joining the New York Giants fresh out of Fordham University. The aggressive, talkative Frisch sparked the Giants to pennant wins in his first four regular seasons in the '20s. He had a robust sense of humor and was especially popular with fans, intrigued by his flashy play and outgoing personality.

Legendary Walter Johnson played in the first World's Series of his illustrious pitching career in 1924; he is still respected for his incredible speed and control and loved because of the humble, modest, farm-boy image he projected. Similarly, right-hander Grover Cleveland Alexander topped off his great career with a dramatic relief appearance in the 1926 World Series when he struck out the Yankees' Tony Lazzeri in a pinch while struggling with a world-class hangover.

The late '20s witnessed the appearances of a number of future greats. The potent Ruth-led Yankees of the late '20s showcased durable, powerful Lou Gehrig and smooth, line-drive-hitting catcher Bill Dickey. The Pirates introduced the talented brothers and outfielders Paul and Lloyd Waner. In the mid–'20s the Giants introduced Bill Terry, an accomplished hitter and highly-skilled first baseman, juvenile Mel Ott who would carry the Giants' offense for many years, and screwballing lefthander Carl Hubbell, Ott's counterpart on defense. As the '20s ended, Connie Mack's Athletics were in the midst of three straight pennant wins spearheaded by such popular fan favorites as bullet-throwing left-hander Lefty Grove, the extremely competent field leader and catcher Mickey Cochrane, and power-hitting greats Jimmie Foxx and Al Simmons.

The two most memorable managers in the 1920s, were the Giants' John McGraw and the Athletics' Connie Mack. The stocky, explosive McGraw was an upstate New York native who managed the Giants to four straight pennants from 1921 through 1924. After that his clubs remained in the running during most of the remaining years of the '20s but he was less successful because of a combination of health problems and player rebellions against his tyrannical, overpowering, managing style.

McGraw had a genius for inciting enemy fans both on and off the field. Hostile fans around the National League responded by pelting the

Giants with rocks and bottles as his club left the field after road games. McGraw also had his share of fights with fans off the field. The most famous brawl occurred in August 1921 after McGraw drank bootleg whiskey for the better part of a night at the Lambs Club, a famous New York theatrical club and watering hole.

The doughty little manager fought with a fellow member and was escorted home around breakfast time by two other club members. As the men were leaving McGraw's apartment, one of them heard a sickening thud as his companion, actor John C. Slavin, fell face down on the pavement. Although it was never firmly established that McGraw had caused Slavin's resulting fractured skull and other injuries, Slavin brought suit against McGraw for $25,000 damages in a case settled out of court. McGraw's membership in the Lambs Club was summarily withdrawn.

Frank Graham wrote that, to the amusement of the fans, New York newspapers printed McGraw's "ring record" in his fights on and off the field. Their glee was heightened when McGraw added to his record a few weeks later by fighting with another fan. But McGraw had the last laugh in the Slavin matter the following May when he was acquitted by a district court jury and happily reinstated by the Lambs Club.

Completely different from McGraw in personality, physical appearance, and demeanor, Connie Mack (nee Cornelius McGillicuddy) resembled McGraw only in his importance as a manager and in their shared Irish heritage. A lean, dignified New England native with an accent to match, during games Mack sat in the dugout in his street clothes with his signature derby hat and starched collar in hot or cold weather. The fans were intrigued by his habit of positioning his players in the field by waving his ever-present scorecard. A sweet-faced man who rarely resorted to profanity, he was beloved by his players, all baseball men, and the fans. This adoration continued even in Mack's managerial dotage in his 80s when he dozed frequently on the bench during a game while an assistant coach served as the Athletics' de facto manager.

After many highly successful years from 1903–14, Mack was forced to sell his stars for financial reasons and it was not until the mid–'20s before his teams became respectable again. After several near-misses, Mack's assemblage of such great players—Lefty Grove, Jimmie Foxx, Mickey Cochrane, and Al Simmons—won pennants from 1929 to 1931. The up-and-down performance of his teams during his 53-year managerial career was largely attributable to a perennial shortage of money and his resulting need to sell star players. As a result, Mack wore out his welcome with many Athletics fans over the last several years of his managerial tenure because his teams were not competitive. But his status with the fans was irrelevant as he had the ultimate job security — the "Tall Tactician" was the Athletics' principal owner.

Brooklyn Dodgers manager Wilbert Robinson was another fan favorite in the post–World War I period. The well-loved Robby was a portly man with a baseball knowledge extending back to his playing days with the famed Baltimore Orioles in the 1890s. He possessed a lovable personality, endearing him to the long-suffering fans of the hapless and helpless "Daffiness Boys" Dodgers in the 1920s. Harold Seymour, a Dodgers batboy for a season during this period, wrote entertainingly of the fans' love affair with Robinson, a man with none of McGraw's imperious, pugnacious style or Mack's austere, gentlemanly manner, in running his team and dealing with his club's rooters. Harold Seymour wrote:

> Robbie's warmth and simplicity made the fans feel that they had a personal share in the fortunes of the team and in helping him run it. He was always ready to argue strategy with them under the stands or in the street, and he accepted taunts as personal challenges. More than once I saw him step in front of the dugout to shout back at some particularly loud-mouthed heckler.... That Brooklyn fans continued to come out to Ebbets Field, if only for laughs, testified to their unshakable attachment to "their" team. Just as for children it is sufficient that candy be sweet, so for local fans the flavor of Brooklyn baseball satisfied, regardless of quality.

Fans in the 1930s enjoyed the differing styles of play between the two leagues. American League pitchers tended to favor the fastball while more National League pitchers were curveball specialists. National League pitchers were more aggressive in pitching inside to hitters and there were more brawls ignited by perceived bean balls in the older league. More than in the American League, it was standard procedure for National League pitchers to knock down the next hitter after a home run was hit.

There were more traditional rivalries between National League teams than in the American League. Most celebrated was the continuing enmity between the Dodgers and the Giants and their fans. The long-standing interborough rivalry became especially important in 1934 when the second-division Dodgers knocked off the Giants who led the league until the last weekend of the season. The Giants, of course, returned the favor in 1951 on Bobby Thomson's last-ditch home run. By comparison, the rivalry between the Yankees and the Red Sox, of more recent vintage, lacks some of the intensity felt by the players and fans when the Giant played the Dodgers.

During the rollicking '20s, both leagues emphasized the offensive game. But, after witnessing sky-high offenses in 1930 (a league batting average of .303, Bill Terry's .401 batting average, and Hack Wilson's 191 RBIs), the National League had its official baseballs deadened. As a result, until the ball was enlivened a few seasons later, National League games resembled more the game played before World War I than those played in the '20s. The liveliness of American League baseballs apparently remained unchanged through the decade.

Through the '30s, the tighter National League races were dominated by great pitchers—Dizzy Dean, Carl Hubbell, Lon Warneke, Paul Derringer, Bucky Walters, and Hal Schumacher—and the American League by powerful, strapping sluggers—Babe Ruth, Lou Gehrig, Jimmy Foxx, Hank Greenberg, Al Simmons, Joe Cronin, Joe DiMaggio, and later, Ted Williams. During the '30s, the American League significantly outscored the National League in every season. In 1933, the American League scored an average of almost five runs a game, one run a game more than in the older league. During that season, Carl Hubbell, for example, led the National League with an impressively low 1.66 ERA.

Before World War II, American League races were dominated by overpowering Yankees teams while the National League provided fans with more competitive pennant races. From 1930 to 1939, the National League champions won over the second-place team by an average of 4.5 games compared with American League pennant winners' average 10.7-game margin. The Bronx Bombers won five pennants in the '30s, three of them by overwhelming margins, and fans and writers began referring derisively to the eight-team American League as the baseball version of the then-popular movie *Snow White and the Seven Dwarfs*.

The Cardinals, Cubs, and Giants won all of the pennants in the '30s until the Reds improved to win the pennant as the decade ended. From the fans' viewpoint, the most entertaining clubs of that era were the high-spirited, colorful "Gas House Gang" Cardinals, a group of hungry, largely unlettered, country boys. They were the cream of the players developed by the Cardinals general manager's far-flung farm system. Second baseman-manager Frankie Frisch, the leader of the entourage, managed to keep his high-energy charges under more or less control.

The boisterous Cardinals featured several noteworthy players. Jerome "Dizzy" Dean and his quieter pitching brother Paul were standout right-handers. Rough-hewn, infielder-outfielder Pepper Martin was an unusually high-spirited player, noted for his head-first slides. Abrasive but highly skilled shortstop "Lippy Leo" Durocher (so nicknamed because he rarely had an unuttered thought), was the best fielding shortstop in the league. And slugging outfielder Joe "Ducky" Medwick was a high-octane competitor and a terror at the plate, not at all averse to brawling with teammates during a game. In the mid–'30s, sweet-swinging first baseman Johnny Mize became one of the premier National League hitters. And outfielders Enos "Country" Slaughter and skillful center fielder Terry Moore also thrilled the fans.

The Cardinals' hellbent playing style was matched by their off-field antics. The clowning of Dizzy Dean and Pepper Martin was most famously illustrated when they donned workmen's clothes in a Philadelphia hotel and broke up a welfare workers luncheon meeting, insisting they had to paint the walls of a packed banquet room.

The fun-loving 1936 Gas House Gang Cardinals were a joy to watch in pregame practice. Early in the drills, Pepper Martin customarily blew a whistle and the players immediately formed two opposing squads for a short, spirited touch football game. This off-the-wall tomfoolery especially delighted New York fans who never saw such madcap antics during the managerial regimes of Giants managers John McGraw or Bill Terry and certainly not under the stern leadership of Yankees manager Joe McCarthy.

Chicago Cubs fans of the '30s watched their favorites (the endearing term "Cubbies" had not yet come into wide use) win three pennants every third year beginning in 1932. The Cubs made up in sheer ability what they lacked in color with the exception of short, heavyset, outfielder Hack Wilson, who terrorized National League pitchers and red-faced catcher Gabby Hartnett, a hard hitter with a rifle arm. Other Cubs stalwarts were young first baseman Phil Cavaretta, a highly proficient double-play combination of smooth second baseman Billy Herman and aggressive shortstop Bill Jurges, ever-smiling third baseman Stan Hack, and speedy outfielder Augie Galan. And the Cubs had excellent pitching from lefty Larry French, intimidating right-hander Charley Root, and curveballing right-handers Lon Warneke and Bill Lee.

The Giants under Bill Terry were the antithesis of the Cardinals, a quiet, no-nonsense team. Terry was a bright man who saw no reason to ingratiate himself with the Giants writers and fans and who paid the price with a highly antagonistic press. Terry's persona was that of an impersonal businessman who happened to be a great hitter and first baseman and a first-class field leader. Left-hander Carl Hubbell, possessor of a wondrous screwball with exquisite control and pitching savvy to match, was a taciturn man who had little to say off the field. Mel Ott, the Giants' offensive bellwether before, during, and after the '30s, was as quiet as Hubbell but the fans found the sturdy little Louisianan especially appealing because he joined the Giants as a young teenager and because of his pleasant, modest personality. Terry, Hubbell, and Ott were the three baseball figures who carried the Giants to three pennants in the 1930s.

At the end of the '30s, the Reds emerged as the best team in the National League, winning the 1939 and 1940 pennants under manager Bill McKechnie. He was a highly respected field strategist, nicknamed "the Deacon" because he had a restrained, sober manner and he sang in the church choir in his native Wilkinsburg, Pennsylvania. Catcher Ernie "The Schnozz" Lombardi, considered the slowest player in the league but a murderous hitter, was a beloved figure in Cincinnati with his easygoing nature and his Jimmy Durante-sized nose. The Reds' fundamental strength was their pitching staff led by right-handers Paul Derringer and Bucky Walters, who won 48 percent of the Reds' victories during their consecutive pennant wins.

Fans remember the '30s for a number of highly publicized events. One was Babe Ruth's "called" home run in the 1932 Yankees–Cubs World Series. Actually, Ruth's pointing toward the outfield between hard-bitten Charley Root's deliveries was given little attention until some time later when *New York World-Telegram* sports editor Joe Williams speculated, possibly tongue-in-cheek, that Ruth was pointing out to the center field stands in which he deposited his homer on the next pitch. Many knowledgeable fans, writers, and players refused to believe that Ruth had indeed called the home run. Perhaps most telling was the comment Ruth himself made to a team trainer years later: "I may be dumb, but I'm not that dumb. I'm going to point to the center field bleachers with a barracuda like Root out there? On the next pitch they'd be picking it out of my ear with a pair of tweezers."

Fans were deeply impressed by Carl Hubbell's feat in striking out in a row future Hall of Famers Ruth, Gehrig, Foxx, Cronin, and Al Simmons in the 1934 All-Star game. John McGraw's voluntary stepping down as the Giants' manager in June 1932 after 30 years was a momentous day as was Babe Ruth's departure from the Yankees after the 1934 season. There were other seminal events during the decade.

With Cincinnati Reds executive Larry MacPhail the driving force, the first major league night game was played at Cincinnati between the low-attendance Reds and the Phillies on May 24, 1935. By the outset of World War II, night ball was being played in most major league ballparks and, just after the war, in all stadiums except Wrigley Field. The Hall of Fame opened in Cooperstown, New York, in 1939 shortly after Lou Gehrig's tragic departure from the game. Fans also remember the '30s because of the emergence of three all-time greats— Bob Feller, Joe DiMaggio, and Ted Williams.

The historic 1941 season is well remembered by older fans. Ted Williams, hitting .405 at the midseason break, won the All-Star game at

Fans look on at the dedication of the Baseball Hall of Fame in Cooperstown, New York, on June 12, 1939 (Transcendental Graphics, Boulder, CO).

Detroit with a dramatic two-out-in-the-ninth home run. Given the option of sitting out the season-ending double-header with a .400 average, Williams came through in style with a six-hit day to finish with a .406 average. DiMaggio hit in 56 straight games. And, to the consternation of Dodgers fans, the Yankees pulled out a pivotal game of the World Series after Brooklyn catcher Mickey Owen permitted a third-strike pitch from reliever Hugh Casey to elude him. The play deprived the Dodgers of a win and the Yankees went on to win the series and Lou Gehrig died at 37 from the disease which bears his name.

Baseball fans received a small taste of the future impact of World War II as early as 1940 with the institution of the military draft. Tigers first baseman Hank Greenberg and Phillies right-hander Hugh Mulcahy were the most prominent players to be drafted. Even at ballgames, important war news was provided first hand to fans. With the Giants and the Boston Braves tied at 1–1 in the fifth inning of a night game at the Polo Grounds on May 27, 1941, the game was stopped. For almost an hour, the crowd sat in engrossed silence as President Franklin D. Roosevelt's solemn voice boomed out of the loudspeakers atop the center field clubhouse. FDR announced an unlimited emergency and the U.S. intention of resisting further Nazi attempts to stop or destroy Allied vessels. The fans listened intently and players sat on the stairs leading to the clubhouse or leaned out of the clubhouse windows overlooking the field. The game was completely ignored as the national emergency commanded attention. The Japanese attack on Pearl Harbor occurred a little more than six months later.

As soon as the shock of the attack wore off and fans had taken stock of their own wartime situations, they wondered how the war would affect baseball. Responding to Commissioner Landis's request regarding base-

Transportation shortages during World War II forced major league teams to hold their spring training near their home cities. New York Giants player-manager Mel Ott shakes hands with great left-hander Carl Hubbell as the Giants opened their 1943 training camp in Lakewood, New Jersey. The enthusiastic welcoming fans' reference to "1943 Champions" was not an accurate prediction as the Giants finished a disastrous season in last place, 49½ games off the pace (Transcendental Graphics, Boulder, CO).

The traditional conflict between fan and umpire was at fever pitch in this June 1944 scene as American League umpire Bill Summers traded epithets with a Cleveland Indians fan (Transcendental Graphics, Boulder, CO).

ball's status, President Roosevelt gave the game a go-ahead, expressing the view that the game was a morale-booster and that it should continue operating. However, FDR indicated there would be no special concessions granted baseball, such as draft deferments for players or transportation privileges. As a result, spring training camps were held near team's home cities. But the major leagues continued to operate through the war largely because the fans supported the game in sufficient numbers.

The call-up of players by the military increased rapidly in 1942 and intensified for the next two years. The Yankees and Cardinals won pennants in 1942 and 1943 on the strength of the relatively large number of able players remaining in their farm systems but only the Cards had the manpower to repeat in 1944. By that season, there was a 60 percent reduction in player personnel from the previous season. The key determinant had become the availability of players classified 4-F (physically unfit for military duty) or deferred for other reasons. As able players left for the service, draft rejects, Latin American players, and players too old or too young to be called up were at a premium. Still, the fans ignored on-the-field deficiencies as attendance increased to then-record levels in 1944–45 after slipping the previous two years.

Fans agreed there was a significantly lower level of play during the 1942–1945 seasons. But they had few complaints, hungry as they were for baseball and with higher defense-related wages to buy tickets. Fans learned to accept the deficiencies of wartime baseball along with lowered quality in other aspects of their daily lives. And they still had fun at games. David Voigt wrote:

> Often gaiety was mingled with little acts of wartime coverage. At Wrigley Field in 1945, a reporter noted the brave humor of crippled soldiers who shouted, "No foul balls this way." Such sights and sounds were sobering, but were balanced by opportunities for the "innocent flirting" of soldiers

The long wait for a limited number of bleacher seats before the first game of the 1946 World Series finds these hardy bleacher fans waiting patiently at Sportsman's Park in St. Louis (Steve Milman).

Cardinals fans bundle together during a drizzle before gates are opened before the first game of the 1944 World Series (Steve Milman).

and young ladies.... Some observers noted less yelling, but one reporter insisted that ladies made up for it by learning to whistle male-style with their fingers in their mouths.... Since violent former fans found themselves in military uniform alongside players, it was inevitable that some player [in the military] would confront a former heckler.... [Phillies outfielder] Morrie Arnovich met the fan who once had hit him in the face with a hot dog complete with mustard and relish. Although Arnovich had vowed to maim his tormentor, their common plight made them friends instead.

The 4-F–laden Cubs and the Tigers played the 1945 World Series in what many fans considered the worst series ever. The Cubs proved to be a worse team than the Tigers who won the series, led by Hank Greenberg, newly released from the service. Before the first game, writers sat in the press box trying to predict the winner. Veteran Chicago writer Warren Brown refused to join the discussion. He looked down at the nondescript group of players warming up and said, "I'm not doing any predicting. I don't think either team can win."

The fans felt somewhat the same. With the war just over, following the dropping of two atomic bombs on Japan in August 1945, baseball fans were more interested in 1946, the first postwar season. And so with the war over, the fans eagerly awaited the new season. In the words of a popular song of the time, the "lights [had] come on again all over the world."

4

Post-World War II Expansion

With the war over, baseball was back in full swing in 1946. With the established players back in uniform, fans followed the intense competition for the remaining roster spots. Teams brought the largest squads in memory to spring training camps. Several clubs had as many as 25 pitchers in camp, and the Philadelphia Phillies looked over 30 pitchers. A number of teams had more than 15 infielders fighting for a roster spot, and the Detroit Tigers had 19 outfielders in camp. Several teams had as many as 60 aspirants for their 25-player rosters.

The hectic spring activity was further intensified by a new factor — the emergence of the Mexican League, an "outlaw" league not subject to regulations applied to teams and leagues in "organized" baseball. Operated by wealthy Mexican customs broker Jorge Pasquel and his brother Bernardo, the Mexican League approached a number of major leaguers to induce them to jump to teams in Mexico. The salaries offered were well in excess of those paid in the States and several players took the bait and went to Mexico — most notably Cardinals pitcher Max Lanier, Giants star reliever Ace Adams, and catcher Mickey Owen. But the Pasquels were unable to snag Cardinals superstar Stan Musial, the biggest potential catch of them all. After a few months, the threat to the major leagues presented by the Mexican League faded and baseball fans rejoiced as major league baseball returned to its pre–World War II mode.

In retrospect, the 1946 season provided a welcome but short-lived return to the "normal" game baseball fans had missed through the war. DiMaggio, Williams, Feller, and the other familiar stars resumed their great careers and the fans returned to major league stadiums in record numbers. But the game was shaken to its roots in 1947 by two profound developments — the color line was broken by Jackie Robinson's historic entrance into the Brooklyn Dodgers lineup, and player unions became an irreversible element of the major league scene.

The postwar changes in baseball reflected massive adjustments taking place in the United States. There were demands for the eradication of racial inequalities of which Robinson's appearance was baseball's first step in righting a century-old injustice. Robinson's herculean achievement in establishing the proper place of African-Americans in major league baseball, supplemented by Larry Doby's emergence later in the season as an American League star, is one of baseball's and the nation's enduring postwar milestones. The numbers of black players accelerated to well over 100 players by the end of the 1960s.

The tremendous increase in economic prosperity during and after World War II and the resulting increase in Americans' disposable income available for recreation led to record attendance and club revenues. The increased union activity in the nation reflected workers' desire to claim their share of the expanding economic pie. As a result, the unionization of the players beginning in 1947 mirrored the aspirations of all U.S. workers to improve their economic lot.

Unlike the failure of the short-lived Players League in 1890, this time the baseball union was here to stay. At the time baseball fans seemed largely oblivious to the existence and implications of the new baseball union. But in the decades to come, fans would become well aware of the impact of the players union as players moved from club to club and gained progressively higher salaries under contract changes put in place by the union.

The commercial development of television in the late 1950s was another profound factor in baseball economics and communications, its effects still being felt more than a half century later. The astronomical television-related profits experienced by wealthier teams relative to teams representing smaller areas has intensified concerns that many clubs are hopelessly outgunned in competing with teams with much larger TV contracts. And, of course, television revenues are a main reason for the out-of-sight salaries paid modern players. These developments could not have been predicted in the 1960s.

David Q. Voigt discussed the impact on the baseball fan of increased postwar leisure time. He wrote:

> With working hours in 1950 averaging just under 41 a week, most of the 150 million Americans enjoyed weekends free from work.... With half of the population now clustered in metropolitan areas, Americans were spending $11.3 billion a year on ... [diverse] leisure pastimes.... Television viewing became the most popular outlet.... Thus, the 1950s saw the marriage of television and [baseball].

Major league baseball's income from television rights rose to more than $20 million a year by 1950 before falling below that level for several years as other sports became more competitive for TV time. Major league teams received significant television revenue even during this period but many fans in minor league communities saw their teams forced out of business. Led by innovative baseball entrepreneurs, notably Bill Veeck, baseball teams instituted a variety of marketing schemes utilizing television to stimulate attendance.

Baseball owners viewed with keen interest the increased population shifts to the West after World War II. St. Louis was the farthest western major league city in the earlier '50s. In 1953 the Braves became the first franchise to move during baseball's modern era, shifting from Boston to Milwaukee. The next year saw the habitually downtrodden St. Louis Browns move to Baltimore and in 1955, with Connie Mack long out of the picture, the Athletics abandoned Philadelphia and set up operations in Kansas City.

The biggest surprise of all came in 1957 when the Dodgers left Brooklyn and moved to Los Angeles. At the same time, the once-proud Giants moved from Manhattan to San Francisco. To the present day, many pre–1958 Dodgers and Giants fans have not regained the deep attachment to the game they knew before their favorites departed for California. From 1953 to 1958, five old-line franchises shook loose from their traditional surroundings, leaving many local baseball enthusiasts disillusioned and disgusted. In the final analysis, many fans had to recognize an inescapable fact — there is no sentiment in baseball when money is involved.

Bill James provided a balanced perspective on the franchise shifts of the 1950s:

> People were afraid to go to ball games [because of decaying slums, rising crime rates, and poor transportation].... The true story of baseball in the 1950s is not a story about greedy men who betrayed the trust of loyal rooters and brought the golden age of sport crashing down as they foraged for even greener pastures. It is a story about fear and urban decay, about a panic-stricken industry scrambling for survival. It is a story about old ballparks that had come to symbolize the rotting neighborhoods in which they rested.

Despite these profound off-the-field changes, baseball fans witnessed a high level of competition and achievement on the field after World War II. In 1946, the St. Louis Cardinals finished the regular season dead even with the Brooklyn Dodgers and the Cards won a best-of-three playoff series to win the pennant. The World Series between the Cards and the Red Sox was billed as a contest between superstars Stan Musial and Ted Williams. But diminutive Cards lefthander Harry "The Cat" Brecheen stole the show, winning three games. His last win came in the game fans remember best for Enos Slaughter's dramatic dash for home from first base to score the winning run for the Cardinals in the deciding seventh game.

The year 1947 is remembered, in addition to Jackie Robinson's entrance into the majors, for Leo Durocher's year's suspension for involving himself with unsavory people, and for two memorable plays in the seven-game World Series between the Bucky Harris-managed Yankees and the Dodgers. The Dodgers tied the series 2–2 in a remarkable game in which Yankees righthander Bill Bevens held the Dodgers hitless through 8⅔ innings only to lose the game 2–1 on Harry "Cookie" Lavagetto's last-ditch two-run double. Later in the series, Yankee Stadium rocked as Dodgers substitute left fielder Al Gionfriddo made a remarkable catch of a long drive by Joe DiMaggio near the Yankees bullpen fence 415 feet from the plate. Fans were struck by the unusual sight of the normally impassive DiMaggio kicking the dirt near second base in his frustration.

The Indians won the 1948 Worlds Championship over the Boston Braves in a more routine six-game series. And then came the remarkable era of the inimitable Casey Stengel. After a career in which Stengel had filled every baseball role except that of a successful major league manager, the colorful Casey was hired by Yankees general manager George Weiss to replace the efficient but less demonstrative Bucky Harris. Stengel's appointment was announced after the 1948 World Series to a skeptical gathering of New York writers.

In addition to his confusing doubletalk and clownish mannerisms, Stengel was criticized for his unorthodox managing strategies. As Robert W. Creamer described it:

> Casey introduced a radical departure in spring training procedures that didn't sit too well at first. He split the squad into several groups and had different coaches [and veteran players] work with each group: an infield specialist with infielders [and so on].... That sort of seminar approach to training is fairly standard today, but it wasn't back then.

Stengel himself was one of the primary instructors. He loved to tell a story concerning Mickey Mantle's rookie season in 1951. The Yankees played the Dodgers in Ebbets Field in the final exhibition games before that season opened. Mantle had never been in Brooklyn before and Stengel, who had played the outfield in Ebbets Field for the Dodgers 40 years before, instructed Mickey on playing the outfield in that ballpark. Stengel reported later, "Mickey listened to me but I could tell he didn't really believe I knew the park because he seemed surprised, asking me, 'You played here?'" The grizzled Stengel chuckled and cracked, "The kid must have thought I was born old and wrinkled."

Stengel also was one of the earliest managers to platoon his players on a daily basis. He made exquisite use of all of his players, depending upon who was pitching and what the game situation required. Stengel was a master at deploying his players in a way calculated to maximize their playing strengths and minimizing their weaknesses. He was a fan favorite but he was not beloved by all of his players. Stengel had the ability of making his reserves feel equally important to team victory as his starting players.

The remarkable Casey Stengel era as Yankees manager began in 1949 and the Yankees put together a string of five Worlds Championships, a feat never accomplished before. In 1949, the Yanks held off the Red Sox with two close wins to end the season, and then defeated the Dodgers handily in the series. The 1950 Yankees won the pennant with five straight wins near the end of the season. Then they polished off the "Whiz Kids" Phillies in the World Series in four straight games.

The year 1951 was the rookie year of two brilliant New York center fielders, Mantle and the Giants' Willie Mays. The Yankees won their third straight pennant largely on the strength of an improved (24 shutouts) pitching staff. But this was the year of the Giants' "Miracle Under Coogan's Bluff" season, when the Giants tied the Dodgers for the pennant at the end of the regular season. The Polo Grounders won the pennant playoff on Bobby Thomson's historic, come-from-behind home run in the bottom of the ninth. The Yankees trumped that achievement by overpowering the emotionally drained Giants in a six-game series. Stengel's club fought off the Indians in a close race in 1952, then outlasted the Dodgers to win a seven-game series.

The 1954 Yankee club was Stengel's strongest, winning 103 games. But manager Al Lopez's Cleveland Indians were even better, winning a record 111 games. Incredibly, the seemingly invincible Indians lost the World Series in four straight games to Leo Durocher's New York Giants. Fans remember the Series for Willie Mays' signature over-the-shoulder catch of a 440-foot drive by Vic Wertz, cutting short a first-game Cleveland rally. Knowledgeable fans recognized that equally impressive as the catch was Mays' magnificent throw to the infield holding the runners in check before his momentum sent him sprawling on the outfield grass.

Stengel's Yankees rebounded with four consecutive pennant wins from 1955 through 1958. His rebuilt teams were the class of the American League, yet the Yankees won only two of these four seven-game World

Series. In 1955, less than two seasons before the Dodgers left Brooklyn, the ecstatic Dodgers fans saw their heroes defeat the hated Yankees in a series highlighted by Dodgers left fielder Sandy Amoros's rally-killing catch of a Yogi Berra drive in the deciding game.

The Yankees rebounded with a smashing pennant win over the Indians in 1956, sparked by Mantle's Triple Crown year — a .353 average, 52 home runs, and 130 RBIs. The series with the powerful Dodgers featured Yankees right-hander Don Larsen's perfect-game masterpiece after a well-publicized night on the town. The Dodgers kept their rooters' hopes alive by coming back to square the series at three games before the Yanks won the clincher convincingly.

The Yankees won the 1957 pennant easily but lost to the Milwaukee Braves in another seven-game series as Braves right-hander Lou Burdette won three games, two of them shutouts. Stengel's club repeated with another easy pennant win the next year but it was a different story in their second straight seven-game series with Milwaukee. Down 3–1 in games, the Yanks thrilled their fans, fighting back as right-hander Bob Turley won a shutout and then saved the sixth game. In the decisive seventh game, the Yanks attacked Burdette with a four-run burst in the eighth inning to put the game out of reach. Stengel had won his seventh and final World Championship.

The year 1961 saw the American League expand from its long-standing eight teams to a 10-team circuit. Calvin Griffith moved the Washington Senators to Minneapolis where they became the Minnesota Twins. Washington fans at least received a consolation prize, an expansion club also called the Senators. California fans had the new Los Angeles Angels to root for.

The National League expanded to 10 teams in 1962, with New York Mets and Houston Colt .45s (now Astros) fans having teams to call their own. The fans' enthusiasm for the new clubs was tempered by the handicaps facing their new favorites. Each new team paid a sizeable fee to join the league and then had to pick players from an expansion draft. The available players were the 15 most expendable spares from each established team's 40-man roster.

Baseball's 10-club format continued through 1968. Two years before that, the Milwaukee Braves moved to Atlanta to take advantage of a new, low-rent, publicly owned stadium. And the Kansas City club transferred operations to Oakland for the 1968 campaign. Another big change came in 1969 when both leagues expanded to 12 teams, a six-team Eastern Division and a six-team Western Division. The American League accepted the Seattle Pilots and the Kansas City Royals, and the Montreal Expos and San Diego Padres joined the National League.

The league schedules were expanded to 162 games from the long-standing 154-game schedules with the creation of the 12-team leagues. Fans had to adjust to new intra-league setups and schedule changes. Under the divisional system, each league was divided into two divisions with the winners of each division playing for the league championship. The extended regular season, the playoffs, and then the World Series stretched the season out well into late October.

It was like old times for the Yankees fans during the first half of the 1960s. Stengel won his last pennant in 1960 but he made the mistake of turning 71 during the season and losing a seven-game World Series to the Pirates on Pittsburgh second baseman Bill Mazeroski's dramatic ninth-inning home run in the last game. Both Stengel and George Weiss were fired unceremoniously after the season because, as Stengel put it, "They think we're too old."

Ralph Houk replaced Stengel and the Yankees did not miss a beat. They won the 1961 pennant easily, powered by Roger Maris's record-breaking (and asterisk-producing) 61 homers and Mantle's 54 blasts, and overpowered the Cincinnati Reds in a five-game World Series. Houk's club won again in 1962 and eked out a win over the San Francisco Giants in an exciting seven-game series. The Bombers won the deciding series game 1–0 when, with two out in the bottom of the ninth and men on second and third, Willie McCovey smoked right-hander Ralph Terry's pitch directly at Yankees second baseman Bobby Richardson for the final out.

Houk won his third straight pennant in 1963 but lost the series to the Dodgers in four straight games. The Yankees' hitters were immobilized by the superb pitching of Sandy Koufax, Johnny Podres, and Don Drysdale. Yogi Berra, succeeding Houk in 1964, managed the Bombers to a fourth straight pennant, but the Yankees lost a seven-game series to the Cardinals. Berra was fired the day after the series ended by CBS, which had purchased the Yankees in August. The reasons for Berra's dismissal after leading his club to a pennant were never clearly explained to the fans.

There was irony in the purchase of the Yankees by a major broadcasting corporation. A few years earlier, as the Yankees ran roughshod over other American League teams, the popular wisecrack was "Rooting for the Yankees is like rooting for U.S. Steel." There was added irony as the Yankees became also-rans immediately after the corporate purchase. The Bombers would not become a truly competitive team again until a decade later, after a syndicate headed by George Steinbrenner purchased the team from CBS.

Fans in other American League cities rejoiced over the demise of the Yankees and in the leadership of their favorite teams. With the hated Yankees in a tailspin, the leadership role in the American League devolved among the Twins, the Orioles, the Red Sox, and the Tigers. Fan interest was stimulated around the American League.

The amateur free agent draft instituted in 1965 triggered an important change in player recruiting. Wealthier teams like the Yankees, Dodgers, and Cardinals had been consistently successful in acquiring top prospects for their farm teams. The availability of free agents to all teams had the effect of establishing a more competitive balance between teams and making more likely dramatic improvements in teams successful in drafting young players who would not have been available before the draft was instituted.

The dominant National League teams in the 1960s were the Dodgers, Giants, and Cardinals. The Dodgers and Giants dueled all of the 1962 season, the Dodgers relying upon the brilliant pitching duo of Koufax and Drysdale and the Giants on right-hander Jack Sanford and powerful hitting by Orlando Cepeda, Felipe Alou, the still incandescent Willie Mays, and Harvey Kuenn. The teams were in a tie after 162 games, and in the best-of-three playoff, it was 1951 revisited as the Giants came from behind to pull out the third and deciding game.

In response to the explosive offenses in 1961 and 1962, Baseball Commissioner Ford Frick took steps to help out the pitchers. He convinced club owners to expand the strike zone for 1963 to the top of the armpit to the bottom of the knee—dimensions used before 1950. Predictably, from 1962 to 1968, American League batting averages dropped from .255 to .230, strikeouts increased from 8,535 to 9,641, walks dropped from 5,671 to 4,881, runs scored dropped from 7,183 to 5,532, home runs decreased from 1,552 to 1,104, and the league on base percentage dropped from .328 to .299. National League averages showed the same offensive downtrend.

The Cardinals and the Dodgers between them captured the next six pennants. The Dodgers edged out the Cards in 1963. In that low-scoring year, the Dodgers hit a mere .251 as Los Angeles outfielder Tommy Davis led the league with a modest .326 average and shortstop Maury Wills stole a league-leading 40 bases. But the key was the pitching staff's excellence (2.85 ERA), led by the brilliant Sandy Koufax, who had 25 wins and a sparkling 1.88 ERA. In a four-game World Series sweep of the Yankees, Dodgers pitchers dominated, holding the New Yorkers to a .171 average as the victorious Dodgers averaged a pallid .214.

Manager Walt Alston's weak-hitting Dodgers slipped all the way down to sixth place in 1964 despite having the best pitching in the league. This race still produces heartburn in older Phillies fans. Manager Gene Mauch's Phils, leading the league by 6½ games with 12 games left, lost 10 straight games to blow the pennant to the Cardinals by one game. The Cardinals' surprise win precipitated a bizarre managing situation. The Yanks, unsatisfied with rookie manager Yogi Berra, retained Berra for the rest of the 1964 season but signed Cardinals manager Johnny Keane in midseason to manage the Yanks in 1965. To complicate matters, the Cards, led by their lame-duck manager, met and defeated the Yanks in a seven-game World Series.

Keane's unusual departure worked out poorly for both teams in 1965. The World Champion Cardinals fell to seventh place and the Yankees slipped to sixth place. And who replaced the Cardinals? None other than the powder puff, .245 hitting Dodgers, without a single .300 hitter, but with their customary superb pitching staff led by Koufax's 26 wins and Drysdale's 23 victories.

Dodgers fans supported their heroes royally as evidenced by the club's home attendance which had exceeded 2 million in every season since the Dodgers moved to Los Angeles in 1958. Koufax and Drysdale, realizing their contribution to the Dodgers' success, conducted a successful joint holdout to force the club to reward them. It was never clear whether or not Dodgers fans favored the pitchers' bargaining tactics. Most likely, the fans were largely oblivious, their only interest being the continued success of the Dodgers. And Koufax delivered for the Dodgers and their fans in 1966 with 27 victories and a 1.73 ERA, leading the perennially weak-hitting club to a close pennant win over the second-place Giants. But even Koufax and Drysdale, who had a mediocre year, were unable to hold off the Baltimore Orioles, who steamrollered the Dodgers with four straight series wins.

After the 1966 season, Koufax was forced to retire prematurely with chronic arthritis in his pitching arm. With his loss, the Dodgers floundered and the Cardinals came on strong to win pennants easily the next two years. Cards star right-hander Bob Gibson returned from an injury-hampered 1967 season to win three superbly pitched complete games as the Cards defeated the Red Sox in a seven-game series, despite the heroics of Sox right-hander Jim Lonborg.

Enthralled by a healthy Bob Gibson's 22 wins and 13 shutouts and outfielder Lou Brock's league-leading 62 steals, St. Louis Cardinals fans watched their heroes win the 1968 pennant easily despite a .249 club batting average in a year when National League hitters averaged .243. Gibson fanned a record 35 hitters in the World Series against Detroit but he was trumped by left-hander Mickey Lolich who won his third game of the seven-game series. The ultimate in this low scoring era came when Red Sox left-fielder Carl Yastrzemski led the American League in 1968 with a .301 average.

The first year in which both leagues operated under the new 12-team format was 1969. Baseball fans took readily to the new format despite a year in which none of the four divisions, two in each league, provided a close race. In that first expansion year, the well-balanced Baltimore Orioles won the pennant, powered by first baseman Boog Powell and outfielder Frank Robinson and with the league's best pitching staff. The underdog "Amazin' Mets" rewarded their fans' impassioned cries of "Let's go, Mets!" by taking the World Series from the Orioles, winning the last four games of the series.

The new teams began operations in 1969 at a severe competitive disadvantage in comparison with the established teams. In the National League, the new Montreal Expos and San Diego Padres remained mired in the lower echelons of their divisions for 10 seasons. Seattle's new Pilots finished last in 1969 and the bankrupt club was sold to a Milwaukee group. The most successful new franchise was the Kansas City Royals, finishing fourth in their first season, second in their third campaign, and winning four division titles and a league championship over the next 10 seasons.

Bill James wrote about increased fan interest in the 1960s:

> Three things happened to make baseball much more competitive by 1970 than it ever had been before. One was the collapse of the Yankee dynasty [1965], which opened the American League up to the kind of competition the National League had periodically enjoyed. The second was the amateur free agent draft ... which began in 1965. The third was expansion, which made the races more competitive simply because a twelve-team league is inherently more difficult to dominate than an eight-team circuit.

The year 1970 was not remembered for close division or pennant races, but for the World Series between Baltimore and Cincinnati won by the Orioles in five games. This was the "Brooks Robinson "Series as Robinson thrilled the fans time after time with miraculous stops and throws at third base and, for good measure, led his team offensively with six RBI and a .429 batting average. The first close division race of the decade came the following year when the Giants nosed out the Dodgers for the division by a game. But the Giants were stopped in their tracks after that, losing the pennant playoff to the Pirates. Pittsburgh, sparked by the brilliant Roberto Clemente, went on to defeat the Orioles in a seven-game World Series.

In 1972, Cincinnati's "Big Red Machine," featuring catcher Johnny Bench, outfielder Pete Rose, second baseman Joe Morgan, and first baseman Tony Perez, defeated the Pirates to win the National League pennant.

They lost to Oakland in a magnificent seven-game World Series in which six of the games were decided by a single run. Journeyman Athletics catcher-first baseman Gene Tenace surprised fans by driving in nine of the A's 16 runs as right-hander Jim "Catfish" Hunter and relief ace Rollie Fingers excelled. As 1972 ended, baseball fans mourned the tragic death of Roberto Clemente in a plane crash on New Year's Eve on a mercy flight to aid earthquake victims in Nicaragua.

National League attendance had far exceeded American League attendance for several years and, after the 1972 season, American League owners took a unilateral step to juice up their offenses and thereby attain attendance parity; they installed the designated hitter. Used successfully in the minor leagues, the DH allows a designated hitter to bat in place of the pitcher in the batting order. The DH has successfully increased the offense of American league teams, increasing the league batting average from .239 in 1972 to .259 the following year. Since that time, American League batting averages have consistently exceeded the National League's. By 1977, the fifth year after the DH was installed, American League attendance finally drew even with that of the National League. Ignoring any other factors improving attendance, the DH has achieved its major purpose.

The availability of a DH provides the American League teams with an additional offensive specialist compared with National League teams. However, this has not been a significant factor in World Series competition. In the first eight years the DH was used in World Series (1973–1980), each league won four times and each league's representatives won 24 games. Apparently the DH has not given the American League any competitive advantage in head-to-head competition.

The National League has pleased many fans by continuing to resist employing the DH. Baseball purists decry the reduced strategy involved when the DH is used and concern has been expressed that the DH distorts comparisons of past and present players' careers by permitting aging sluggers to prolong their careers after they are unable to field a position satisfactorily. Other fans are pleased with the DH because it enhances offensive play. From 1973 through 1985 the DH has been used in alternate World Series. Since that time, the DH has been used only in World Series games played in American League parks. Thirty years after its employment in the American League, fan sentiment remains split on using the DH, and there is no sign that the American League will abandon the DH or that the National League will consider adopting the controversial rule.

The prices fans paid for attending a ballgame were raised by large increases in player salaries in the 1970s. The players union was strengthened immeasurably during the 1970s and players' salaries soared. Players were paid an average of $34,000 in 1970 but the average salary increased each year until it reached $185,000 in 1980. The effective leadership of Players Association director Marvin Miller was the primary factor in the vast improvement in player status. Miller threatened the owners with a strike in 1969 and was able to negotiate a basic agreement leading to increases in players' minimum salaries and their pension fund, and gaining the right for player salaries to be negotiated by their agents.

When negotiations for a new basic agreement stalled in 1972, the players staged a 13-day strike. As a result, players gained the right to have their salary demands decided by an arbitrator. This was the key to the ensuing dramatic salary increases. Three years later professional arbitrator Peter Seitz delivered the deciding vote in a landmark case involving Dodgers pitcher Andy Messersmith. He had refused to sign his 1975 contract and, after playing that season under his 1974 contract, claimed his free agency. The decision bypassed the longstanding reserve clause and led to an agreement providing for free agency to players after six years of major league service.

Powerful Oakland Athletics teams won three straight pennants beginning in 1972. In 1975, the Red Sox dethroned the A's by defeating them in three straight games in the American League championship series, setting up a monumental, seven-game World Series against the Reds. Five of the series games were won by a single run, and two of those came on sudden-death rallies in extra innings. Almost every game was a seesaw affair, with the games retied or the lead reversed 13 times. In six of the seven games the winning team came from behind.

With the Reds leading three games to two, the sixth game was the contest most fans remember. It was played under almost continuous tension as one team, then the other, appeared to have the game in hand only to fall back. The Sox were losing 6–3 in the bottom of the seventh when unsung utility outfielder Bernie Carbo tied the tense, nip-and-tuck game with a pinch-hit three-run homer. Three Red Sox relievers held the Reds in check through the top of the 12th. Pete Rose, leading off the top of the 12th turned to catcher Carlton Fisk and said excitedly, "This is some kind of game, isn't it?"

Fisk led off the Boston half with a drive down the left field line. The transfixed Fenway Park crowd, and millions of television viewers, watched Fisk as he stood on the first base line, waving at the ball and frantically applying all the body English he could to keep his drive fair. The ball landed barely in fair territory and the hysterical home team crowd roared for several minutes at the dramatic end to the game. To this day, the vision of

Fisk waving his home run fair is vivid in many fans' memory. But in an anticlimax, the Red Sox lost the series the next day.

The power-packed Big Red Machine overpowered the resurgent Yankees in four straight games in the 1976 World Series. But the Reds failed to win the pennant the next year while the Billy Martin-managed Yankees repeated. They played the Dodgers in a series dominated by outfielder Reggie Jackson as he gained the sobriquet "Mr. October." As the Yankees clinched a series win, Jackson thrilled Yankee Stadium fans with his third, fourth, and fifth home runs of the Series, all hit on successive pitches.

The American League expanded to 14 teams in 1977, adding the Seattle Mariners and the Toronto Blue Jays. The new Seattle entry came in response to lawsuits filed by Seattle business interests and local fans after the Seattle Pilots were forced out of the American League following the 1970 season. The inclusion of the Blue Jays, placed in the Eastern Division with Seattle in the Western Division, balanced out the two American League Divisions at seven in each division. The National League remained with six teams in each division.

The Yankees capped off a tumultuous 1977 regular season with a third-straight six-game series victory, again over the Dodgers. Trailing the Red Sox in midseason, George Steinbrenner fired the volatile Billy Martin and replaced him with easygoing Bob Lemon. The Yanks fought back to gain a tie with the Red Sox for the division title and force a sudden-death playoff game. In a game which still drives some Boston fans into a deep depression, Yankees shortstop Bucky Dent, a .247 hitter with a modest eight home runs that season, homered over the 315-foot "Green Monster" left field wall to drive in the winning run. Reggie Jackson characteristically led the Yankees to a World Series win over the Dodgers with five homers and eight RBI.

The decade ended with manager Chuck Tanner leading his Pirates to a seven-game World Series win over Earl Weaver's Orioles. The Pirates were sparked by first baseman Willie Stargell, the much-loved orchestrator of the club's "We are family" approach to the game. Down three games to one, the Pirates roared back to win three straight games and finish off the decade in style.

The increase in minority group players continued during the 1970s. By 1974, black players amounted to 26 percent of all major leaguers although the percentage dropped to 20 percent by the end of the decade. By that time, 10 percent of major leaguers were of Hispanic descent, an early indication of the future increase in players representing that ethnic group in the years to follow.

The 1970s saw the construction of nine new ballparks, five in the

National League and four in the American League, plus a major refurbishing of Yankee Stadium. The new locations were built to benefit fans by providing more comfortable seating and easier parking and to lower maintenance costs. Nevertheless, many fans longed for the old, idiosyncratic ballparks, their sites now converted to housing developments and industrial sites.

The postwar and expansion periods witnessed profound changes in players' backgrounds, playing styles, and in the structure of the game. But most important, the game's essential beauty and unpredictability remained unchanged as the '70s passed into history.

5

Since Then

The 1980s was the first full decade of the free agent era. Conventional wisdom among fans and writers held that free agency would drastically reduce the future competitive balance between teams as players presumably would be drawn inevitably to the wealthier clubs. However, this did not prove to be the case, at least in the short run. On the contrary, the '90s including some extremely competitive years, was a decade of high achievement by the small-market teams. The Cardinals won three pennants. And two pennants were won by both the Kansas City Royals and the Oakland Athletics, and the Milwaukee Brewers and Minnesota Twins each took one flag.

The labor contract between the owners and players expired on December 31, 1979, and baseball fans saw ominous signs that the new decade would begin with another players strike. This could precipitate a more serious confrontation than the 1972 strike and perhaps result in one of the magnitude of the 1890 impasse which gave rise to the Players League. The underlying issue was the redraft concession which owners felt would undercut the reserve clause.

The redraft provision would permit a player to enter the free market and the club with which he signed would be required to provide his former club with a draft choice. This would have the effect of freeing players to move unimpeded and with a resultant increase in players' salaries. But the 1980 season began on schedule and the full season was completed after conferees narrowly avoided a last-minute work stoppage in late May.

Failure to agree on the new work agreement led the players to walk off their jobs for 50 days at the height of the 1981 season. At this point, even the most avid fans (especially those to whom comparability of season-to-season statistics is a near religion) were disgusted with the game's inability to solve its problems fairly and quickly and avoid a strike. Influenced by newspaper stories, a slight majority of the fans favored the players. A *New York Times*/CBS poll indicated that younger, poorer, less-educated fans supported the players while the owners' position was favored by older and wealthier fans. About a third of those polled either resented both sides equally or did not care how the strike played out.

There were other problems hurting the game in the fans' eyes. The drug problem faced by the nation was reflected in the increased numbers of players found to be using drugs. And late in the '80s, the Pete Rose gambling matter came to light. Commissioner Bart Giamatti's expulsion of Rose was followed by Giamatti's sudden death. And there were other disasters, most notably the 1994 season when the players struck on August 12, wiping out the rest of the regular season, the playoffs, and the World Series. Looking back, it is a testimony to the game's continuing appeal that it survived the series of unhappy events. John Thorn commented on the 1994 strike:

> As fans, we were presented with a dilemma: to side with the players, who went on strike hoping to extend their gains of the two previous decades. Or to side with the owners, who stood fast in insisting upon a balance between costs and revenues? As fans, we tried to side with the game of baseball, and wish that its most intense contests would soon reconvene to the field of play.

The year 1980 was a great one for Phillies fans as their favorites won their fourth division title in the last five years and won the worlds championship over the Kansas City Royals. The season featured brilliant seasons by free-agent Pete Rose and future Hall of Famers third baseman Mike Schmidt and lefthander Steve Carlton. This was an especially gratifying season for the local fans as the Phils had been the only one of the original 16 major league franchises never to have won a World Series.

It was also a fan-pleasing year of first-rate performances. George Brett hit .390 and two other players hit over .340. Mike Schmidt hit a then-outstanding 48 home runs. Led by Rickey Henderson's 100 stolen bases, speedsters Ron LeFlore and Omar Moreno exceeded 96 steals. And there were strong pitching performances during the season as Steve Stone won 25 games, one more than Steve Carlton, who won his third Cy Young award.

With the 1981 season shortened by 50 days because of the players strike, Commissioner Bowie Kuhn pushed a plan to salvage what he could of the disastrous season. But the plan had serious faults easily detected by the fans, faults which could easily taint the integrity of the pennant race.

5. Since Then

Under the plan the four prestrike leaders were considered the first-half winners who competed against the four winners of the poststrike games for regular season honors. The problem was that none of the first-half winners were eligible to repeat, thereby removing any incentive that any first-half winner had for playing well in the second half except against stronger teams most likely to be encountered in the postseason. Fans also expressed concern that a team which had played poorly in the first half might win the second half and unfairly remain in the running to compete for final honors.

Predictably, angry fans stayed away in droves when play resumed. There were close second-half races in each division, but attendance slumped for 17 of the 26 major league teams. The combination of the reduced playing schedule and the fans' unhappines resulted in a drop in major league attendance in 1982 of some 16.5 million compared with 1981 figures. Eventually the pennant-winning Yankees and Dodgers met in the World Series and the Dodgers won 4–2. Sportswriter Red Smith summed up the dismal year as "baseball's dishonest season."

Baseball rebounded smartly over the next several years. The ever-forgiving fans returned to the ballpark in the same volumes as in prestrike days and in increasing volume later in the '80s. And owners and players prospered in part because of healthy attendance but even more from increasing television revenues. But drug abuse became an increasingly serious problem, and the Players Association admitted that a significant percent of major league players might be drug abusers. In 1983 three Kansas City players were jailed as convicted users and other players were suspended or traded because of involvement with drugs. Fans were shocked again two years later when 17 players were named as drug users during two court trials in Pittsburgh.

No team dominated the game over the rest of the '80s. But there were several noteworthy individual achievements to thrill the fans. Rickey Henderson set a new stolen base record with his remarkable 130 stolen bases in 1982. Cincinnati Reds player-manager Pete Rose (reinstalled as a Reds player the year before to accomplish the feat while with the Reds) obtained hit no. 4,192 on September 11, 1985, to break Ty Cobb's record. Knuckleballer Phil Niekro, Gaylord Perry, Don Sutton, and Tom Seaver each won game no. 300. Orel Hershiser broke Don Drysdale's major league record with his 59 consecutive scoreless innings on September 28, 1988.

On the negative side, Baltimore fans moaned as the Orioles lost 21 consecutive games on April 28, 1988, to break the major league record shared by the 1906 Red Sox and the 1916 and 1943 Athletics. Red Sox first baseman Bill Buckner gave his club's franchise-long jinx a new dimension on October 25, 1986, when he permitted a ground ball to go through his legs as the Mets came from behind to pull out a playoff game win. And Bart Giamatti, former president of Yale University and of the National League, became the game's seventh commissioner on September 8, 1988.

The '80s ended on a somber note. In August 1989 Commissioner Giamatti banned Pete Rose from baseball for Rose's alleged gambling on major league games. Then Giamatti died suddenly a few days later. A judge issued a finding of collusion by the owners to undermine the free agent market. And the World Series sweep of the Athletics over the Giants was delayed for 11 days after an earthquake struck the San Francisco area before the start of Game 3.

Again contrary to the expectations of fans, free agency had no discernible impact on the competitive state of major league baseball during the first half of the 1990s. None of the big-market teams (Yankees, Mets, Red Sox, Cubs, White Sox, or Dodgers) won a pennant from 1990 through 1995, although the Yankees, White Sox, and Dodgers were leading their divisions when the 1994 season was aborted with nearly 50 regular season games remaining. The well-run Atlanta Braves, with a moderate salary structure, was the most consistently winning team during the first six years of the '90s. But in 1996, the high-salaried Yankees broke through and won the World Series from the Braves.

Yankee fans have seen their favorites consistently been the team to beat since then. One exception came in 1997, when the Florida Marlins won a surprise worlds championship. After the 1996 season, the Marlins hired established manager Jim Leyland and, within a three-week period, signed six free agents including high-priced outfielders Bobby Bonilla and Moises Alou. The downtrodden Florida fans went crazy over their wild-card Marlins as they fought their way to the National League pennant and a seven-game World Series win over the Indians.

Many older Yankees fans compared the 1998 Bombers to the fabled 1927 "Murderers Row" club and the 1936 Yankees, who finished 19½ games ahead of the second-place Tigers. Joe Torre's 1998 team broke the American League record with 114 wins in the regular season, and finished the post season in style with seven straight wins, the last three games of their championship series with the Indians and a four-game World Series win over the San Diego Padres. The Yankees won the next two World Series to close out the decade with three consecutive worlds championships.

The Yankees' 2000 series win over the Mets was a baseball fan's delight even though it lasted for only five closely played games. The American Leaguers won the first game in 12 innings but the second game was the one fans would remember. In the opening inning at Yankee Stadium, Mets

5. Since Then

catcher Mike Piazza stood in against right-hander Roger Clemens. The big Texan characteristically put in his unmistakable claim on the inside corner of the plate by throwing two high and tight pitches to the slugging Piazza, who stared out angrily at Clemens. Piazza shattered his bat on the next pitch and the jagged bat barrel sailed out to the pitching mound, landing at Clemens' feet. The pitcher picked up the splintered bat and inexplicably flung it back past the first base line, narrowly missing Piazza who stood on the line glaring angrily in disbelief at Clemens.

The partisan Yankees and Mets fans shouted as Piazza took a step toward Clemens and then thought better of it and stopped. With that, both teams raced out of their dugouts and the shouting in the stands and on the field did not subside until the umpires and peacemakers on the field calmed things down. Piazza returned to the plate as Mets fans shouted for a retaliatory home run and Yankees partisans rooted loudly for a strikeout. But Piazza grounded out and the unruffled Clemens went on to hold the Mets scoreless for eight innings and win the game. The Yankees went on to win two of the next three games to take the series. But any fan who saw the incredible Clemens-Piazza episode is not likely to forget it.

The 1990s was a decade marked by a record number of strikeouts, homers, and relief pitchers used in games. The strikeouts can be explained in part by Ralph Kiner's classic rationale, "Singles hitters drive Chevies, home run hitters drive Cadillacs." Since the 1990s, almost all hitters have been swinging like would-be Cadillac owners. And long-ball hitters naturally tend to strike out more frequently than contact hitters.

In the pre–World War II years, and for many years after, each team typically had a few long-ball hitters—large, muscular, men who hit home runs and who usually were positioned in right and left fields and at first base, and occasionally in center field or third base. The middle infielders tended to be smaller, more agile, men selected for their defensive abilities, and very few catchers hit with any authority. But since the early 1980s, powerful hitters have occupied every position. For example, tall and robust Cal Ripken was one of the original hard-hitting middle infielders, a breed that now includes such powerful hitters as Alex Rodriguez and Nomar Garciaparra. Johnny Bench and Mike Piazza were two of the hardest-hitting catchers ever to play the position.

Unlike the lineups 30 years ago, there are fewer soft-hitting spots in lineups. As a result, to the delight of most fans, the practice of pitching around a hard hitter has been largely abandoned because the next hitter often is equally dangerous. The American League's designated hitter position has intensified this trend. One exception to this trend was Barry Bonds of the late 1990s and early 2000s whose murderous hitting led to a record number of intentional and semi-intentional walks.

Fans have been aware that homers have become more plentiful and theories abound as to the reasons for it. The newer ballparks are smaller, the players are bigger (there was a time when many major league players weighed less than 170 pounds), and there are suspicions that a livelier ball is in use. Another reason for the increase in home runs is that the increased size and bulk of today's players has made it less necessary for hitters to pull the ball to reach the stands. The older hitting theory held that hitters should try to pull pitches only on the inside half of the plate. Outside pitches were not to be pulled because doing so would more likely than not result in balls hit up the middle and within range of middle infielders. But the increased size and strength of today's players has made it easier for homers to be hit into any outfield sector.

No less an authority than veteran right-hander Greg Maddux has commented on the prevalence of opposite field home runs since he became a major leaguer in 1986. Maddux attributed this to the increased number of hitters who stand much closer to the plate than in the past. This has made it easier for batters to hit outside pitches with authority. Maddux noted that in his rookie year he saw possibly a half-dozen opposite-field home runs all season. Research shows that since the 1980s, opposite-field home runs have become commonplace, nearly tripling since 1987. Over the same period, the number of hit batsmen has more than doubled as pitchers have attempted to retain their right to the inside corner of the plate. Hitters have responded by wearing such protective equipment as helmet ear flaps and padded material on their arms.

Occasional fisticuffs do spice up baseball games. Although statistics are not available on brawls precipitated by brushback or knockdown pitches, hitters also have responded by charging the mound more often than in earlier years. This trend has continued despite league policies of automatically expelling players for charging the mound, and pitchers who throw suspiciously close to a hitter after being warned by the plate umpire. Fans are well aware that the American League's designated hitter rule emboldens pitchers who do not bat and therefore do not face the possibility of being subjected to retaliatory close pitches.

There is some valid basis for each of these theories but the lighter, thinner bats in use today may well be an equally important factor behind today's power hitting displays. The theory, of course, is that the speed with which a bat moves through the strike zone is a major determinant of the distance a drive will carry. The lighter bats used today make it possible for the hitter to whip the bat faster through the zone and therefore to hit the ball further. The reported use of such chemical aids as steroids may be the most important factor of all but, at this writing, the impact of steroids has not been determined definitively.

One of the reasons baseball fascinates its fans is its continuing change in tempo. The beauty of a baseball game, unless it is a blowout, is its continuing series of built-up tensions, each culminating in a temporarily decisive action such as a hit, an out, or a double play in a clutch situation. Delays in the game interfere with these alternating tension and relaxing periods unique to baseball. The time required to play a nine-inning game has increased significantly over the last two decades, frequently affecting the pleasing flow of the game.

There are a number of reasons for the longer games. One obvious source of delay is the irritating habit many hitters have adopted of unnecessarily stepping out of the batter's box after every pitch. The existing rule does not permit the hitter (or any other player) to call time; that is the umpire's responsibility alone. Texas and Cleveland first baseman Mike Hargrove was perhaps the worst offender. Hargrove was in the habit of stepping out of the box after every pitch and going through a long, unfailing ritual including smoothing and adjusting his uniform and cap, tapping his spikes with his bat, stretching his arms over his head, and finally stepping in to hit. It was an exasperated Indians fan who fastened the apt nickname "Human Rain Delay" on Hargrove.

In an earlier era batters, including such great hitters as Joe DiMaggio and Ted Williams, wasted little time after entering the batters box. They stepped up to the plate and did not step out until they hit a fair ball, walked, or were retired. There are, of course, times when it is appropriate for the hitter to step out of the box, most justifiably to obtain signs from a coach or to deal with a special situation. But otherwise this is an unnecessary game delay which, most fans would agree, should be dealt with.

Pitchers are other significant contributors to extending the length of a game. Some pitchers throw multiple times to first base when the base is occupied, a legitimate technique so long as it is done in a realistic attempt to pick off a runner or keep the runner close to the base but not, as is frequently the case, when the runner is within a step of the base if not standing on it. Of course, frequent pitching changes slow the game up perceptibly. As Bill James described it:

> The number of relievers used per game has increased by more than 50% since the mid–1980s.... Almost all of the increase has occurred in the late innings of close games, at a time when baseball is supposed to be most

exciting. This constant shifting of relief pitchers, unheard of a generation ago, has profoundly changed the experience of watching a closely contested baseball game.

The '90s opened on a somber note. In April, less than a year after his banishment from baseball for his illegal gambling activities, all-time hit leader Pete Rose pleaded guilty to two felony counts of filing false income tax returns. Three months later Rose was sentenced to five months in jail and fined $50,000. His subsequent elimination from the Hall of Fame ballot continued to be a bone of contention among fans for many years after his guilty plea.

There were some noteworthy achievements in the 1990s. The Minnesota Twins entertained their fans with two triple plays in one game in July 1990. And there were some stories of special interest to fans who care about baseball families. In August 1990, the Seattle Mariners' Ken Griffeys—Junior in center field and Senior in left—became the first father-and-son combination in major league history to play as teammates. In another familial achievement two years later, Mariners' second baseman Bret Boone played his first major league game, following in the footsteps of his father, catcher Bob, who played for 19 seasons, and his grandfather, infielder Ray, a 13-year major leaguer. The three-generation record was tied with Indians third baseman David Bell's major league debut in 1995. His father, Buddy, and grandfather, Gus, preceded him in the big leagues.

Two Baltimore Orioles fan favorites—Cal Ripken and Eddie Murray—wound up their careers in style in the 1990s. Ripken broke Lou Gehrig's 2,130 consecutive game record on September 6, 1995, before a capacity Camden Yards crowd and ran the streak to 2,632 straight games before ending it on September 19, 1998. After breaking Gehrig's "unreachable" record, Orioles players pushed Ripken out of the dugout to take a lap around the park, shaking hands and exchanging high fives with fans. On September 6, 1996, Murray, who had returned to Baltimore after a seven-year absence, hit home run no. 500 to join Henry Aaron and Willie Mays as the only players with at least 500 homers and 3,000 hits.

The increasing slugging in the '90s reached a crescendo in the latter part of the decade. The Mariners' Ken Griffey Jr. hit 56 home runs in 1997, a forerunner of things to come. The Cardinals' Mark McGwire thrilled all fans with his historic 70 homers the following year. The Cubs' Sammy Sosa dueled McGwire for much of the 1998 season, finishing with 66 blasts. Fans have always loved the home run but this was unforgettable baseball theater: McGwire swinging his bat as though it were a magic wand, and lofting herculean drives for record distances in game after game. Sosa, doing his characteristic whirlaround just after home runs left his bat, keeping pace with the mammoth McGwire until the very end of the season.

The two men throttled down to McGwire's 65 and Sosa's 63 homers in 1999, as Babe Ruth's earlier record 60 and Roger Maris's 61 were virtually forgotten. The next milestone was reached in 2001 with Barry Bonds's 73 homers. By this time, the fans were ready to concentrate on all dimensions of the game, not only home run totals.

The Yankees' domination continued in the new millennium but these clubs were not the equal of the teams Joe Torre led in the '90s. The Bronx Bombers won pennants in 2001 and 2003 but lost both series. The many fans around the country who were not George Steinbrenner admirers were pleased when the Yankees fell in 2001 to the Arizona Diamondbacks' power-pitching duo of Randy Johnson and Curt Schilling and in 2003 when the underrated Florida Marlins upset Torre's club.

Today's fans are more restrained in their treatment of players and umpires than in the earlier years of the game. Yet during the early 1980s there remained a small minority whose ballpark deportment left a lot to be desired. An ugly incident in Houston in the early '80s galvanized major league clubs into dealing with badly misbehaving fans. Houston outfielder Cesar Cedeno had attacked a fan in the stands in reprisal for vicious insults directed at him over several days. As a result, teams took steps to control alcohol abuse and disruptive fan behavior. Drinking in parking lots was forbidden and policed. Security guards checked bags brought into the ballpark to be sure that glass bottles were kept out of the park. Pregame announcements reminded fans to be considerate of those around them. Beer vendors were ordered to refuse beer to fans who had too much to drink and all beer sales were discontinued after the seventh inning of a game. And security guards moved around the park to eliminate trouble among fans before it got out of hand.

Consequently, fan behavior has been much improved since the early 1980s. As Bill James pungently put it, "After a couple of years, people no longer *expected* to be able to go to ballgames to get drunk and scream at people. A whole generation of fans has grown up now to whom the idea of going to a baseball game to drink until you vomit would seem as foreign as the idea of going to Alaska to test out your new fly swatter."

Since the 9/11 disaster in 2001, of course, teams have had to develop thorough security programs to protect fans against possible terrorist activities. Security in and around ballparks matches that observed at all large gatherings of people throughout the country. In addition to the customary, routine protective practices used widely, patrolling airplanes are often conspicuous in the skies around the ballparks, especially when large crowds are in the stands.

The drug problems arising in the 1980s were a forerunner of the steroid problems blighting the early 2000s. They came to the attention of fans as a result of the prodigious display of power hitting beginning in the 1990s. As many as 10 players hit 50 homers or more in a season between 1995 and 2002 compared with a total of 11 players before 1995. Since 1995 there have been six seasons when a player hit 60 homers. The previously untouched 70-homer mark was reached twice—by McGwire (70) in 1998 and by Barry Bonds (73) in 2001. Incredibly, Sammy Sosa hit 66 home runs in 1998, 63 in 1999, and 64 in 2001, and failed to win the National League home run title in any of the three seasons.

And so the always records- and statistics-conscious fans and reporters have raised the question: Were these home run records chemically enhanced or were they genuine and truly comparable to the earlier records of such home run hitters as Babe Ruth, Roger Maris, Hack Wilson, Jimmy Foxx, and Hank Greenberg? The steroid question came to a head after the 2003 season when Major League Baseball reported that as many as 84 unnamed players (the equivalent of more than two full major league team rosters) had tested positive for steroid use during the just-completed season. The estimate that 6 to 7 percent of major league players had used steroids triggered a requirement that all players be tested for steroid use beginning in the 2004 season.

McGwire, Bonds, and Sosa among other power hitters have long denied taking steroids to help build muscle. But some fans still point to the test results as apparently confirming what many had suspected: that a significant number of major league players have been using illegal, performance-enhancing chemicals, thereby helping them to shatter some of baseball's most revered records. In early 2004, it was unclear how pervasive the steroid problem was and whether it would diminish as more players were intimidated by more intensive testing and threatened penalties. And the ultimate question: What would be the impact on future player performance of these efforts in controlling the steroid problem?

Baseball officials had other matters of concern as the new century began, although most fans tended to focus only on problems of specific concern to them. Equitable revenue sharing is a fundamental issue. Because of the wide disparity in team revenues and, as a result, player payrolls, it has become apparent that in most seasons only a handful of the 30 major league teams have a realistic chance of winning the pennant. This is of little concern to fans of the wealthier teams but of real concern to supporters of teams with much lower revenues. Any objective fan would have to agree that equitable revenue sharing is the only long-term solution for attaining better balance among teams.

Bob Costas has suggested that the owners and the players agree to a "floor-to-ceiling cap." Using this arrangement, Costas proposes development of a major league team payroll minimum equal to the per-team average of media revenues (both local and national) and a maximum equal to twice that figure. This ceiling-floor proposal would mean that every major league team would have a payroll at least half as much as the team with the highest payroll. This would not put the teams on a perfectly equal salary basis but it would dramatically reduce present payroll imbalances between teams, which in 1999 found the Yankees' payroll six or more times higher than those of the Expos and the Twins and much higher than any other major league team.

Costas is very much opposed to the wild-card scheme in which the winners of the three divisions in each league compete for the league championship with a fourth team which had the highest won and lost percentage of the remaining clubs in the league. He cited the 1999 pennant race when the Braves and Mets vied for the National League's Eastern Division title before the Braves defeated the Mets several times, forcing the Mets back into the wild-card race. With the wild-card slot for the Mets to fall back upon, much of the urgency was drained from the Braves-Mets games.

The Mets' situation muddied the Central division race between the Astros and the Reds. Without the wild card, either division race would involve a clear-cut, win-or-else drama, irrespective of the outcome in the other division. But with the wild card, Costas described the present scheme as a game of musical chairs in which the regular season eliminates only one, rather than two, of the final four participants. This tends to eliminate some of the fans' excitement as the pennant race progresses, although the point can be made that the divisional and league championship series have injected a new level of competition for fans to enjoy.

There are other issues in which fans have a special interest. The designated hitter rule will continue to be a bone of contention between the traditionalists and those who favor emphasis on the offensive game at the expense of game strategy. Should it be eliminated or utilized by both leagues for purposes of uniformity between both major leagues? In the makeup of all-star game rosters, some fans favor the current rule requiring that each team be represented, thereby eliminating some deserving players. Other fans want the game to be as competitive as possible with winning the game taking precedence over representation by all teams.

There is only one certainty in baseball. As some of these problems are solved, others will come along to replace them.

6

The Writers

The baseball fan needs the writer, a vital source of otherwise unavailable information about the game. And the writer needs the fan who, after all, is his client. But there is very little personal involvement between the fan and the baseball writer despite the fact that they are indispensable to one another. The average fan would not recognize the writer whose product he reads every day. And so, except in the case of celebrated writers and journalists, most baseball fans tend to know or care little about the relatively anonymous people whose material they read so avidly each day.

The baseball fan from 1850 to 1870 followed baseball by one of three means—either by attending a game, hearing a first-hand account of a game from an attendee, or reading a written account of the game. William Cauldwell, editor of the *New York Mercury*, in 1853, was the first person to write about baseball for a daily newspaper. But perhaps his most important contribution to the game was his hiring of Henry Chadwick.

Chadwick was born in England but his family migrated to the U.S. and he grew up in Brooklyn. In 1848, he was a 24-year-old baseball enthusiast whose writings on the game were picked up by several New York sports periodicals. With the increase in his writing output in newspapers and later on in his books on baseball fundamentals, he gained recognition among the kranks as the leading baseball authority and critic of the time. His background as a cricket and baseball player was useful but his real strengths were the close personal contacts he cultivated with baseball people, his deep understanding of the game, and his desire to improve baseball artistically, ethically, and as a spectator sport. By the time Chadwick was 50, he was widely acclaimed as the "Father of the Game."

Chadwick, who wrote in a heavy, stilted prose, did more than merely write about the game. He was considered a leader whose suggestions were solicited and honored by baseball officials, and he worked closely with them to improve and clarify baseball rules. Chadwick also was credited for devising the first box scores. And most important, he was a moral force, decrying the evils of players' involvement in excessive drinking, gambling, and rowdy activities. Chadwick was honored widely both before and after his death. He was elected to the Baseball Hall of Fame after it opened in 1939.

Timothy Murnane, a former player and later an editor with the *Boston Globe,* was another early writer, following on the heels of Chadwick as an influential baseball figure and widely respected writer. After his death in 1917, a large Boston crowd attended a Red Sox game to raise money for his widow's support. Murnane was only one of a number of other early writers who sought to improve the game and edify the fans.

Baseball writing expanded in the 1890s with the formation of full-time sports staffs. Before that, newspaper accounts of baseball games were provided fans by such biased or otherwise unreliable sources as team employees and part-time correspondents who had little knowledge of the game. But newspaper editors responded to the developing public interest in sports, and especially baseball, by hiring skilled reporters who understood and cared about the game. And these reporters gained their own followings, similar to the players. The New York papers were the first to establish sportswriting staffs, followed by papers in other major cities.

The approach to covering games varied among cities. Veteran sportswriter Jack Lang wrote:

> In New York and Boston the style of baseball writing emphasized expert knowledge of the game. In Chicago and other [midwestern] cities, the style involved more humor and cynicism.... [In Chicago] such writers as ... Ring Lardner, Hugh Fullerton, and Charles Dryden were winning over readers with their humorous accounts.

Ring Lardner was a columnist for the *Sporting News* in 1911. He later covered sports in Chicago and Boston before abandoning the baseball scene for a career as an outstanding short story writer. He continued to delight baseball fans with his tales of wide-eyed, nearly illiterate baseball players in "You Know Me Al" and "Alibi Ike." He remained proud of his sportswriting background even after little attention was paid him at a baseball writers meeting years after he left the baseball scene. He remarked, "What's the matter with you boys? I belong here. I am still a baseball writer and always will be."

Hugh Fullerton was a 16-year-old cub writer in Cincinnati before becoming a major baseball columnist in Chicago, New York, and Philadelphia. Fullerton arrived at the Polo Grounds press box to cover the famous 1908 playoff game between the deadlocked Giants and Cubs. Typical of the disrespect baseball officials accorded writers in that era, Fullerton discovered that actor Louis Mann, a friend of John McGraw, occupied Fullerton's assigned seat and Mann refused to vacate the seat. The furious Fullerton was forced to move elsewhere and that inconvenience, combined with other indignities imposed upon reporters, led Fullerton to join with other writers in forming the Baseball Writers Association after the 1908 season. As a consequence, working conditions improved for the writers as unauthorized visits to press boxes were banned, and writers were provided with complete control of their working area. Fullerton was considered something of a seer with remarkable abilities in forecasting the winner of important games. To many fans he is best remembered for his major role in exposing the fixing of the 1919 World's Series.

Fans in the late 1890s and early 1900s were entertained by the wit of early baseball writer Charles Dryden. After writing baseball in several cities, Dryden, who had little formal education, settled in Chicago in 1905 where he gained national fan recognition for nicknaming players and teams—Charles Comiskey became "The Old Roman." The light-hitting 1906 Chicago White Sox became "the Hitless Wonders." And a succession of poor Washington Senators teams precipitated Dryden's descriptive "Washington, first in war, first in peace, and last in the American League."

Many discerning fans enjoyed Dryden's slightly off-color wit. Fred Lieb wrote:

> I never could understand how Dryden could write so well and so interestingly, for he had little education.... For Dryden, writing baseball was a constant battle of wits ... with editors and proofreaders.... He was constantly trying to work into his sentences double-entendres, innocent-sounding phrases that would shock Aunt Nellie if she understood them.... Ever so often Charley would slip through a good one.... The Cleveland club came up with a pitcher named Eugene Krapp. The name intrigued Dryden. He was proud of this one, which got by the editor: "Krapp squeezed his way out of a tight hole when, with the bases full, he induced [the next hitter] ... to line out for an inning-ending double play."

John McGraw had a mutually beneficial relationship with a number of sportswriters. He fed the writers stories intended to further his own purposes while satisfying their reportorial needs, and the writers recognized McGraw as a constant source of good material for their stories. The fans benefited because the stories provided by McGraw were interesting and colorful. The fiery McGraw's first years as the Giants' manager came after he angrily left Ban Johnson's infant American League. The New York writers—Sid Mercer, old McGraw cronies Sam Crane and the wonderfully named Bozeman Bulger among them—helped McGraw keep alive his continuing feud with Johnson by printing McGraw's derogatory comments regarding Johnson.

The writers also defended McGraw when Pittsburgh Pirates president Barney Dreyfuss accused McGraw of defaming him. The congenial relations continued for several years until McGraw and the highly respected Mercer crossed swords when McGraw committed a classic journalistic no-no, denying his printed inflammatory comments to reporters after encouraging them to print his comments. McGraw had gotten into a violent disagreement with National League president John Tener. McGraw had told Mercer that Tener favored the Philadelphia Phillies and was unfair to McGraw and the Giants. McGraw encouraged Mercer and the other Giants writers to print his views after Mercer gave McGraw time to reconsider his accusation. The stories triggered predictably heavy counter fire from National League officials and, as a result, McGraw repudiated his published statements, claiming he had never made them.

The outraged writers were up in arms and demanded that the National league investigate to determine who was telling the truth. As a result, the league fined McGraw $1,000. Mercer was so incensed at McGraw's betrayal of the writers that he refused to cover the Giants any longer. The two men remained on the outs for many years after that. Other writers, not in a position to be as independent as Mercer, also had reason to question McGraw's reliability as an information source after his serious breach of faith.

McGraw knew the writers' motivations and weaknesses as well as he knew those of his players. Frank Graham described the dismay of the Giants writers in 1926 when they learned McGraw had left the club during spring training, hoping to sign star outfielder Edd Roush, without informing the writers he was leaving. They complained to McGraw that their editors would accuse them of negligence if they were not aware that McGraw was not with the club. A furious writer told the manager, "Don't you think that if you had told us you were going, but asked us not to print it, we would have done as you asked?"

Graham wrote:

> A reporter left the room without a word. Shortly after, McGraw told another writer, "I just want to give you a tip. You were giving me hell for not trusting the newspapermen. It might be a good idea ... to find out if

[you fellows] can trust each other. You know what that bird who went out a while ago is doing, don't you? He's in his room calling his office on the telephone so he can scoop the rest of you on the Roush story." The angry writer darted out of the room heading for the departed writer's room. But he thought better of it and decided not to go to his colleague's room. He was afraid he'd discover McGraw was right.

By 1910, New York City fans had daily access to a number of excellent writers working for the dozen or so local newspapers covering the Giants. The New York writing contingent included writers—gifted men like Grantland Rice, Franklin P. Adams, Heywood Broun, and Damon Runyon—who graduated from the Polo Grounds beat to more prestigious journalistic heights.

Grantland Rice covered sports in Nashville and Cleveland before moving to New York with the *Evening Mail* and later with New York's *Herald-Tribune* and *Daily News.* After that he became a highly successful syndicated columnist. He was famous for a few lines of verse preceding his columns on all sports, notably baseball, football and horse racing. Baseball fans of his era, less critical of sports figures than those of today, enjoyed the gentle, largely uncritical, tone of his writing. Many fans and colleagues considered him the greatest, and most beloved, sportswriter of the pre–World War II period.

Franklin Adams, writing under the byline "F.P.A," was a sophisticated writer and poet who, before moving on to greener journalistic pastures, was remembered for his poetic salute to the 1908 Chicago Cubs' double play combination of shortstop Joe Tinker, second baseman Johnny Evers, and first baseman Frank Chance. The poem was largely instrumental in leading to the induction of the three players into the Hall of Fame. Written during a famous Cubs–Giants series when the Giants were turned back by short to second to first double plays, it read in part:

> Ruthlessly pricking our gonfalon bubble,
> Making a Giant hit into a double,
> Words that are weighty with nothing but trouble,
> Tinker to Evers to Chance.

Brooklyn-born Harvard graduate Heywood Broun began covering baseball with the *New York Tribune* in 1912. Hardly a fashion plate, Broun always wore unshined shoes and unpressed and ill-fitting suits. He remained on the baseball beat until World War I when he began his highly opinionated, controversial column entitled "It Seems to Me." Even after leaving the sports beat, Broun's fascination with baseball remained and he still found time to write wry, witty pieces on the game.

Broun's lead comment on a World Series game in which Babe Ruth led the Yankees to victory was, "The Ruth is mighty and shall prevail." When the Giants' great left-hander Carl Hubbell pitched an 18-inning, complete game win in 1933 without walking a hitter, Broun (referring to the baseball myth that left-handers are more unpredictable than right-handers) commented in the press box: "Such control in a lefthander is incredible. There must be a skeleton in Hubbell's closet somewhere, perhaps a righthanded maternal grandmother."

Broun was the founder and first president of the American Newspaper Guild. New York City mayor Fiorello LaGuardia said of him: "The forces of reaction did not hate Broun because he was a radical, nor did they dislike him because he was a liberal; but how they feared him because he was truthful!"

Damon Runyon covered the New York Giants for the *New York American* during the same period that Broun reported on baseball. Runyon was as much at home with rough-hewn gangsters, boxing figures, and baseball fans as he was with cultured patrons of the arts. He was best known for his wonderful short stories about unsavory members of society. Runyon's stories were converted into such successful musicals and movies as *Guys and Dolls* and *Little Miss Marker,* masterful interpretations of the slangy language spoken by denizens of Broadway and the underworld.

Fred Lieb broke in as a baseball writer with the *New York Press* in 1911 at the Polo Grounds and, unlike press box companions Broun and Runyon, was perfectly content to travel the baseball beat for more than 60 years. He worked for several other New York newspapers and for the *Sporting News,* covering more than 8,000 major league games and every World Series for 47 years beginning in 1911. He wrote numerous books, the most important of which is his *Baseball As I Have Known It,* a marvelous literary tour of the baseball people and events he encountered over his long career. He was noted for his objectivity and his willingness to accept changes in the game and for his willingness to reject "good old times" thinking, despite his longevity as a writer.

In the years preceding and following World War II, the New York baseball scene included a number of other excellent journalists who spent all or part of their careers covering sports, and especially baseball. The most popular writers with the fans included Frank Graham, Dan Daniel, Joe Williams, Dan Parker, Jimmy Powers, Tom Meany, Sid Mercer, Ken Smith, John Kieran, Jimmy Cannon, Red Smith, and Dick Young.

Frank Graham began covering the New York Giants for the *New York*

Sun as early as 1916. Fans remembered him as one of the most effective early practitioners of the reporting style of today in which the actual conversations of players and managers are interspersed with the reporter's description of the game action. In those days before the tape recorder, Graham displayed his perfect ear for dialogue and his virtual word-for-word recall of the conversations he heard and digested. Instead of incorporating his personal opinions into his column, Graham helped his readers develop their own opinions by "escorting" the fan into the dugout or clubhouse so that the reader could learn the conversation for himself. In this way, the reader could "see" and "hear" the intimate details that did not reach the grandstand or the bleachers.

Graham's tasteful columns and books were never written in the first person. Instead he would write "Someone asked…" when that questioner, of course, was Graham himself. He was a special favorite of the fans as he made them feel as though they were in the dugout listening to the conversation. Graham utilized his masterful use of simple, declarative sentences in his splendid biographies of John McGraw and Lou Gehrig and other informal histories of the New York-area teams.

Dan Daniel was an amazingly prolific writer who began his sportswriting career as a 19-year-old with the *New York Herald*. He later became a beat reporter for the *New York World Telegram and Sun* and an anonymous reporter for the Sporting News, for which he wrote 5,000 words a week for many years. Daniel was a recognized authority on the Yankees, covering the club from the pre–Babe Ruth period before World War I through the Mickey Mantle era. He was known for his major scoops; in one case, he personally talked Babe Ruth into signing with the Yankees for $80,000 in 1930, pointing out to the Babe that holding out for $85,000 was inappropriate considering the Depression bread lines at the time.

Daniel's detailed interests and curiosities extended well beyond baseball. A colleague saw him in a food store one morning when the Yankees were in Detroit. Daniel was examining a head of lettuce, shaking his head in disbelief, and was heard to mutter "Twenty five cents a head; in the Bronx, it's a nickel." And his analyses of players, in a popular column for the *Telegram* under the heading "Daniel's Dope," were no-nonsense critiques which told the story to fans in an easily understood manner. Long, involved questions about his player evaluations were answered with crisp, unmistakable authority—"Terry Moore over Vince DiMaggio, better arm and speed; Lon Warneke over Johnny Vander Meer—better control more important than speed."

In a way, the usually dead-serious Daniel was something of a throwback to Henry Chadwick. Jerome Holtzman wrote, "He was baseball's high priest, alternately reporting and analyzing, and constantly issuing encyclicals for present and future [baseball] conduct." St. Louis writer Bob Broeg remembered, "When a story moved him to take the time — or when he rose to speak in his rasping voice — the old baseball writer best demonstrated the wit and warmth he kept covered under a gruff exterior."

Joe Williams was the longtime sports editor of the *New York World-Telegram* and Dan Parker (*Daily Mirror*) and Jimmy Powers (*Daily News*) were his opposite numbers on the two New York tabloids of the 1930s. Williams was a clever wordsmith with a well-developed wit which could be cutting at times. He feuded with Giants manager Bill Terry in the 1930s because Terry refused to give writers his home phone number under the theory that his time away from the ballpark was his own. Interestingly, Peter Williams, Joe's son, in his *When the Giants Were Giants*, wrote about Terry most flatteringly as if to make amends for the Terry-Joe Williams feud, long after the senior Williams's death. Joe Williams was best-known to baseball fans as the first reporter to write about Babe Ruth's "called" home run in the 1932 World Series.

The *Daily Mirror*'s Dan Parker had a gentle satirical wit. New York fans loved his columns, especially his amusing poems about Dodgers fans. *Daily News* editor Jimmy Powers' lighter octane "Powerhouse" column seemingly was devoted more to fueling well-recognized fan likes and dislikes than to providing original information. Powers is remembered for fastening the nickname "El Cheapo" on Branch Rickey following Rickey's economy moves after he took over management of the Brooklyn Dodgers. Also many fans derided Powers' columns because it was widely rumored that many of them were ghostwritten.

Tom Meany's baseball writing career began with the new Brooklyn edition of the *New York Journal* in 1922 when he was a teenager. Subsequently, he covered baseball for several New York newspapers including the *World Telegram, Star, Morning Telegraph, and PM,* and published articles in large-circulation magazines such as *Collier's*. He was a gifted writer with a sharp, entertaining wit, enjoyed by fans everywhere but especially in his native New York. The Brooklyn-born Meany had his career scoop on July 2, 1932, when he was the first writer to discover and publish the fact that John McGraw had resigned as the Giants' manager after 30 years at the Giants' helm.

Similar to Joe Williams, Meany was among the New York writers who feuded with Bill Terry, many of them finding the businesslike Terry a brisk, sometimes cold, man. Terry, in turn, privately referred to some of the writers contemptuously as "25 dollar-a-week ribbon clerks." When it was learned that Terry owned a large cattle farm near Memphis, Meany offered the thought that Terry probably raised white-faced cattle. Asked why he suspected that, the quick-witted Meany replied, "So Terry can count their faces at night."

Sid Mercer wrote sports in the St. Louis area in his early 20s before joining the St. Louis Browns for a year as the club's road secretary. He returned to sportswriting in New York, writing for the *Evening Globe* and the *Evening Journal* and later wrote for the *New York Evening Journal* (*later the Journal-American*) where his syndicated columns on baseball, boxing, and other sports brought him national fame. He was a man of great integrity and firm convictions as he proved by his willingness to stand up to John McGraw.

Ken Smith was a diminutive, extremely popular, baseball writer whose gentle disposition, gracious personality, and knowledge of the game won him the admiration of the fans who read the *New York Mirror*. Smith was as much a fan as he was a writer even after long years in the press box. His loyalty to his favorites was legendary and Mel Ott was one of his particular favorites. After Leo Durocher replaced Ott as the Giants' manager in midseason of 1948, an unhappy Smith approached Durocher and told him, "Leo, I love Mel and I can't promise that I'll be as objective with you as I should be." Durocher responded with uncharacteristic feeling, "Kenny, I understand and I appreciate your frankness and loyalty to Ottie."

The likable Connecticut-born Smith started in baseball as a batboy for the Danbury club when he was 11, beginning his professional career at 23, covering the Giants for the *New York Graphic* in 1925. He switched to the *Mirror* two years later and remained with the newspaper until its demise in 1963. He then joined the staff of the Baseball Hall of Fame and Museum as its public relations director where he remained until his retirement in 1979, and he was extremely well-liked by baseball fans visiting Cooperstown.

John Kieran was the erudite author of the first bylined "Sports of the Times" column in the *New York Times* after covering sports for the *Times* and other New York newspapers beginning in 1916. Kieran was a man of varied and extensive interests. An accomplished ornithologist and naturalist, he was head of the National Audubon Society for several years. While on the road covering baseball games, he spent much of his spare time in local libraries pursuing his interests in ornithology and art. Kieran proved to baseball fans that baseball writers have interests over and above the press box and clubhouse and it was no surprise when he exhibited his wide knowledge as a regular on the famous *Information Please* radio show beginning in 1938.

Jimmy Cannon was a quintessential native-born New Yorker. He had a distinctive, street-smart style, always at the ready to attack hypocrisy and perceived social injustice. Cannon began his sportswriting career at 16 with the *Daily News* and he later moved to the *Post* and the *Journal-American*, writing a syndicated sports column for both newspapers.

Cannon had no illusions about the baseball writing profession. In Jerome Holtzman's *No Cheering in the Press Box* Cannon set forth his credo:

> I don't want sportswriters being fans.... The worst thing a sportswriter can be is a fan. A baseball writer's relationship with a ballplayer is a cop-and-crook relationship. You're not there as his buddy, as his fan, as his teammate. It's an adversary relationship. A lot of writers think that ballplayers love them. But ballplayers are amused by writers and consider them necessary evils.

Walter "Red" Smith is considered one of the best sports columnist-reporters ever and many baseball fans feel he is *the best*. Baseball fans found his columns completely informative while written with a rare literary elegance. Born in Green Bay, Wisconsin, Smith worked for newspapers in Milwaukee, St. Louis, and Philadelphia before gaining nationwide prominence in New York with the *Herald Tribune* and later with the *Times*.

Smith never took himself too seriously which, along with his naturally graceful writing style, contributed to his writing success. His goal was to give his readers a little pleasure and entertainment along with the basic facts on the subject. Smith believed fans attending a game can enjoy the same game again, reading about it the following day.

Fans considered Dick Young as one of the most influential, and yet controversial, sportswriters of his time. He was respected for his baseball knowledge, his crisp, breezy style, and for his leadership in the fight for improved working conditions for those covering baseball. But he annoyed some fans and players as he became increasingly more conservative and disproportionately supportive of baseball management at the expense of players. He catered to the conservative tastes of some of his readers, complaining in print about the players union, its demands for higher player salaries, and modern players' habits and mores.

Young began his career with New York's *Daily News* as a messenger boy, eventually becoming the newspaper's sports editor and a syndicated columnist. He was one of the first baseball writers to develop the reporting technique used widely today of breathing life into his game accounts by incorporating player comments directly into his account of the game.

Young was one of the first of the so-called "chipmunks," a term applied to writers who specialized in asking players and managers tough, impolitic, and impolite questions. Answers to irreverent questions often advance the writer's knowledge and make for an eye-catching story for the fans but they also can lead to controversies as the answers may show up in the writer's story in a form embarrassing to the person being interviewed.

Fans in all baseball cities have had their own favorite writers. In Washington, D.C., it was Maine native Shirley Povich. He began his career with the *Washington Post* in 1923 when he was 17, and a few years later he became the youngest sports editor of a major newspaper in the country. Povich worked for the *Post* until he retired at 74. Actually, Povich continued to write his sophisticated, beautifully crafted stories for the newspaper until his death at 92 in 1998.

Povich was an excellent raconteur, speaking in a gentle New England accent. Other than his extensive baseball knowledge, especially involving the Senators, Povich's talks always included a humorous description of honors he had received from womens organizations given him under the assumption that *Shirley* Povich was an eminent lady sportswriter. But Povich was indeed a treasured Washington institution. Ben Bradlee, former executive director of the *Post*, stated, "Shirley Povich was why people (and the fans) bought the newspaper. You got the *Post* for Shirley and the sports section. For years, he carried the paper."

In Detroit, it was Harry G. Salsinger, a dignified baseball expert, who enlightened Tigers fans for the *Detroit News* for over 50 years. In Chicago, the distinguished press box group comprising Ring Lardner, Hugh Fullerton, and Charles Dryden was replaced by such fan favorites as Warren Brown, John Carmichael, and Edgar Munzel. James Isaminger was a Philadelphia institution from 1905 through the 1940s. And other fan favorites in that era included Harold Kaese (Boston), J. Roy Stockton and Bob Broeg (St. Louis), Gordon Cobbledick (Cleveland), Si Burick and Earl Lawson (Cincinnati), and Tommy Holmes (Brooklyn).

Baseball coverage changed slightly before major league teams began to play a small portion of their games at night, but the baseball beat changed drastically after World War II. Prewar baseball writers had a choice sports assignment. Dick Young referred to the baseball beat at that time as the "crème de la crème," choices of the sportswriting assignments. Writers covered spring training beginning in mid–February in then-sleepy southern areas, removed from wintry weather up north. Regular season games started at a civilized 3 p.m. time except for double-headers, continued for six months during the day through the regular season, and on into the World Series.

Writers for morning papers had ample time to prepare their reports for the next morning's papers. After most games there was no need for the writers to interview managers or players unless there was a play or situation of special interest to fan-readers requiring clarification. Writers for afternoon newspapers usually had only the relatively simple task of writing a lead paragraph or two where the early innings of the game were reported in late editions of the newspaper. The only exception to this leisurely pace occurred when the morning papers (in New York, for example, it was the *News* and the *Mirror*) published an early edition which fans snapped up eagerly from New York City newstands at about 10 P.M., the day before.

Postseason games were played usually in more temperate weather than today when the season is extended with two postseason series preceding the World Series, and with all games played at night through late October's chilly days and nights. After the series ended, pre–World War II baseball writers had a relatively easy off-season, covering trade rumors and completed trades, the winter meetings, and contractual matters preceding spring training.

Since World War II, night games have become the norm and writers find themselves working much longer hours. They write pregame dispatches, postgame reports, and follow-up stories in a routine especially difficult for reporters with morning papers. And the assignments have become far more complicated with increasing numbers of off-season issues, some requiring special expertise.

Traveling has become more wearing with baseball's expansion to the West Coast and the need to travel by air rather than by trains or cars. Before the expansion, trains usually left after a game around midnight, permitting writers to sleep en route and spend relaxed time with the players. Reflecting on the changes over the last half century, well-traveled writer Jack Lang observed that few writers remain on the baseball beat for any length of time, attributing this to the exhausting travel, the long hours, and the night games. Before the television era, most writers remained on the baseball beat for many years. But many of today's baseball writers burn out after a few years. And there probably are fewer openings for baseball writers today on the major newspapers than there were 50 years ago simply because there are fewer major newspapers today. On the other hand, baseball writers do not remain on the same job as long as they had formerly and there is a faster turnover.

Baseball writing styles have changed over the years. The earlier baseball journalists wrote in the stilted sentences, phrases, and words typical of the 1800s but that changed with the gifted, colorful writers on the baseball beat in the early 1900s. They wrote in imaginative, sometimes fanciful, prose. They entertained the fan reader with the nicknames they gave players and with the fresh, innovative way they described plays, players, managers, and the fans themselves.

Baseball writing styles varied depending upon the newspapers' readers. In the 1920s and 1930s, the tabloids and the Hearst-type papers were slanted at the everyday working public. They were written in simple, direct, and uncomplicated language, some written in a pedestrian, humdrum style and others written in lurid detail. These papers were replete with photos and sensational, attention-drawing headlines, the hallmark of the Hearst papers and the tabloids.

The newspapers aimed at the better-educated, more opulent fans were written in more restrained language. The *New York Times*, for example, printed only the baseball news considered "fit to print." Stories were written in an objective style, with no attempt at sensationalism. And the writing style of the *Times* was downright traditional, using proper old English spelling; for example, as late as 1938 the *Times* referred to Joe DiMaggio as the Yankees' *centre* fielder.

Baseball coverage was presented somewhat more informally in the years after World War II and, reflecting the times, much more informally in the free and easy days of the 1970s. The new group of writers frequenting press boxes in the 1970s had more journalism training than their predecessors and most of them were unwilling to accept the formal, professional niceties favored by their elders. Their increased informality went hand-in-hand with the emergence of the "chipmunks," who wrote with the same irreverence they accorded the baseball people with whom they dealt. And that attitude continues through the present day.

The writer's off-the-field proximity to the players has changed drastically over the years. Teams traveled by sleeper trains until after World War II and writers and players travelling together had ample opportunity to get to know each other well. Other than to sleep, eat, and play cards, players were readily available to writers, especially on long sleeper train trips to and from the East Coast to St. Louis, then the farthest western city in which major league teams played. Also, when teams were on a road trip, many players were in the habit of sitting in hotel lobbies, some to idly watch people walk by, others, more purposefully, to scan the crowd for young women seeking "companionship." In any event, players were on the scene to talk with reporters. Today, time is at a premium after a short plane trip and players have less time or inclination to make themselves available to reporters. Furthermore, some reporters encounter a language communication problem with the many foreign-born players.

Fans received little or no information about the players' personal lives

30 or 40 years ago. For example, before that time, descriptions of Babe Ruth's excesses with liquor, food, and women were never discussed except for relatively innocuous stories about the Babe's pregame consumption of numerous hot dogs, soda pop, and bicarbonate of soda. Fred Lieb described an illustrative Babe Ruth escapade in the early '20s and the writers' reaction to it:

> We [the writers] were on the Southern Pacific Express from Shreveport to New Orleans when the train stopped at Baton Rouge.... I was in a card game. Suddenly the front door of our car opened violently and a panting Babe Ruth came rushing through ... pursued by a dark-haired, dark-eyed woman [later to be identified as the wife of a Louisiana legislator] carrying a knife.... [Ruth managed to escape her before the train pulled out.] I still wonder why we newspapermen acted as we did. There were eleven of us sitting there and no one said a word. We just went on typing, reading magazines, and playing cards. A writer put it best when he said whimsically, "Well, if she had carved up the Babe, we really would have had a hell of a story."

Today such a story would have been reported to the fans in graphic and complete detail.

There is a general consensus among publishers, journalists, and fans that baseball is the American sport best suited for literary efforts. There are good reasons for this. The history of baseball is more deeply interwoven into America's history than any other commercial sport. Baseball also has been an important factor in the history and growth of individual cities and smaller towns. More Americans, certainly older Americans, as youngsters played some form of baseball in comparison with other sports. And the leisurely pace of baseball lends itself best to the characters and the description which make for good literature.

The numbers of books of special interest to baseball fans have increased greatly over the years. The first nonfiction baseball books of significance were written before the early 1920s by baseball pioneer Albert Spalding, and New York Giants luminaries John Montgomery Ward, Christy Mathewson and John McGraw. Fans in the 1930s and 1940s read the first of the classic baseball books, comprising team histories and player biographies, most of them written by Frank Graham and Fred Lieb.

Lieb's books provided the fan with an unvarnished view of the players Lieb covered over his seven-decade writing career. His coverage of Casey Stengel in his *Baseball As I Have Known It* includes his personal observations of Stengel at the start of Casey's playing career. Every Stengel biographer has described Casey's inimitable use of double talk to inform and confuse, and his glory years when he managed the Yankees. But who but Lieb could write a story of Stengel's depression as a young Brooklyn outfielder before World War I. Stengel told Lieb that he was contemplating jumping off a bridge because "[Brooklyn manager] Wilbert Robinson doesn't like me. And I've got [gonorrhea]."

The first scholarly series of baseball history books arrived in 1960, beginning with Harold Seymour's epic three-volume set. David Quentin Voigt also published an excellent three-volume history of the game. Both sets provide fans with a comprehensive account of baseball from its origin. Seymour's work runs through the 1970s and Voigt's the 1980s. Two other classic books gaining large-scale fan acceptance in the 1960s were Eliot Asinof's *Eight Men Out* and Leonard Koppett's *Thinking Man's Guide to Baseball*. Asinof's book provides the most authoritative coverage of the 1919 Black Sox scandal, and Koppett's gem presents expertise on a variety of baseball issues, all supported by a wealth of historical data.

Fans have greatly enjoyed reading the many books containing retired players' recollections of their playing days. The first of these invaluable oral histories became available in 1966 with the publication of Lawrence Ritter's classic *The Glories of Their Times*. Donald Honig followed Ritter's lead in 1975 with his *Baseball When the Grass Was Green*. In the next four years Honig wrote three more oral histories, and these four books were so successful that they were published by Simon & Schuster as part of their Fireside Sports Classic series. Fans were pleased to read oral interviews with former players and the technique has been used by baseball authors since that time, most effectively by Peter Golenbock in his histories of several major league teams.

A number of groundbreaking baseball books were published in the 1970s. Roger Angell's *The Summer Game,* the first collection of his elegant *New Yorker* pieces, was published in 1972. Roger Kahn, who covered the Brooklyn Dodgers beat in the Jackie Robinson era, hit the jackpot with his classic *The Boys of Summer* in 1972. This marvelous book was loved by fans primarily for its emotional description of how time has treated the Dodgers of Robinson's era after their playing careers were over. But it also spawned a number of books by other authors on a subject dear to the hearts of many fans—what happened to their old heroes after they left the game.

John Holway's writings have provided an important contribution to baseball fans' knowledge by recounting the feats of the black stars before their entrance into the major leagues His first of several collections of interviews of the old Negro Leaguers was published in 1975 as *Voices from the Great Black Baseball Leagues*. He since has written on several other baseball subject areas.

George Will is a devoted baseball fan who has written superb books in the 1990s on baseball, a subject unrelated to his impact on political subjects resulting from his columns, articles, books, and television appearances. Will's baseball books have been enjoyed by fans (regardless of their political views) for their sophisticated analyses of technical baseball subjects. Also, David Halberstam, heretofore known as an important writer on political matters, entertained fans in the 1990s with books on baseball in the 1950s and '60s.

Robert W. Creamer and Charles C. Alexander have written the most fan-friendly biographies of the last few decades. Creamer's biography of Babe Ruth, *Babe: The Legend Comes to Life*, was published in 1974. *Washington Post* book critic Jonathan Yardley called it "the best biography ever written about an American sports figure." Alexander, a college history professor, has written highly successful biographies of such unforgettable baseball figures as John McGraw and Ty Cobb.

John Thorn has been a potent force in baseball literature since the early 1980s. His most important contribution has been his major involvement in producing and updating *Total Baseball*, a 2,500-page publication which includes records of every major leaguer to play in the major leagues along with articles on a wide range of baseball subjects. Thorn also has edited, authored, and co-authored a number of other well-received books.

Thomas Boswell, a nationally syndicated columnist, has been producing incisive, beautifully-written, baseball pieces for the *Washington Post* since the early 1980s. Boswell has been described as an astute observer of the human condition with the knack of relating those observations to baseball situations and players. George Will has described Boswell as "the thinking fan's writer about the thinking person's sport."

Players have written many books (some ghostwritten) over the years. Christy Mathewson is credited with the first of such books with his *Pitching in a Pinch* in 1912. Since then, many books have been bylined by players, the most substantive of which have been Jim Brosnan's *The Long Season* in 1960 and Jim Bouton's *Ball Four* written 10 years later.

Bill James is arguably the most influential baseball writer of today. He can be properly classified as a baseball writer even though he is not a baseball beat reporter nor does he write a syndicated column or publish articles on a regular basis. But James is a triple-threat baseball communicator. He is the author of several excellent, groundbreaking, and entertaining baseball books. Moreover, he has been an expert participant in owner-player arbitration cases. And most important to the sabremetrician and fan, James has been a key figure in developing and promoting more sophisticated and reliable methods of analyzing and predicting player performance.

The Kansas-born James began his writing career by self-publishing his *Bill James Baseball Abstract* before it was published commercially. Although much of his work is statistically based, baseball fans enjoy his witty, innovative writing, employing an expository-historical, rather than a statistical, approach. Recognized by baseball aficionados in general and fellow members in the Society for American Baseball Research in particular, James's progressive ideas on measuring and predicting player performance have captured the attention of major league teams.

In 1990, *Baseball Magazine* listed the 10 baseball writers best known to the fans and considered most influential at that time. The list included Dick Young, Jack Lang, Bob Broeg (a master in producing historical sketches and pleasantly nostalgic pieces) of the writers already discussed. It also included Phil Pepe, of the *New York Daily News*; Murray Chass, of the *New York Times* (especially skilled in writing interpretive analyses of baseball's labor and legal issues); Peter Gammons, of the *Boston Globe*; Jerome Holtzman, of the *Chicago Sun-Times*; Joe Falls, of the *Detroit News*; Hal Bock, of the Associated Press; and Milton Richman, of United Press International. If the list were updated to the first decade in the 2000s, it undoubtedly would include Boswell and James. Even in a communications world dominated by television and computers, these writers provide the reading fan with literary style and information in the best traditions of past and present "knights of the Keyboard."

7

Radio

Baseball announcing on the radio began slowly in the '20s, but encompassed all major league cities by the end of the '30s. Televising games began after World War II and, by the '50s, all major league teams had some or all of their games on the tube. By the time television arrived, most radio announcers also had begun broadcasting games on television.

This chapter focuses on several prominent baseball radio announcers during the pretelevision era, several of whom developed devoted fan followings. Before the 1930s, most baseball fans followed major league baseball either by attending games, trading information with other fans, or reading written accounts of the games and the players. The first play-by-play radio account of a major league game was broadcast on Pittsburgh Station KDKA on August 5, 1921. The game, in which the Pirates defeated the visiting Phillies, was transmitted from Forbes Field by local announcer Harold Arlin from a ground-level box seat.

More than 60 years later, Arlin remembered the first baseball broadcast (referred to at the time as "wireless telegraphy") as a catch-as-catch-can arrangement conducted as something of a one-time stunt with no expectation that game broadcasts would become a future staple of baseball information. Arlin recalled that during his broadcast the transmitter worked only sporadically and that the transmission was drowned out from time to time by the shouts of nearby fans.

Two months later, the first Subway World's Series between the Yankees and the Giants was broadcast by famed writer Grantland Rice in an unschooled but witty and authoritative manner. Over the next decade, the series were broadcast by smooth-talking Ted Husing, who knew his baseball, and Broadway singer Graham McNamee, whose mellifluous voice was far more impressive than his knowledge of baseball. (After a series game, Ring Lardner wrote of McNamee, "I don't know which game to write about—the one I saw today, or the one I heard.") But McNamee shook off press criticism, proclaiming that he had succeeded in carrying out what is still one of the basic functions of the play-by-play or color man, to "make each of your listeners, though miles from the spot, feel that he or she is there with you." Fan interest in his broadcasts was evidenced by more than 1,700 fan letters of approval to New York's Station WEAF after McNamee broadcast the 1923 World's Series. Red Barber, eminently qualified to judge baseball broadcasting, said decades later that McNamee was "the greatest announcer we ever had."

Chicago fans were the first to hear radio broadcasts of games on a continuing basis, followed by listeners in Detroit and Boston. During the late 1920s, Cubs home games were transmitted over five local stations. Curt Smith wrote that baseball team owners earlier had differed in their views as to whether radio broadcasts helped or hurt attendance. Smith reported that most team operators, with the notable exceptions of the Cubs' William Wrigley and the Reds' Larry MacPhail, believed that broadcasts might dim incentive for fans to pay to attend games when they could hear the game description on radio at no cost.

By the mid-'30s, fans in all major league areas, except the New York City area, heard daily broadcasts of their teams' games. However, some Giants game developments apparently were being broadcast by some clandestine means. There were indications that live reports of games had been pirated out of the Polo Grounds without the Giants' permission. After the 1935 season, the Giants filed suit to restrain bootleg broadcasts of all sporting events from the Polo Grounds. The suit was filed against several communication companies, although the Giants admitted that "the method of acquiring simultaneous description of baseball games is unknown."

The Yankees, Giants, and Dodgers originally had banned all game broadcasts from Yankee Stadium, the Polo Grounds, and Ebbets Field, including all broadcasts and re-creations to the visiting team's home cities. The three New York teams had signed a pact in the early '30s prohibiting broadcasts of their games through 1938. The powerful Yankees and Giants were concerned about losing attendance and the Dodgers, bogged down by ineffectual front-office leadership, went along with the arrangement. But the situation changed when aggressive Larry MacPhail took over the Dodgers after the 1938 season. One of his first moves was to pull the Dodgers out of the pact and hire the talented Red Barber away from the Cincinnati Reds to broadcast all Dodgers games, at home and on the road.

Originally there was some concern about broadcasting both home and away games in two-team cities. Most owners had come to think of home game broadcasts as good advertising. But, in a two-team city, broadcasting away games of one team could conflict with a game in the home city and provide an opportunity for a fan to stay home and listen to the away game rather than to attend the local game. This was no problem where one station broadcast both teams' games but it represented a problem where games were broadcast by different stations.

For economic reasons until after World War II, most away games were not broadcast live but rather were re-created via Western Union wire from the ballpark. Older fans will remember the clicking sounds signifying dots and dashes which the announcer translated into sketchy descriptions. Depending upon the announcer's predilection, the results might be presented as a simple relay of the result ("ball one, strike two,") or the results might be presented with added, if fictional, descriptive embroidering. Former president Ronald Reagan, who announced Cubs games in the 1930s for Des Moines station WHO, described a re-creation broadcasting experience to Curt Smith:

> In those days a team didn't have its own announcers, and so there were about five or six of us doing the same game. We had to compete for the audience.... I'd get something that [indicated only ball or strike].... So, I would say, "[Dizzy] Dean comes out of the windup, here comes the pitch, and ... it's a called strike breaking over the outside corner to a batter that likes the ball a little higher."

Reagan told of the time that he announced that a pitch was on its way to the plate when his assistant receiving the wired information shook his head and passed Reagan a note. It informed the future president that "The wire's gone dead." So the unflappable Reagan stalled, reporting that the pitcher had stepped off the mound to grab the resin bag, had shaken off a couple of signs, and then delivered a fictitious pitch. Reagan went on to announce that the batter had fouled off a pitch and that a fight had broken out between two fans over the baseball. Reagan slowly described the scuffle in minute detail. Finally, the report from the field arrived and Reagan laughed when he learned that the batter had popped out on the first pitch. The irrepressible Reagan chuckled after recounting the tale to Smith and commented: "But maybe I shouldn't tell that story. People are suspicious enough of those in politics."

The re-enactment of a local game in the evening after the game was a prevalent practice in the 1930s. In the New York area, for example, at dinnertime fans usually did not know the score of the Yankees or Giants game played that afternoon. To satisfy the lively interest in obtaining scores before the next morning's newspaper, New York station WOR sports announcer Stan Lomax reenacted the afternoon home game each night between 6:45 and 7 P.M. With a canned recording of crowd noises backing him up and a recorded crack of bat against ball, Lomax provided a realistic account of the game, pitch by pitch.

Red Barber refused to fake a broadcast of a re-created game. He told Curt Smith:

> I never tried to fool anybody. I couldn't be — didn't intend to be — like most guys. They deceived by omission. They didn't tell their listeners that this was a game based on cold type. They'd try to convince their audience that they were somehow at the ball park.... I couldn't go for that dishonesty. To me, the audience should know the truth. So what I did was intentionally arrange for the sounds of the wire service to be in close proximity to the mike. At home, you heard the dots and dashes — the sounds of the operating receiver typing away. I *wanted* the sounds to be heard — nobody was going to con the fans. I always felt that even with a re-creation, if you were a professional, if you had the talent, the audience would be pleased.

Ernie Harwell said of Barber: "Red was the first to take broadcasting out of the era of getting a scorecard and just being a fan. He turned it into studying players, supplying information, and taking folks behind the scene." Barber spoke with a soft, crisp, rhythmic southern accent in sharp contrast to the Brooklyn version of New York-speak of his audience. At first blush, it appeared that Brooklyn fans either would take a long time to become accustomed to his tart "foreign" speech or never become accustomed to it at all. But the Floridian's direct, no-nonsense approach and his unsurpassed knowledge of the game caught on quickly. He became an immediate favorite of Brooklyn fans quick to recognize genuine quality when they saw or heard it.

Fans enjoyed Barber's use of terms which had never been heard in Brooklyn — such as his down-home "sitting in the catbird seat" or "rhubarb" (dispute), and his typically vivid description of a line drive base hit as a "pistol shot single." It has been said that, in the Dodgers' pennant-winning season in 1941, it was unnecessary for a Dodgers fan to own a radio to hear a local game. All the fan had to do was to walk down any Brooklyn street and hear Barber's broadcast coming from each open window or hear the game from cars' open windows at traffic lights.

Barber was equally fond of the Dodgers fans as they were of him. He contributed his talents to raising money for the World War II effort and participated in local civic programs. He became so well-liked that a couple of years after he arrived in Brooklyn the Brooklyn Chamber of Commerce cited him as "the young man who has made the largest civic contribution to Brooklyn's betterment." Barber would say years later with quiet pride, "Brooklyn had 3 million people who needed a voice, and the fates had made me that voice."

Many fans rated famed Yankees announcer Mel Allen as Barber's equal and both men were voted into the Hall of Fame in August 1978. Allen, a precocious law school graduate born in a suburb of Birmingham, Alabama, was hired during the 1939 season to assist in broadcasting Yankees and Giants home games. He was an instant fan favorite, becoming the primary announcer for the Yankees in 1940. Allen possessed a clear, bell-like voice with a slightly slurred southern accent. New Yorkers found Allen's free-flowing style, exuberant enthusiasm, and baseball knowledge as appealing as they had Barber's more precise, less relaxed, delivery.

Allen loved everything about the Yankees and his announcing reflected it. He fed off the ambience and atmosphere of Yankee Stadium and he greatly enjoyed Yankees fans' enthusiasm and their appreciation of the game. And Allen was inspired by his association with the great Yankees— manager Joe McCarthy, Lou Gehrig, Bill Dickey, Joe DiMaggio, Red Ruffing, Lefty Gomez, Mickey Mantle, and others. He was so devoted to the players that he gave them loving nicknames, most famous his inspired reference to DiMaggio as "the Yankee Clipper."

Curt Smith compared Barber and Allen. He noted that Barber was the critics' choice; the average fan favored Allen. The elegant Barber was "white wine" and Allen was "beer." Barber was a "poet" while Allen was a "balladeer." Barber was less dramatic and prone to biblical allusions compared with the more down-to-earth Allen. But both men were considered the best in their profession. Paralleling their local stature, Barber and Allen also were national fan favorites as well. Both men were widely recognized by fans throughout the country and the world, chosen regularly to broadcast World's Series and All-Star games. But fans in each major league city also had their local announcer favorites.

Graham McNamee, despite his limited understanding of baseball, delivered such a vivid, colorful description of World's Series goings-on, both on the field and among the spectators, that it became apparent to radio station operators that broadcasts during the regular season would appeal to fans. In April 1924, Hal Totten, a Chicago *Daily News* writer, described a play-by-play of a Cubs–Cardinals game with wireless-provided information. Unlike McNamee, Totten had a quietly authoritative, laconic style apparently appealing to Chicago-area fans who had at least as much interest in the game itself as in the broadcaster's histrionics. Totten played a long, important role in developing radio broadcasts in

Chicago. He was the first to broadcast Cubs games, over five stations at one time, and White Sox games over two stations. He broadcast baseball in Chicago through the 1950s before he left the booth to become president of the Three-I League.

Curt Smith wrote that in that earlier era, "stations competed for broadcast *listeners*, not broadcast *rights*." In Chicago, for example, Cubs owner William Wrigley's idea was to obtain as many outlets as possible to tie up an entire city's fans. This was especially important in a two-team city like Chicago. Of course, in today's world, and especially with the advent of television, the shoe is on the other foot. Clubs' current incomes from their sales of broadcasting rights have become one of their largest revenue sources.

As other major league teams realized the potential commercial value of radio broadcasts, other cities followed the Chicago example — first Philadelphia, then St. Louis, Boston, and Cleveland. France Laux took over the microphone in St. Louis in 1929, and remained there for the next 18 years, extolling the on-field exploits of the colorful Cardinals, before and after the Gashouse Gang era, and struggling with the local fans through the ineptitude of the terminally dull Browns. Laux, an Oklahoma country boy in manner and style, broadcast the 1934 All-Star game, remembered for Carl Hubbell's feat in striking out five future Hall of Fame hitters in a row. Laux enjoyed telling the fans that he had batted against Hubbell in a sandlot game.

Laux was a quiet, low-key man, well-liked by the fans and players who were appreciative of his fairness and complete impartiality. But he had to overcome his flat delivery and aloof personal style. St. Louis sportswriter Bob Broeg said of him: "The truth was that when France had the field to himself, he could just be himself ... just tell the facts, and he could do that well. But when he had to entertain — jazz up the re-creations or be flashy like his competitors — he couldn't do it. People said he was too old-timey."

As a youngster, Tom Manning had boomed out the announcement of the pitchers and catchers at Indians games in the intimate confines of Cleveland's League Park, armed only with a megaphone. He broadcast Indians games sporadically beginning in 1925 for three years before becoming the club's regular announcer for the next four years. The redheaded Irishman was the direct opposite of Laux in style and manner. He had a loud, rasping voice, accentuating his outgoing, jocular manner. Jimmy Dudley, who broadcast Indians games for 20 seasons beginning in 1948 described Manning's impact on Indians fans: "What had been cold newsprint, Tom brought alive." Manning vacated the radio booth after the 1931 season, eventually moving into television before returning as a co-announcer for the Indians for a couple of years in the late '50s to the delight of his old fans.

Fred Hoey, a well-established sports official and sportswriter in the Boston area, was the original Boston baseball broadcaster beginning in 1925. A New Englander to the core, he broadcast Red "Sawx" and Braves games through the 1938 season, doing double duty as a well-respected sportswriter for a number of those years. Hoey had a drinking problem of which fans were aware but, in testimony to his close relationship with his listeners, they chose to ignore it. He was selected as one of the announcers for the 1933 World Series but he encountered some difficulty before the game struggling up the stairs to the radio booth.

New York sportswriter Til Ferdenzi, who grew up in the Boston area listening to Hoey, recalled the incident. "He was bombed. In the second or third inning, they had to yank him off the air with the explanation that he had a "bad cold."

In his *The Broadcasters,* Red Barber wrote of Hoey's close relationship with his fans.

> In 1937, at the height of his popularity, the sponsors and the station decided to fire Fred. This news was met with a deluge of protests to the radio stations, [and] newspapers. The firing was front-page news, and a boycott grew and grew. The protest culminated in the picketing of the two [Boston] ball parks. As far as I know, his dismissal occasioned the first pickets to march around a ball park in protest of the firing of a play-by-play announcer. In fact, the protest was so effective, Hoey was rehired and wasn't fired again until March 18, 1939.

Ferdenzi remembered, "Fred was a home-town boy, and he became a hero, a regional giant. He helped make fans of thousands of people — men, housewives, young kids. He was excitable — not trained ... and very much applauded." Hoey's success was all the more commendable considering he was covering a succession of inferior Red Sox and Braves teams.

Many older fans have a fond recollection of the special enjoyment baseball radio provided them when they were youngsters. After the advent of the small transistor set, it was common practice for a young fan to hide a set under the sheets of his bed and listen to a game while ostensibly obeying a parental order to go to sleep. After all, what better way to fall asleep than to relax to the dulcet tones of an Ernie Harwell or Vince Scully, or to stay awake to enjoy the exultation or disappointments each batter, inning, or game provided?

Actually, many fans consider radio to be the most entertaining means of following a game other than seeing the game in person. A radio broadcaster provides the basic facts—ball, strike, groundball, line drive, etc.—leaving the listener to visualize the scene in his individual way. And, the listening fan's enjoyment is enhanced further by a broadcaster with the ability to skillfully weave his own perceptions and anecdotes into his account of the game. By comparison, television zeroes in on the individual pieces of action but provides little or no room for the fan's imagination.

Edwin Lloyd "Ty" Tyson, a down-to-earth Pennsylvanian, broadcast the first Tigers game on April, 19, 1927, over Detroit station WWJ. Similar to several announcers of that early era, Tyson discarded any pretense of objectivity. He was an unapologetic "homer," an enthusiastic Tiger rooter who also happened to be the announcer of the Tigers games. Tyson had the ability to make the listening fan feel so much into the game as to feel that he was seated next to Tyson as Ty called the game. A veteran Tigers fan from a rural area 60 miles north of Detroit remembered how much Tyson's broadcast meant to rabid Tigers fans in his little hometown. He told Curt Smith:

> Ty was so vivid, he made games come alive. It was new, naturally, but it was his voice too—it was graphic. There was an *excitement* about him. Ty talked real slow, but he had an urgency inside him and he transmitted that to us.

It is of interest that station WWJ viewed its coverage of Tigers games as a public service, a concept difficult to grasp in today's heavily commercialized broadcasting world. The station had no sponsors in Tyson's first seven years of broadcasting which freed him to concentrate completely on the game. Finally, in 1934 when the Tigers won the pennant, the station accepted a sponsor. Even then, Tyson had to mention his sponsor—Mobil—only twice during his broadcast. At the game's start, he intoned, "This game is brought to you by Mobil Oil" and he finished the broadcast with "This game has been brought to you by Mobil Oil."

Byrum Saam was a long-time radio announcer for the Phillies and the Athletics, beginning in 1938. The personable Fort Worth, Texas, native did not have an especially distinctive style or a flamboyant personality but he was an extremely competent announcer. He is remembered fondly by Philadelphia-area fans for his laid-back style and longevity in the booth.

Any announcer who broadcasts thousands of games is bound to issue an occasional slip of the tongue, if not a downright malapropism, given the immediacy of description required in describing live action. Saam had his share. For example, he opened nervously on his first major league game broadcast in 1938, "Hello there, Byrum Saam, this is everybody speaking." Then there was the time he was introduced during a World Series by Mel Allen who said, "And now here's the very fine announcer from Philadelphia, the very engaging Byrum Saal." The congenial Saam, who did not hear Allen, responded with, "Right you are, Mel." In 1969, his non sequitur of the year came in his first broadcast from Montreal when he commented, "You know, 85 percent of the people up here speak French, but they're nice people anyway." But his most unconsciously titillating comment came in a late-night broadcast from San Francisco when, exhausted from his hectic life on the road, he wearily began his explanation of a complicated play with, "And now, for all you guys scoring in bed...."

The overpowering ineptitude of the Philadelphia clubs whose games Saam broadcast is a major reason Saam has been relatively unheralded. Connie Mack's Athletics had a miserable 1,057–1,553 (.405) record in the 17 years during which Saam broadcast their games and the Phillies were barely better with a 2,182–2,842 (.434) record in the 32 seasons when he covered them. In his 49 seasons behind the microphone, none of these teams won a pennant and, to add insult to injury, the Phillies' Whiz Kids won the pennant in 1950, the year that Saam left to handle the A's broadcasts.

There were few former players moving into the broadcast booth before World War II. Jack Graney, a retired journeyman outfielder with the Indians, was the first. He replaced Tom Manning in Cleveland for the 1932 season. Graney, an articulate speaker who was especially skilled at re-creating games, usually broadcast from an automobile showroom when not covering live action from the ballpark. Baseball commissioner Landis selected him as one of the announcers of the 1935 World Series, the first ex-player to announce a series.

Hall of Fame right-hander Waite Hoyt was generally considered the most effective former player-announcer of the pre–World War II period. The Brooklyn-born Hoyt was an extremely bright, urbane player who never let his sense of propriety stand in the way when he joined teammate and fellow Yankees mainstay Babe Ruth in spending riotous evenings on the town in the '20s. Quick on the verbal trigger, Hoyt was well-equipped for his eventual radio role, having spent time on the vaudeville circuit during off-seasons. The washed-up Hoyt quieted a group of opposing Pirates players as he struggled through his last few games with the Dodgers in 1938. When several Pittsburgh players began to needle him mercilessly, he stepped off the mound and, recalling the Yankees' overpowering four-game World Series sweep over Pittsburgh in 1927, responded loudly, "If you fellows don't pipe down, I'll put on my '27 Yankee uniform and scare you all to death."

After his retirement as a player in 1938, Hoyt worked on New York radio station variety shows and pregame announcing chores. He was a great storyteller with a virtually inexhaustible supply of baseball tales. There were times during the 1940–41 seasons when Dodgers games on New York station WOR were delayed by rain. During the breaks, Hoyt effortlessly told fascinating baseball stories of games and personalities without pause until the game resumed or was called. Many fans enjoyed his time on the air as much as they did Red Barber's live play-by-play accounts.

Hoyt was hired to do the play-by-play of Cincinnati Reds' games in 1942, and he remained there for the next 25 years interspersing his game accounts with his wonderful anecdotes. He broadcast all of those years from ancient Crosley Field and his perch was a small, rickety open booth which swayed in the wind. But Hoyt was comfortable. He remembered fondly, "You were *close* to the fans, you recognized a lot of the people there, and they'd be calling up to you."

The Pirates began broadcasting their games in 1936 and their messenger was Albert Kennedy "Rosey" Rowswell. The gnomelike Rowswell's broadcasting style was the direct opposite of that of serious, businesslike Waite Hoyt. To Rosey, his Pirates were putting on a show and he considered himself a vital part of the production. He did an adequate job of reporting the nuts and bolts of a game but a completely off-the-wall job of dramatizing the action.

Rosey had a close rapport with his listeners. And he had his own expressions for many occurrences on the field, all of them designed to please his legion of fans. When the Pirates loaded the bases, the bags were "FOB," for full of Bucs. Any Pirates base hit was inexplicably referred to as a "doozie marooney." After a Pirates double play, Rosey summed up the play with a triumphant "Put 'em on and take 'em off." And Rosie could be as hammy as Harry Caray many years later when a Pirate homered. Rosey would jump to his feet and shout, "Get upstairs, Aunt Minnie, and raise the window! Here she comes." Rosey's broadcasting sidekick, Bob Prince, then would come into play, creating a shattering noise by dropping a large, loaded tray on the floor while standing on a chair. It was corny, but Pirates fans loved it. They also loved his blind devotion to his Bucs; he was the ultimate "homer."

Rosey talked constantly during his broadcast of anything that came into his head, a useful diversionary tactic during many of his 19 years touting the virtues of poor clubs. Bob Prince remembered:

> He'd be [talking about] *anything* but the game.... [He'd say] "Bob, we have sponsors that deserve fans, and we've got listeners that deserve a show.

Now, if I just sit up there and talk about the facts, we ain't gonna have — fans or a show." And ... he was right. You can't just ho-hum it; you have to *entertain*.

Jerome Herman (or Jay Hanna, take your pick) "Dizzy" Dean was the best-known player turned broadcaster. The Hall of Fame right-hander was an irresistible *force*, both on the mound and in the radio booth. The rangy, loose-jointed Dean retired as a player in May 1941, his career shortened prematurely by an injury in the 1937 All-Star game. He began announcing games immediately after his retirement as a player. The uneducated and grammar-challenged Dean was hired by a St. Louis radio station where he became an overpowering fan favorite within a few months. He broadcast the always-contending Cardinals games through 1946, then covered the lowly Browns for three years before moving out of the St. Louis radio scene into national television.

Speaking in a hillbilly drawl, Dean did not only abuse the King's English, he absolutely fractured it. In his uninhibited style, runners "slud" into bases, hitters "swang" at the ball, pitchers "thowed" the ball, an infielder was given a "'sist" (assist) and other easily pronounced words became barely distinguishable; that is, until the listener was able to put his every-sentence malapropisms into proper context. Just as pitcher Dizzy thumbed his nose at Cardinals manager Frankie Frisch's dictates, he skirted the government requirement during World War II that weather could not be reported. Said Dizzy during a rainstorm delay, "I cain't tell you why this here game is stopped but you'll know why if you jes stick your head out the window."

Dean's outrageous language forced Commissioner Landis to banish him from the broadcasting booth during the all–St. Louis World Series in 1944. Dizzy responded with the thought, "How can that 'commissar' say I ain't eligible to broadcast? I ain't never met anybody that didn't know what ain't means." Yet, with Dizzy's misuse of his native tongue, there were indications that his abuse of the language was partially intentional. He realized that fans expected him to play the part of the shrewd hillbilly. His poor grammar had become something of a trademark, and he was heard on occasion to use the word "slid" and quickly change it to "slud."

Former major league infielder Buddy Blattner worked with Dean for five years on television. Blattner, who knew Dean's strengths along with his tendency to overpower his colleagues, nevertheless admired him. He felt that Dean related so well to people because they admired his overwhelming ability to back up everything he'd achieved as a player. The possibility of failure as a baseball player, golfer, or announcer probably never entered his mind.

Ernie Harwell was the TV announcer when Bobby Thomson hit his "Miracle at Coogan's Bluff" homer to win the 1951 pennant for the New York Giants. Harwell was one of the most learned and versatile writers of the great baseball announcers. Most importantly, in a quiet, unobtrusive way he became one of the best-loved personalities in the game. He had a warm, homey, southern accent, and, when asked why so many top announcers were southerners (among them Red Barber, Mel Allen, Russ Hodges), he opined, "We came from a storytelling background." But he was more than that; he also was a teacher whether broadcasting in Brooklyn, New York, Baltimore, and Detroit.

Veteran Baltimore writer John Steadman wrote of Harwell:

> He had more authenticity as an announcer than anyone I've ever heard. Ernie could extrapolate on anything—poetry, history, baseball, manufacturing.... He was highly respected because he didn't talk in cliches.... Plus, Ernie had a wonderful tempo, a great delivery ... just a lot of laudable qualities.

After television came in, most well-established radio announcers began splitting their broadcasting time between radio and TV. Harwell is the only one of the elite radio-TV announcers who, while at the top of his game in both media, desired to return to the radio booth exclusively. He had been doing both radio and TV his first five years in Detroit but the two functions were split and Harwell found that he didn't miss the greater visibility of TV broadcasting at all. As Harwell described it:

> Radio is the best medium for baseball.... Sitting home, you can imagine it all. Everyone knows where the ... bases are, where a shortstop plays for a pull hitter.... The bags, the positions, the batter, the pitcher—they're all definite designations. You start with the bare bones, and your creativity fills in the rest.... which is why the [radio] announcer *matters* more [to the fan] in baseball than in any other sport.

Red Barber agreed with Harwell, writing in his *Rhubarb in the Catbird Seat*:

> Most people don't realize it, but there is a profound difference between doing a play-by-play broadcast on radio and doing the same thing on television.... I would much prefer to do a ball game on radio instead of TV, and I think any baseball announcer worth his salt would agree with me. On radio the play-by-play announcer is the show. He is the artist.... On television, instead of being in control and broadcasting what *his* eyes see and

what *his* brain thinks of, the announcer is the unquestioning servant of the director [who decides what is to be done].

In a misguided move, the Tigers fired Harwell just before Christmas in 1990; their excuse was that they believed the 72-year-old intended to retire anyway. Harwell had no attention of leaving the radio booth and the firing was rescinded after Detroit fans threatened to boycott Tigers games, the radio station, and Tigers owner Tom Monaghan's pizza products. Harwell returned to broadcast games until he retired after the 2002 season. He left to the tributes of his fans in each American League city on the Tigers' last visit of that season.

Many other first rate-baseball broadcasters worked in the years before television. Harry Hartmann was a short, grossly overweight Cincinnati announcer who broadcast Reds games from 1930 until Red Barber replaced him four years later. He was an early version of John Madden, inventing such testosterone-derived terms as "socko," "whammo," and "bammo." Harry Heilmann, a Hall of Fame outfielder with the Tigers, broadcast Tigers games for 17 years. Heilmann's anecdotes and knowledge of the game compensated for his rough delivery.

Jim Britt, a law school graduate and possessor of a magnificent vocabulary, gave up on the law to broadcast Red Sox and Braves games for 12 years beginning in 1939. Bert Wilson, a wildly enthusiastic Cubs fan who was an even more dedicated "homer" than Harry Caray, broadcast from Wrigley Field in the '40s. Bob Elson was another Chicago favorite, remembered best for his laconic style and his introduction of the pregame, on-field player interviews. Earl Gillespie, a colorful extrovert known for his outlandish antics in the booth, recounted the Milwaukee Braves' up-and-down fortunes from 1953 though 1963.

Radio coverage always will have an important place in keeping a fan abreast of a game's progress. It permits the fan to follow a game while driving or to pick up broadcasts of games not otherwise available. It also gives the listener the same opportunity to enjoy the game vicariously as radio did in the '20s and '30s. And, even with the advent of TV, baseball on radio remains a prime source of enjoyment for the baseball fan.

8

Television

Commercial television came on the American scene after World War II ended. The 1946 Yankees club was the first major league team to have a limited number of games televised. A small number of baseball fans owning sets viewed games on small, seven-inch black and white sets. The early imperfections of the medium were reflected in frequent breakdowns in the transmission accompanied by the frustrating phrase "Please stand by." And the views of the game action were limited, usually one from behind the plate and the other from another location, usually from off the dugouts in the first- or third-base stands.

The two foremost radio broadcasters, Red Barber and Mel Allen, announced the 1947 World Series, the first to be televised. The differences in broadcasting philosophy between the two great announcers were illustrated in the fourth game of the series when the Dodgers' Cookie Lavagetto broke up Yankees right-hander Bill Bevens's no-hit bid with a game-winning, two-out-in-the-ninth hit. Allen announced the first half of the game. He refused to report that Bevens had a no-hitter, reflecting a traditional player superstition that no one on the pitcher's team bench is to mention that the opposing team has yet to obtain a hit.

But Barber, a no-nonsense stickler for factual reporting, took over the microphone at midgame and threw tradition to the winds with the clipped words, "For the Dodgers, one run, two errors, and *no hits*." For the rest of the game, Barber continued to report the Dodgers' failure to hit safely. Actually, he was enhancing his listeners' enjoyment by making sure they knew about the no-hitter, thereby maximizing the delicious feeling of suspense and anticipation which accompanies watching a no-hitter.

Chicago area fans had their share of unforgettable baseball announcers, among them Hal Totten, Ronald Reagan, Bert Wilson, Pat Flanagan,

8. Television

Bob Elson, Jack Brickhouse, Charlie Grimm, Lou Boudreau, and Harry Caray.

Jack Brickhouse was the quintessential Chicago baseball announcer, as unabashed a rooter for the Windy City home team as the most avid Cubs or White Sox bleacher fan. A Peoria, Illinois, native, the big, hearty, round-faced Brickhouse joined the Chicago radio broadcasting scene in 1940 with the support of Bob Elson, the well-established lead announcer. After World War II service, Brickhouse announced New York Giants games for a year before returning to Chicago. His television debut came on Chicago's TV station WGN in 1948. At the time, Chicago had a disproportionately high ratio of TV sets, and Brickhouse became a big hit with his spirited, gung-ho style of reporting. In retrospect, and without realizing it at the time, Brickhouse was developing an intimacy between ball club and viewer that decades later made the Cubs a "national" team.

Brickhouse loved everything about baseball in general, and most specifically, Chicago baseball—the Cubs, the White Sox, Wrigley Field, Comiskey Park, and, above all, Chicago fans. Brickhouse gained the nickname "Hey-Hey" because of his habit of saying that to celebrate a favorable occurrence at the ballpark. This was an early version of Harry Caray's subsequent triumphant "Cubs win, Cubs win!" after every Chicago victory.

Since the first radio broadcast and continuing into the TV era, baseball moguls have debated whether broadcasting games results in a net attendance gain or loss. Brickhouse took the view that, on any given day, televising a game could cause a slight drop in attendance but that, in the long run, the fan interest engendered would raise attendance. He believed that those who became Cubs fans as a result of television would sooner or later come out to Wrigley Field.

Vin Scully, Ernie Harwell, and possibly Curt Gowdy are considered by most objective fans as the best of the announcers of their era. The Bronx-born Scully is a dyed-in-the-wool New Yorker who attended and played baseball at Fordham University. As a 22-year-old, Scully impressed Red Barber immediately with his voice, his maturity, and his zest for learning his trade. Barber hired him and Scully's announcing improved steadily under Barber's demanding tutelage.

Scully took over as the Dodgers' primary announcer in late 1953 after Barber left the Dodgers to join Mel Allen in the Yankees' broadcast booth. Scully proved a superb replacement for Barber. He remained in Brooklyn through the 1957 season, then accompanied the Dodgers when they moved to Los Angeles after that season. He had his greatest thrill in baseball when the Dodgers defeated the Yankees in the 1955 World Series. Emotionally devoted to Dodgers fans, after calmly reporting the final out of the series, Scully was asked how he could remain so calm. He responded, "If I'd said another word, I'd have broken down crying."

Incredibly, Scully was still going strong as the Dodgers' announcer 50 years after he started the job. He loved New York and was not thrilled at leaving Brooklyn where he had been very successful and extremely popular with the fans. But he loved being with the Dodgers and, as he put it, "I was like the bride whose husband had been transferred, she might not want to go, but she goes."

In Los Angeles, Dodgers president Walter O'Malley banned all free TV of home games, enabling Scully to capture on radio many fans who formerly had watched the Dodgers home games on TV. And so Scully flourished even more in Los Angeles than he had in Brooklyn. He was credited with increasing sales of transistor radios in his station's listening area. Even during games, the sounds of Scully's radio broadcasts can be heard echoing throughout the Chavez Ravine stands. Apparently, Dodgers fans cannot do without Scully's commentary even when they are watching the game he is broadcasting. Ernie Harwell has written, "Vin is generally regarded as the premiere baseball announcer."

As an announcer, the redheaded Scully has it all. He has a great voice, exquisite command of the language, and a passion for detail but with the ability to separate meaningful detail from minutiae. He has the knack of putting words together to draw a precise picture of the action, thereby providing the radio listener with the mental tools to process the game in his mind. And, on the personal side, all of his announcing colleagues, as well as his fans, regard him as a classy man.

Curt Gowdy was another radio booth giant. He did not have the eloquence of Barber, Harwell, or Scully but he was considered their superior in his versatility in describing several sports. Most baseball announcers also have called other sports, most often football or basketball. Gowdy was considered the most solid, the most knowledgeable, as evidenced by his well-received description of such events as Super Bowls, college football bowls, NCAA basketball championships, and Olympic events. Well before the National and American football leagues merged into today's NFL, and before Gowdy became a kingpin in broadcasting national baseball events, he was the AFL network's primary play-by-play announcer.

Gowdy was called "the Cowboy" because of his Cheyenne, Wyoming, background. In his broadcasts, he came across to fans as a down-to-earth, regular guy from the western plains. Curt Smith wrote that Gowdy's broadcasts were filled with "numbers, anecdotes, and … fact; and if less poetic than Scully, or exciting than [Pittsburgh's Bob] Prince, or dependent on punch-lines than [Joe] Garagiola, revealed a natural, honest delivery that ... [could be called] *meticulous, professional,* and *fair.*"

Red Sox fans remember Gowdy's years with the Red Sox for the Sox's great players rather than for their futile chase of the Yankees. Gowdy recalled, "We didn't do much in the standings—but what personalities we had! The [Mel] Parnells, the Bobby Doerrs ... and the Williamses. That's why broadcasting the Red Sox was so fascinating. In a way, they were *like* baseball. It's not really a team game, like football. It's a game of individuals."

Gowdy was the foremost baseball announcer of the '70s. Beginning in 1966 through 1975, he broadcast the play-by-play of every All-Star game and every World Series game. All fans agreed with Gowdy's straightforward credo on broadcasting: "The one who remembers that the game is the most important thing is the one who will make it."

Russ Hodges was born in Dayton, Kentucky, and, like many of the broadcasters, he was a college athlete. His radio career began at 21 when he took the first of a series of on-the-air jobs, a broadcasting trail that took him through Covington, Kentucky, Rock Island, Illinois; Charlotte, North Carolina; Chicago; and finally to Washington, D.C. in 1938. The New York Giants job opened up in 1939 and the easygoing Hodges moved in and began his 33-year broadcasting career with the Giants, the first 20 in New York and then 13 after the club moved to San Francisco.

Hodges, who died unexpectedly in 1971, was a warm, friendly, universally liked man whose direct, unpretentious, relaxed broadcasting style reflected his personality. He had a gentle voice, always dispassionate, and sometimes droll. Hodges relied completely on his ability to describe the action as accurately and fairly as possible. His signature "Bye, bye, baby" told fans that a baseball had been hit out of the park. Fans remember best his famous radio call on Bobby Thomson's "miracle" home run over the Dodgers on October 3, 1951:

> [The Dodgers' Ralph] Branca throws.... There's a long drive! It's going to be, I believe! The Giants win the pennant! The Giants win the pennant! The Giants win the pennant! The Giants win the pennant! Bobby Thomson hits into the lower deck of the left-field stands! The Giants win the pennant! And they're going crazy! Oh-ho! ... I don't believe it! ... The Giants win by a score of 5 to 4 and they're picking up Bobby Thomson and carrying him off the field!

Lindsey Nelson had a 40-year career behind the microphone in several cities but fans remember him best as the first New York Mets announcer, a post he retained from 1962 through 1978. Actually, to many sports fans, the Pulaski, Tennessee, native was as highly respected for his college football work as for his baseball announcing. When the Mets hired him in 1962, a number of TV critics, not aware of his baseball background, asked, "What the heck are the Mets hiring a *football* guy for?"

Before beginning his baseball announcing in 1950, Nelson had taught English in high school, and, after an Army stint, was a news reporter in Knoxville. TV network executive Tom Gallery said of the erudite Nelson:

> He shouldn't have been called a *professional* announcer — he should have been called a *professor* of announcing because when you [hired] him, you got a writer, an editor, an educator, a guy who would study an event from top to bottom — he was a damn perfectionist. The incompetent broadcasters on the air today — they should hire Lindsey to coach 'em from the ground floor up.

Nelson was known for his large collection of outrageously colorful, plaid sports jackets. But, more substantively, he was extremely knowledgeable with a vibrant, pleasant, faintly southern accent and the ability to excite Mets fans, although he was not a "homer" in the Chicago tradition. In expressing his preference for radio over TV broadcasting, Nelson said, "There's no radio sport better than baseball to do stream-of-consciousness — the slow pace, the time to improvise." Nelson was extremely popular, not only with the fans, but with his fellow broadcasters, worth mentioning in the highly competitive, frequently cutthroat world of broadcasting.

Bob Wolff broadcast the Washington Senators' games for 15 years beginning in 1947. His early background resembles that of Vin Scully — a New York City native, extremely bright and ambitious, and a college athlete. Wolff played baseball at Duke University, and earned a Phi Beta Kappa, but his dream of a professional playing career ended abruptly after he broke an ankle while sliding into a base in his sophomore year.

Wolff, a handsome, cerebral man, was an artistic success as the "Voice of the Senators," which is more than could be said for the inept clubs he covered. The Senators finished in the second division in every one of Wolff's 14 years with the club for a miserable .410 record (883–1270). Wolff tried to maintain his sense of humor and he recalled: "Did I have a *choice*? No, I couldn't laugh it off when the shortstop kicked one that let in the winning run — although I was laughing inside. But believe me, there were plenty of times it was tough to keep a straight face and tell the fans, "Now, the Senators need eight runs in the last two innings to pull it out."

There has never been a closer kinship between a baseball announcer and the baseball fans than that which existed between Harry Caray and the fans living by his words in St. Louis, Oakland, and Boston. It was one of a kind. Harry, nee Harry Christopher Carabina, had a voice like a drunken stevedore, a propensity for "telling it like it is" which put Howard Cosell to shame, and an extensive knowledge of the game and the players.

After broadcasting minor league games, he made his major league announcing debut in 1945 in St. Louis. From the start, Caray broadcast games with the direct bluntness of an impassioned fan. He would say later in his career:

> My whole philosophy has always been to broadcast the way a fan would broadcast. I'm tough on my guys [players] because I want them to win so much. I've often thought that if you gave the microphone to a fan, he'd sound a lot like me. The disappointment, the hurt, the anger, the bitterness, the love, the ecstasy — they'd all be there.... The way I broadcast — I sound the way I do because I'm just an inveterate fan who happens to be behind the mike.

Caray was a showman as well as a fan with a microphone. His deep, booming voice was replete with such patented expressions as "Holy Cow," "It might be ... it could be ... it is!" (signifying a home run), and his gleeful shout after a home team victory, "Cardinals [Cubs] win!" Another familiar part of the Caray shtick was his belting out "Take Me Out to the Ball Game" in a lusty, off-key voice before the home club's half of the seventh inning. And he was not above diverting fans' attention during a losing Cubs effort by attempting to catch foul balls near the broadcast booth with a net.

Of all of the prominent broadcasters, Caray had the most interaction and identification with his listening fans. New York Mets announcer Lindsay Nelson told Curt Smith:

> His impact [on the fans] was enormous. People love him or they hate him, but they always listen.... I'd go to dinner with Harry. *I'd* be ignored — *he'd* be mobbed by fans from the Midwest. People'd crowd around, "Hey, Harry. Hey, Har-ry! Sign this, autograph that!" I was absolutely amazed. I'd never seen anything like it. Nobody had, I think, the kind of following Harry did when he was with the Cardinals — they totally idolized him.

Caray broadcast games from the bleachers, a gambit bringing him closer to the fans and, at one time, attendance bonuses. As Curt Smith described the scene when he broadcast White Sox games,

"By late April 1971, he was welcomed by his first banner reading, "Holy Cow!"; by late May, he was broadcasting from the center-field bleachers, encircled by hundreds of fans.... [He just raised a beach umbrella when it rained].... By early October, the Sox had lured 833,891 paid admissions [338,000 over 1970] and Caray [earned] attendance bonuses of $30,000.

His broadcasts were peppered with references to friends passing by his booth or responses to fans from throughout the country who had left him phone messages. While on the air, he talked constantly with his director about matters unrelated to the game. When you listened or watched Caray, you felt you were being entertained by a continuous sideshow along with the play-by-play. And you were not alone as the entire country witnessed the Caray show, courtesy of the cable TV exposure afforded him.

Caray was a throwback to an earlier era, perhaps the days when Rosey Rowswell put on his fan-pleasing private show while broadcasting a game. But Caray was even more outrageous. He hid his deep knowledge of the game behind his show business antics. He exuded confidence and was highly opinionated, fully aware that the fans liked outspokenness, whether justified or not. Caray was prone to getting on errant home team players because, he would say, "That's what fans do." He exulted, mourned, ripped, praised, questioned decisions, and above all, he agonized. All of these qualities accounted for Caray's extraordinary popularity.

Harry Caray also is remembered, along with Dizzy Dean, for being the only broadcaster to overshadow the players whose actions he described. Some fans were put off by his overly subjective broadcasting, but others were enamored of his showmanship, his large, black-rimmed glasses, and intrigued by his very un-private, private life. He earned the title "Mayor of Rush Street"— a nightclub section in downtown Chicago. After games his drinking and taste for night life on Rush Street were legendary. And he had a Babe Ruth-like reputation for his womanizing, including a reported affair with a daughter-in-law of Cardinals owner Gussie Busch when Harry was employed (and immediately fired) by Busch. Also like Ruth, Caray's legendary style, persona and impact on the fans are unlikely to be seen again.

Harry Caray's son, Harry Jr. (Skip) has been the major TV and radio voice of the Atlanta Braves. Skip shares his father's name, bulky physique, and the status of being a lead announcer on a cable TV superstation. Otherwise, the two men are completely dissimilar in broadcasting style and persona. Harry had a loud voice and an earthy, man-in-the-street, broadcasting manner. Skip has a soft, tart, sophisticated voice. Harry Sr. was completely subjective in discussing players, especially their shortcomings;

Skip is more analytical and impersonal in discussing players. And the elder Harry was a showman as well as a reporter. His son relies completely on his broadcasting ability and it is hard to think of him as a showman working to build up gate receipts or playing up to the fans.

Skip Caray admits that he had an advantage in rising to his high-level announcing post. He began his announcing career with the Braves in 1976 at age 35 and is well accepted by Braves' fans and highly rated by his announcing peers. Before that he paid his dues with a background as a radio writer, director, and producer. A third generation of Caray sports announcers has taken wing as of this writing. Skip's son, Chip, broadcasts Chicago Cubs games on TV superstation WGN, following in his grandfather's footsteps.

Joe Garagiola was closely associated with Harry Caray after Joe deserted the playing field for the broadcast booth. Joe was brought up in a heavily Italian section of St. Louis. Garagiola and Yogi Berra grew up together. They played sports together and, as Garagiola loved to recall, shared one glove and played on the same sandlot team. And Garagiola, more than anyone else, has been a leader in inventing "Yogi stories." Playing in the minor leagues before World War II, scouts rated Garagiola as a better prospect than Berra. Joe joined the Cardinals in 1946 but had a journeyman career with St. Louis and later with the Pirates, Cubs, and Giants.

Always a wisecracker and raconteur, Joe became interested in broadcasting in 1950 while listening to Harry Caray's Cardinals broadcasts. The Cardinals picked him to join Caray in 1955 after his playing career ended and he remained with Caray and Jack Buck for eight years before NBC hired him for its *Major League Baseball* program. Garagiola was an immediate hit when he started announcing; his quick wit, amusing stories, and baseball smarts compensated for an average speaking voice and his unpolished delivery at the time. The versatile Garagiola authored *Baseball is a Funny Game*, one of the all-time best-selling baseball books.

Garagiola has a virtually inexhaustible collection of one-liners and a wonderful knack for ad libbing equally funny lines. Many of his earlier funny anecdotes involved Yogi Berra, but Joe realized that the Yogi joke routine was getting old and he has moved on to more generic gags. For example, he had a series of good-natured one-liners about his Italian heritage. There was the time Joe was on the Johnny Carson show with fellow Italian-Americans Kaye Ballard and June Valli. At the time a Mafia investigation was under way on Capitol Hill. Joe cracked, "This is the first time a group of Italians have gotten together without a senator present." He also loved to reminisce of his time with the awful 1952 Pirates team, Joe remembered, "It was the most courageous team in baseball. We had 154 games scheduled, and we showed up for them all. We lost eight of our first nine games, and then we went into a slump."

But Garagiola's comedic talent is just one reason for his success. He is unflappable, extremely alert, and is a quick study. Garagiola has a remarkable memory. Bob Wolff recalled working with Garagiola: "Joe would amaze me with his recall. We'd be driving home from the airport on Sunday night [after a game broadcast], and he'd say, 'You know, Bob, you said "so and so" in the third inning today and I came back with "such and such," and I think it would have worked out better if I'd said "this or that" instead.' He had the sequences memorized word for word. His concentration was absolutely stunning."

Jack Buck was a popular member of the Cardinals broadcasting team along with Caray beginning in 1954, a year before they were joined by Garagiola. Born in Holyoke, Massachusetts, Buck had a variety of odd jobs before attending Ohio State University. He broadcast games in Columbus, Ohio, and Rochester, New York, before joining Caray in the Cardinals booth. He became the Cardinals' lead broadcaster when Caray was fired unceremoniously by Gussie Busch. He replaced Caray in the minds and hearts of the Cardinals' large following throughout the Midwest for many years.

Buck had a more subtle style than Caray and he had a skeptical, satirical bent, well-suited to the tastes of fans in the Midwest. He had an easy-going manner and a whimsical approach to life, and especially baseball. To the delight of his fans, he said he had a "racket" as a baseball broadcaster. As he described his daily routine, "You golf, swim, or shoot pool during the day, go to the park and b.s. with the manager and players a little before the game, do the game, b.s. some more, and go home. It's tough, real tough."

Buck died in the summer of 2002 and his fans throughout the Midwest went into deep mourning. But the Buck name is still prominent in the announcing game. Before he died, he had the satisfaction of seeing his son Joe become one of the foremost sports broadcasters.

Best known for covering *Monday Night Football,* Al Michaels was a fan favorite when he broadcast Cincinnati Reds games in the club's halcyon years in the early '70s and Giants games subsequently. A native New Yorker like his idol, Vin Scully, he patterned his broadcasting technique on the Scully style. Michaels grew up in Brooklyn and Los Angeles at the time Scully broadcast games in those cities and some Michaels listeners feel that Al even sounds exactly like Scully. To other fans, Michaels's voice sounds even more like Alan Alda's.

Michaels became a prime favorite in Cincinnati because of his baseball knowledge and blunt intensity that wore well on Reds fans who take their baseball very seriously. Michaels' aggressiveness did not wear as well with the Reds' front office and he moved into the Giants' broadcasting booth after three years in Cincinnati. Unlike the Reds, the Giants were a lackadaisical, mediocre team and, in his two years in San Francisco, Bay Area fans appreciated Michaels's unvarnished criticism of the goings-on at Candlestick Park. On the air, he accused Giants players of being lethargic and showing little respect for manager Charley Fox. As a result, the highly provocative Michaels was unpopular with the players but a huge success with the fans. San Francisco writer Wells Twombly wrote, "It has been said — not altogether humorously — that the reason the Giants are last in home attendance in the major leagues, is because everybody stays home and listens to Michaels."

Bob Costas, a native New Yorker like Vin Scully, Al Michaels, and Bob Wolff, shares their deep, abiding love for baseball above other sports and this feeling comes through to his listeners. Costas graduated from Syracuse University in 1974 and began his broadcasting career with TV-radio station WSYR in Syracuse. He joined NBC in 1980 and, in addition to studio hosting and reporting, has become one of the network's primary announcers for a wide variety of sports, including baseball league championship series and World Series games, pregame Super Bowl shows, NBA games, and the Olympics.

Costas's broadcasts are a wonderful blend of clearly stated prose and whimsical overtones, incisive opinion, and a pleasing self-deprecating sense of humor. Unlike other sports, baseball is characterized by a deceptive sequence of relatively little action building into a tense situation. This pace is perfectly suited to Costas's subtle, gentle, warmlyexpressed announcing style. As Costas described it: "Baseball is the greatest hanging-around game ever invented. You hang around the batting cage, in hotel lounges or bars after the game, talking to baseball people. There's a romance and mystique to baseball that nothing else can match."

Costas has won many awards, one of them for his eloquent tribute to his boyhood idol, Mickey Mantle. After Mantle's death, Costas talked lovingly of Mantle at his funeral service. Costas said, "I guess I'm here, not to speak so much for myself as to simply represent the millions of baseball-loving kids who grew up in the '50s and '60s." In 1990, Costas did speak for himself, providing sensible suggestions for dealing with major league baseball's problems in a thoughtful, well-received book. To many of today's fans, Costas represents the conscience of the game, a throwback to Henry Chadwick.

Jon Miller is considered baseball's best TV announcer. Miller is from the Oakland area where his first broadcasting stint came when he announced his high school's basketball games. (This excludes his private broadcasts at age nine of toy baseball games during which he imitated the voices of such luminaries as Vin Scully and Russ Hodges). His first major league broadcasting job was in Oakland, followed by moves to broadcasting booths in Texas, Boston, and Baltimore, where he gained national recognition.

The round, robust, balding Miller has every requisite for announcing greatness and he utilizes them all. His voice is just right for baseball — elegant, deep and resonant, with a touch of gentle, bantering humor, especially pleasing to fans on his weekly game broadcasts with Joe Morgan on ESPN. He has a thorough knowledge of players and personalities in both leagues. Miller is a remarkably talented mimic; his subjects range from fellow broadcasters, notably the well-measured tones of Scully, to public address announcers like Fenway Park's dour-sounding Sherm Feller or Yankee Stadium's ethereal-voiced Bob Shepard. Miller's broadcasts enhance the relaxed pleasure of baseball listening.

And then there is ESPN, to which many baseball fans are absolutely addicted. It has been an invaluable information source for baseball fans unable to wait to obtain ball scores from the 6 and 11 P.M. network news broadcasts. ESPN is a special boon to fans craving up-to-the-minute scores, especially of late West Coast games. The station has a large stable of professional announcers including the inimitable Chris Berman, best known for twisting players' names for comic effect, and a coterie of very glib young announcers. Other regulars are authoritative baseball writers like Peter Gammons and Tim Kurkjian and well-respected former players like Harold Reynolds. And, of course, ESPN broadcasts several baseball games each week of the season, employing top-notch announcers like the redoubtable Jon Miller-Joe Morgan team. Watching ESPN is a must for millions of baseball fans.

TV coverage of baseball has improved dramatically since 1948. Announcers have become more authoritative, especially with expanded utilization of former players as announcers, most of whom have invaluable knowledge and insights of the action, game strategy, and players. The development and use of color has given televised games a beauty and vividness over the earlier black-and-white coverage.

The original use of one or two TV cameras has given way to the use of many cameras, enhancing the enjoyment of fans at home. Availability of improved videotape has made a significant improvement in picture quality and facilitated the use of instant replay. The development of portable cameras has made possible especially interesting and revealing camera views. And directors have devised more creative views of picturing individual players, managers, and spectators than were possible in the earlier days of TV coverage.

There are two primary points for viewing game action on TV. The most obvious is the view from the stands behind home plate. This is the view most often used in the first years of TV coverage. But, equally important to many fans, is the view from center field. In the early days of TV coverage, the technology did not permit running a camera cable to center field. Since its use in the late '50s, the view has given the fan a special feeling of involvement in the game as he sees the pitcher, batter, plate umpire, and location of the pitch, as the center fielder sees it.

Watching a game on television is a completely different experience from watching the game in person. The camaraderie with other fans is lacking as well as the sounds, smells, and the nothing-like-it feeling of a ballpark. But, in the absence of the electricity the players and fans generate at a ballpark, television fills a need. And fans have learned to adapt to television. Many experienced TV viewers can determine unerringly how a play will turn out before it is completed, for examples, whether a pitch will be called a ball or strike, if a long drive or Texas Leaguer can be caught, or whether a catcher will be able to reach a ball popped up behind the plate.

Television announcing differs from radio announcing in the way field action is described. Television requires less description because the viewer can see the action. The picture is more important than the accompanying description. Adjusting to these differing needs can be a problem for announcers who shift back and forth between radio and TV. Some fans can be irritated by an overly detailed description of what they themselves can see on TV.

As indicated in the previous chapter, older broadcasters, notably Ernie Harwell and Red Barber who had done considerable radio work before moving to TV, prefer to cover a game on radio rather than TV. Radio gave them an opportunity to be in charge. It permitted them to paint a picture in rich detail as they saw fit. By comparison, the television producer or director decides on the pictures to be shown and that choice dictates the announcer's comments, with one exception. Dizzy Dean did not differentiate between radio and TV as his fanciful monologues often bore no relation to the action on the field or to the TV picture shown. But to the more orthodox, more disciplined announcer, the TV picture limits the scope of his remarks.

Lindsey Nelson, who loved the freedom radio provided him, appreciated the fact that mistakes made on radio were not apparent to the listening fan. He felt that when announcers switch from TV back to radio, they use the same bland, mechanical style that works on TV but reduces the effectiveness of radio play-by-play broadcasts.

Baseball umpires make mistakes. Bill James expressed the view that modern sportswriters dislike second-guessing umpire errors and generally do not do so unless reporting the error is unavoidable. He wrote that broadcasters do not have the same compunction and TV broadcasts even highlight umpire mistakes by showing them repetitively.

It is axiomatic that we tend to remember better the things we see than the things we are told. This appears to be the case in following baseball. Bobby Thomson's miracle home run in 1951 is remembered mostly for Russ Hodges's radio account than for Ernie Harwell's description on TV. The reason: TV had not yet fully caught on with baseball fans. Just three years later, Willie Mays's classic catch of Vic Wertz's blast to center field in the 1954 World Series was seen, and is remembered, by millions because they saw the play on TV. And since that time, TV coverage has dominated the attention of the baseball fan.

9

Player Popularity

Conventional wisdom holds that fans usually are more concerned with the status of their favorite team than individual players. Yet, many fans become as interested in the doings of a favorite player as a favorite team. And so it is interesting to examine the reasons fans become attached to certain players and who these popular players are.

Performance and perception of the player as a person are the most important determinants of player popularity. Cal Ripken is a classic example of a player whose excellent playing was matched by his exemplary personal characteristics. Ripken's career symbolizes the best in a baseball player over and above his ability — his dependability, durability, friendly treatment of fans, avoidance of controversy, and the perception that he played the game as it is meant to be played. And who can forget his sharing the celebration of his consecutive game record with the fans with his triumphal, postgame jog around the field? Ripken's feat has been credited as a major step in recapturing the fans' affection for baseball lost after the disastrous 1994 players strike. Ripken was preceded by third baseman Brooks Robinson. The sweet-fielding and equally sweet-tempered Robinson was as popular with fans throughout baseball as Ripken.

Albert Belle, another great player — at least with a bat in his hands — is the direct opposite of Ripken and Robinson. Belle was as much a menace to other players and fans as he was to the pitchers he terrorized. As a base runner he is remembered for using a flagrantly aggressive elbow on an unsuspecting infielder. He was heartily disliked by his teammates because of inconsiderate conduct in the clubhouse. But best remembered was his thuggish treatment of fans. On one occasion he threw a ball into the stands in an attempt to bean a fan. He also attempted to run down an unruly fan with his car. Belle has not been missed since his retirement.

Obtaining autographs has been a traditional way in which fans connect with their favorite players. But players vary in their patience for accommodating autograph-seeking fans. Cal Ripken, for example, went out of his way to sign autographs for every waiting fan after games as he approached his consecutive game streak record. Other players are far less gracious and some rudely push away young fans seeking autographs.

A tasteless practice has come on the scene in recent years—sports memorabilia shows in which fans pay significant amounts for player autographs. This has provided a bonanza for older players who did not receive the sky-high salaries paid today. But collecting autographs has become something of a commercial gambit and, with some justification, players are loath to sign an autograph for a fan who they feel will sell it for the fan's benefit.

Players, of course, cannot sign autographs during regular season games. But one friendly player practice has emerged since the disastrous players strike in 1994 to mollify fans angered by the untimely end of that season. Outfielders frequently toss the game baseball to the fans after making the last putout of an inning.

Most fans do not know players personally. And so good press relations obviously are important in establishing a player's popularity. Sometimes press relations with a player change and the player's popularity with fans can change with them. Eddie Murray is a good case in point. He became an immediate star after he joined the Orioles in 1977 and Murray and the Orioles flourished over the next seven years. The quiet, self-contained Murray, revered by his teammates, bantered with the writers as Orioles fans cheered him on with rhythmic clapping accompanying affectionate shouts of "Eddie, Eddie."

But something happened beginning in 1984 as the Orioles fell back and Murray's relations with the press cooled. It seems that Murray deeply resented stories written about him and his close-knit family and, proud and blunt by nature, he reacted by sharply reducing his contacts with reporters. Murray's worsening relations with the press resulted in negative stories and the fans, unhappy with the Orioles' poor performance, unfairly began accusing Murray of being lazy and not staying in shape. To make matters worse, Orioles principal owner Edward Bennett Williams, in a clumsy, misguided attempt to motivate Murray, expressed the view that Murray was partially responsible for the club's failings.

Murray asked to be traded and was dealt to the Dodgers in 1989. He helped the Indians win the pennant in 1995 and was traded back to the Orioles in midseason of 1996. Eddie returned to the Orioles in time to hit home run no. 500 before a capacity crowd of wildly cheering fans. Another nice touch came during the opening game in Baltimore in 2003 when newly minted Hall of Famer Murray, then an Indians coach, threw the ceremonial first pitch to the Maryland governor. His relations with the fans and the Orioles had come full cycle. The warmth between Murray and the fans was further evidenced at Cooperstown in August 2003 when he was inducted into the Hall of Fame.

Fans understandably become fond of players with an ethnic background similar to their own. African-Americans, like all Americans, were profoundly affected by the emergence of Jackie Robinson and the other great African-American players who followed him. Within a few years the color line became essentially nonexistent, except in the eyes of a small number of fans unable to rid themselves of their prejudice.

Many fans of Italian extraction embraced Joe DiMaggio in 1936 when he joined two older Italian-American Yankees teammates, Tony Lazzeri and Frank Crosetti. DiMaggio received wildly enthusiastic greetings during his rookie year from Yankee Stadium bleacher fans as he trotted out to his center field position after hitting a home run. He was greeted with shouts, long applause, and fans waving Italian flags. And this was well before DiMaggio had become firmly established as one of the game's greatest players.

For many years John McGraw sought to find a good Jewish player with special appeal to New York's large number of Jewish fans. After Rogers Hornsby wore out his welcome at the Polo Grounds in just one year, 1927, the Giants replaced him with relatively untried second baseman Andy Cohen in 1928. In the first month of the season, Cohen was a revelation, far outhitting Hornsby (now with the Braves). Cohen became a hero to his coreligionists who treated him royally, all the while proclaiming, "Who needs Hornsby, we've got Andy Cohen!" But baseball cream always rises to the top, and when the season ended, Hornsby's .387 batting average dwarfed Cohen's .274.

Hank Greenberg was the fans' favorite Jewish player of the 1930s and 1940s. He was widely respected by all fans of all faiths, appreciative of his powerful field performance and his courage in overcoming religious prejudice. Greenberg was not an especially observant Jew, but Jewish fans nevertheless appreciated his observing the Yom Kippur high holiday, which fell on a day Greenberg's Detroit Tigers were playing the Cardinals in the 1934 World Series.

Sandy Koufax was a special favorite of Jewish fans in the 1960s. They took enormous pleasure in his overpowering pitching, an adoration which was refreshed by Jane Leavy's account of Koufax's career and his premature retirement because of an arthritic problem. Koufax, a sensitive, private man, also declined to play on Yom Kippur. Jewish fans have made less fuss over slugging Dodgers outfielder Shawn Green, except for the multitude of Jewish mothers in Los Angeles who made it abundantly clear that Green would make an exceptionally desirable husband for their available daughters.

The public perceptions of some players change after their retirements. The fan retained their fondness for Babe Ruth to the end. A colossus on the field, Ruth was a continual source of off-field news. The fans enjoyed reading the stories of the Babe's personal lifestyle; that is, the stories that were publishable. Fans could relate to possibly apocryphal stories of his pregame consumption of a dozen hot dogs, washed down by multiple bottles of soda, and dissipated with liberal swallows of bicarbonate of soda. Ruth's legions were regaled with accounts of his delivering home runs he promised to very ill youngsters and his informal dealings with dignified members of high society and royalty.

After his retirement from the game, Ruth's drinking exploits impressed a New York writer who joined the Babe in a tavern. The writer watched in fascination as the big fellow ordered a tumbler filled with vodka on the rocks and downed the glass with a few gargantuan gulps. The scribe reported graphically, "The ice sounded like a load of coal being dropped down a hopper."

Ted Williams was not a fan favorite until late in his career. Bill James wrote of him:

> Ted Williams was despised everywhere in the American League, including Boston for at least the first half of his career.... He splattered water coolers.... He made obscene gestures at fans, carried on decades-long vendettas against selected reporters, sometimes didn't treat his family well... and alternated, in his dealings with fans, between rugged charm and uncharted rudeness.

Williams mellowed somewhat after his retirement and fans viewed him in a more favorable light as they recognized belatedly that he had been a heroic figure in two wars and active in Boston charities. As a highly respected baseball elder, Williams became a hitting guru, and the fans and players cheered him at public appearances in the last few years before his death in the summer of 2002. Then, in a bizarre climax to his legendary career, his children feuded over the question of either burying his body or freezing it.

Joe DiMaggio was more a revered figure to the fans and his fellow players than a beloved one. DiMaggio was a reserved man who, as he grew older, was more interested in protecting his image than in pleasing his fans. In his first years as a player, fans and writers had difficulty deciding whether his aloof demeanor reflected a natural diffidence or simple indifference to matters not of concern to him. After DiMaggio's playing career ended he remained in the public eye with his soap opera-style marriage to Marilyn Monroe. Fan fascination with DiMag continued after their divorce and her death.

DiMaggio appeared at Yankees' old-timers games for many years to the delight of many, although some fans were disenchanted when they learned of his self-centered insistence upon being introduced to the crowd last of all the players. Then, a year before his death an unauthorized biography painted a picture of him as a mercenary, materialistic man, advised by a grasping attorney-adviser, who wanted everything on his terms but who gave back very little. DiMaggio's magnificence as a player has stood the test of time, but in the end it has been not matched by his public persona.

Stan Musial, unlike fellow icons Williams and DiMaggio, has been a fan favorite in St. Louis since he joined the Cardinals in late 1941. That was the beginning of a love affair between Musial and the fans that would keep "Stash" a Cardinals star for 22 seasons. Musial was even popular in Brooklyn, where he was fondly referred to as "Musical." Extremely consistent in field performance and temperament, Musial was one of the most popular men ever to play the game.

Kirby Puckett was one of the most popular of the great players in the game. He endeared himself to the fans with his perpetual smile, relentlessly upbeat personality, and the obvious joy he experienced from playing. His fans were deeply disappointed when glaucoma blinded him in one eye, forcing a premature end to his 12-year major league career when he was only 35. But Puckett's image became tarnished shortly after his 2001 enshrinement in Cooperstown when he went through an ugly marital breakup. Then, in March 2003, he was cleared of charges in the alleged sexual assault of a woman in a restaurant bathroom. Nevertheless, his image has not regained its earlier luster.

Several experts, including Connie Mack, John McGraw, and Ed Barrow among them, considered Honus Wagner the greatest position player of all time. As a player, the square-rigged Dutchman was quiet and shy. But, as a long-time Pirates coach, he changed completely into a gregarious, genial, father confessor to the younger players, and an inveterate spinner of amusing, if improbable, stories. In the sixth edition of *Total Baseball*, Wagner was described:

If his stories were incredible, at least you could tell them to your mother. One estimate puts him as the most beloved man in baseball during the time between King Kelly and Babe Ruth. If so, he deserved the adoration.... He always had time for a friend; he helped rookies ... and he never acted the star. He also refused to let a cigarette company put his picture in their packs because he didn't want to encourage kids to smoke. He made them stop distributing one print, making the few in circulation the most valuable baseball cards in the world.

There have been other great players who have been actively disliked by the fans. Ty Cobb was detested alike by fellow players and the fans. He has been described variously as "mean, vindictive, selfish, vain, a bully, a racist, paranoid, cruel, and hot-tempered." Players hated him because of his intimidating play, his willingness to show them up, and his complete lack of sportsmanship or human feeling. And the fans hated him for those reasons and for attacking unruly onlookers in the stands or away from the ballpark. Cobb presented a completely different picture of himself in his autobiography, *My Life in Baseball*.

Fans have never related to Barry Bonds despite his marvelous play. For all of Bonds's achievements, he is respected but not liked by fellow players, and he has fought openly with teammate Jeff Kent. Bonds has not been a media favorite because of his curtness, incivility, and general unpleasantness, and, as a result, he rarely got a break from the press. And right or wrong, many fans feel Bonds is arrogant. During his record-breaking home run seasons, he occasionally seemed to reach out to the fans but he has not been able to win them over, and there are questions whether he really cares and whether he has been a steroid user.

Adrian "Cap" Anson was the first player to become a universal fan favorite. Anson, the biggest star in the game during the 1880s and 1890s, is credited with being a leader in popularizing the game as it became a truly successful commercial game. The big, gruff first baseman-manager of the highly successful Chicago White Stockings thrilled the fans with his powerful hitting. Additionally, he was a great innovator — the first to use the hit-and-run play, field signals, and preseason training — and he was a master showman.

One of Anson's best-known crowd-pleasing stunts was to march his players onto the field in single file. He also played to the rough-and-ready instincts of some fans by harassing and bullying the umpires, and he played an unfortunate role in refusing to allow his club to play against black players. Regardless, to many fans in that rough-hewn era, Anson was baseball. The renowned poet Vachel Lindsay recalled his early days in Chicago in a poem including the line, "Pop Anson was our darling, pet and pride."

Mike "King" Kelly was Anson's most famous player, a talented outfielder who later became a fine catcher. The handsome, dark-haired Kelly, sporting a luxurious black mustache and a dazzling smile, was a classic matinee idol. A flashy dresser, he rode to the ballpark in a silk hat, ascot tie, in a carriage pulled by two white horses. He was the ultimate matinee idol.

But Kelly was substance as well as form. Fans were enthralled by his hitting, clever fielding, and by his speed and finesse on the bases. After helping Anson's clubs win five flags in his seven years in Chicago, he moved to Boston, his hometown, where he was idolized by the fans. A man who lived the high life, he died penniless of pneumonia at 36. His Boston admirers, faithful to the end, bade him farewell with a royal funeral.

Hard-hitting second baseman Napoleon "Larry" Lajoie was a beloved player for the Indians after spending the earlier years of his career in Philadelphia. A lifetime .338 hitter, he hit .426 for the Athletics in 1901, still the highest American League batting average. Although his large size reduced his fielding range, he was rated the most graceful second baseman of his time. A writer once remarked, "Lajoie even looks graceful chewing tobacco."

Against his better judgment, Lajoie became the Indians player-manager in his third full year in Cleveland and he had some success. But the well-liked Frenchman relinquished the job after five years, claiming that managing responsibilities had reduced his effectiveness as a player. Still, as a measure of his popularity, Cleveland fans nicknamed his team the "Naps" while he was the manager.

Giants right-hander Christy Mathewson was as charismatic and popular as any player in the early 1900s. Voted into the Hall of Fame with the first group of selectees in 1936, Matty was handsome, clean-cut, intelligent, possibly the best pitcher of his day, and certainly the most popular with the fans. They enjoyed his cerebral pitching style, and his ability to outthink hitters as well as to overmatch them with his marvelous control and famous reverse curving fadeaway.

In an era of roughneck players, fans of Mathewson's day especially appreciated his upstanding image as a Bucknell graduate. He had sung in the college glee club, was purported to be a clean-living teetotaler (his wife said he actually was a social drinker), and a model for the Frank Merriwell books designed to mold young boys' characters. Late in his career when he managed the Reds, he held his players publicly accountable when they sold out to gamblers and he worked hard to have Hal Chase, his crooked first baseman, banned from baseball. Bill James wrote admiringly of him, "[Mathewson] said bluntly that the [1919] White Sox were throwing the [World's Series]. He was the Churchill of this crisis, the only man who would stand up and face what was going on."

Walter Johnson was Mathewson's opposite number in the American League. Similar to Matty, Johnson was elected to the Hall of Fame with the first group selected for the hall. Johnson had a legendary fastball (some players claimed they often did not see his pitches but they did hear them). He had a 417–279 record and many fans consider him the greatest pitcher ever. The fans around the American League loved the lanky right-hander with the arms appearing to extend just above his knees. Henry W. Thomas, Johnson's grandson, wrote of the high regard fans throughout the league had for the modest, gentlemanly Johnson. *Baseball Magazine* proclaimed, "It is doubtful if there is a player in either league so universally admired as Walter Johnson."

In the 1920s, the most popular Dodgers were manager Wilbert Robinson and outfielders Zack Wheat and Babe Herman. The rotund, easygoing Robinson had been a highly competent catcher for the famous Baltimore Orioles in the 1890s and a successful pitching coach for Orioles teammate McGraw with the Giants until the two men had a falling out. He left McGraw to become the Dodgers' manager in 1914, a post he held for the next 18 years.

Robby was an immediate hit with the Dodgers fans, raising attendance and improving the club's field performance. But he was deeply beloved by the fans more for his human qualities than for his baseball acumen. His players' children were allowed in the dugout during games, and sometimes he signaled his coaches with a child sitting on his lap. He started a "Bonehead Club" for stupid plays and became its first member when he handed the wrong pre-game lineup to the umpires. Plain-spoken and completely down to earth, he was known to leave his dugout during games to explain a decision he had made to a critical fan. And he told one of his players to stop pounding his bat on the dugout floor during a Dodgers rally because the noise might wake up a dozing coach. The fans' adoration for the lovable Robby was reflected by the club being renamed the "Robins" during his managerial tenure.

Dodgers fans were drawn to outfielder Zachary "Zack" Wheat because he was completely professional, utterly dependable, even-tempered, and also of significance, a lifetime .317 hitter. But Floyd Caves "Babe" Herman was the most unforgettable player of the Brooklyn's "Daffy Dodgers" era in the 1920s. He had a lifetime .324 batting average with two blockbuster years in 1929 and 1930 when, even making allowances for the hitting inflation of that period, he hit .381 and .393. But his deep popularity stemmed from his tendency to become involved in bizarre situations at bat, in the field, or on the bases. His most famous disaster, before his usual adoring fans, came when he doubled into a double play.

> With the bases loaded at Ebbets Field, Herman slammed a drive off the wall, and the ball bounced all the way back to second base. One run scored, and ... [baserunner] Dazzy Vance, halfway home,... scrambled back to third base, where Chick Fewster had already arrived from first base. Herman,... running head down, thought Fewster must be scoring ... so he slid [into third] ... to find the other two already there. They called Fewster and Herman out and gave Herman credit for a double. Ever after, when the Dodgers put three men on base, some wag was sure to ask, "Which base?"

More than once, Herman was hit in the head while attempting to catch a fly ball. He firmly denied the charge. A writer asked him, "How about being hit on the shoulder?" Herman responded, "No, the *shoulder* don't count." Herman left the Dodgers after the 1931 season and the majors after the 1937 season. But at 42, and with the supply of wartime players scraping the bottom, he returned to the Dodgers as a part-time player in 1945. In his first game back, his fans welcomed him back with a rousing hand. He responded by hitting the first pitch on a line to right field. But he tripped and somersaulted running down to first and the right fielder threw him out at first base. The Babe had delivered again for his fans— sort of.

The Dodgers' "Boys of Summer" clubs of the 1950s had several well-loved players. Several books have been written about the reciprocal warm feelings between Brooklyn fans and Dodgers players. First baseman Gil Hodges was a strong, silent, even-tempered man, a deeply respected fan favorite. His loyal fans prayed for him and lit candles as Hodges suffered through an 0 for 21 ordeal during the 1952 World Series. Shortstop Harold "Pee Wee" Reese was a favorite when he came up as a highly touted 22-year-old and the fans' regard for him grew even more over the years as he provided inspired team leadership. He was especially admired for the helping hand the Kentucky-born Reese provided Jackie Robinson when Robinson broke into the majors in 1947.

Robinson had a prickly, take-no-prisoners attitude, and the fans did not so much adore him as they respected him for his profound achievement in integrating baseball. Outfielder Dixie Walker was so popular for several seasons that he was nicknamed "The Peoples' Cherce." But some fans had second thoughts about Walker when they learned of his unwillingness to play on the same team with Robinson. And sweet natured catcher Roy Campanella was a prime crowd favorite. Dodgers fans had trouble adjusting to the loss of Campy after a terrible automobile accident ended his playing career so abruptly.

Frankie Frisch was a great favorite when he came to the Cardinals in 1927, performing impressively as he replaced Rogers Hornsby, who had player-managed the Cards to the worlds championship in 1926. The fans cheered the Fordham Flash enthusiastically as he hit a career-high .337 and set a still-existing record for second basemen of 641 assists. Frisch continued as the toast of the town when the Cardinals won pennants in three of the next four years and his popularity peaked in 1934 when he served as the famous Gas House Gang's player-manager in another worlds championship year.

Frisch's star right-hander, Dizzy Dean, was one of the great pitchers and characters in the game and the fans responded to the colorful Dean's antics and boasts. Center fielder Terry Moore, unsung but the best at his position during the mid–'30s, was another fan favorite. Second baseman Red Schoendienst was a well-liked, post–World War II successor to Frisch. More recently, Mark McGwire has been a tremendous St. Louis fan idol, with his monster, record-breaking home runs. McGwire came to the Cardinals from Oakland without expecting to remain in St. Louis, but the mutual love affair he developed with Cards' fans convinced him to stay in St. Louis until his retirement.

Lou Gehrig and Mel Ott were the two most popular New York players for many years. Gehrig's press coverage was not all that it might have been because he was overshadowed by Babe Ruth in his earlier years and by Joe DiMaggio in his last three years. But New York fans were too knowledgeable not to realize that the piano-legged Gehrig's magnificent power, run production, and dependability were perhaps the most important factors in the Yankees' remarkable success in his years with the Bombers. Pitcher Lefty Gomez, a genuine wit, catcher Bill Dickey, and shortstop Phil Rizzuto also were crowd-pleasers. Rizzuto, a boyish little fellow with a remarkably quick release on throws to first base, was a fan favorite as a long-time player and as an even longer-tenured Yankees announcer.

Since Joe DiMaggio's retirement in 1951, there have been a number of highly talented, popular players with the Yankees, their popularity enhanced by the see-all, tell-all New York press. Mickey Mantle and close friend Whitey Ford were widely loved, with the fans intrigued as Mickey played the part of the Oklahoma bumpkin to Whitey's street-smart New Yorker image. Yogi Berra's considerable popularity was enhanced by his guileless (not really the case) persona and the endless accounts of his malapropisms (most of which were manufactured). Later on, workmanlike first baseman Don Mattingly was a prime fan favorite. Even more recently, shortstop Derek Jeter, a special focal point of younger rooters' adulation, and outfielders Bernie Williams and super-competitive Paul O'Neill have been the premier fan favorites in the Bronx.

Mel Ott was easily the most popular Giants player of his time. The quiet teenage slugger was unusually popular with the fans and writers during his first few seasons as a part-time player. Manager John McGraw insisted on keeping Ott with the Giants so that "no minor league manager can ruin this kid's unorthodox hitting style." A full-fledged superstar at 20, Ott became so popular with Giants fans that many of them preferred to sit in the right field grandstand near him rather than in the usually more desirable seats closer to home plate.

In 1938, a cereal company awarded a new car to the most popular major league player at each position. Ott, alternating between right field and third base, won the fan vote for both positions. With attendance slipping in 1942, Ott became the club's player-manager in an attempt to exploit his popularity. Not a successful manager, Ott nevertheless is remembered fondly by anyone who knew him or who saw him play. Left-hander Carl Hubbell and shortstop-third baseman Travis Jackson were other Giants favorites during Ott's playing days. Jackson was a quiet, businesslike player with a great arm. Frank Graham wrote that Ott and Jackson were "unbelievably popular in Brooklyn," considering that they played for the hated Giants.

The effervescent, supremely talented Willie Mays was a great fan favorite with the Giants in New York but fan ardor diminished after the Giants moved to San Francisco in 1958. Bay Area fans seemed to feel that Mays was a New York leftover and, despite his continued brilliance in San Francisco, they adopted first basemen Willie McCovey and Orlando Cepeda and right-hander Juan Marichal as their special favorites.

When the Braves played in Boston, shortstop Rabbit Maranville, he of the unquenchable taste for fun and booze and the famous "basket catch," was the fans' favorite player. Later on in Milwaukee and in the earlier days in Atlanta, three marvelous Braves players were idolized by the fans— left-hander Warren Spahn, third baseman Eddie Mathews, and Henry Aaron. In addition to Spahn's great pitching, the fans loved him for his dry sense of humor. He gave up Willie Mays' first major league hit, a monster home run over the Polo Grounds roof, after Willie had gone hitless in his first 21 major league at-bats. Years later Spahn said slyly, "I blame myself for the Giants keeping this guy around; if I had struck him out, he might have been sent down for good." Mathews hit 512 home runs and, together with Aaron, frightened opposing pitchers for years. Aaron, over and above the

755 career homers produced by his compact swing, was perhaps the most efficient hitter ever to play the game. The fans were slow to recognize his greatness, but once they did, they idolized him.

The best-liked Braves players of more recent vintage include outfielder Dale Murphy, third baseman-outfielder Chipper Jones, and pitchers Greg Maddux and Tom Glavine. Murphy was admired for his powerful hitting and his squeaky-clean personal image. Jones's popularity has been helped by his cultivation of good press relations. Maddux and Glavine are admired as consistently excellent performers and extremely intelligent pitchers.

Cincinnati fans of the 1930s idolized lumbering, hard-hitting, catcher Ernie "Schnozz" Lombardi. The more recent "Big Red Machine" had an appealing group of players, most notably Johnny Bench, Pete Rose, Joe Morgan, and Tony Perez. The fans were especially fond of master catcher Bench and clutch-hitting first baseman Perez. Morgan was the complete package, brainy (as evidenced subsequently by his excellent broadcasting), and a highly skilled offensive player and fielding second baseman. And Rose was a prolific hitter and hustling hometown favorite before his uncontrolled gambling habit did him in.

Detroit fans loved pre–World War II stars Hank Greenberg, fiery catcher-manager Mickey Cochrane, and quiet second baseman Charley "Mechanical Man" Gehringer, so dependable that a reporter wrote of him, "Ground balls came to him as though he had a magnet in his glove." Since then, the biggest Detroit fan favorites were right fielder Al Kaline and shortstop Alan Trammell. Both men were idolized as classy players and exemplary people. Chicago has had its favorites. The White Sox had right-hander Ted Lyons, a Sunday pitcher for several years after his peak years because he drew the fans to weekend games. Shortstop Luke "Old Aches and Pains" Appling is remembered as a decent fielder and fine hitter, especially adept at fouling off tough pitches. Tough, little second baseman Nellie Fox, with his perpetual tobacco chaw, and flashy outfielder Minnie Minoso were other crowd-pleasing Sox players.

The Cubs favorites in the '20s and '30s were the heavy-drinking and hitting outfielder Hack Wilson and red-faced catcher Leo "Gabby" Hartnett. Gabby was a fan favorite around the National League. For example, some older New-York area fans remember the big, talkative catcher walking slowly to the distant center field clubhouse at the Polo Grounds after games, chatting with fans every step of the way. Third baseman Stan Hack, who had a perpetual smile, was well liked. In recent years, Cubs fans have been enamored with always upbeat shortstop-then first baseman, Ernie "Let's play two" Banks, outfielder Billy Williams, and graceful second baseman Ryne Sandberg. Sammy Sosa has been one of the all-time Cubs favorites with his hop-skip-turnaround-jump act after hitting a homer and his two-fingered kiss blown to the fans after his return to the dugout.

During Ted Williams's heyday, the most popular Red Sox players were first baseman Jimmy Foxx and second baseman Bobby Doerr. The heavily muscled, easygoing Foxx didn't need the friendly Fenway Park left field wall, hitting 534 home runs, many of them monster shots. Doerr was an excellent right-hand hitter and fielder, and a calm field leader.

The earlier Indians' premier fan favorites were efficient right-hander Mel Harder and small but powerful Earl Averill. They were followed by fireballing right-hander Bob Feller and shortstop-manager Lou Boudreau. Boudreau's appeal to the fans was made clear in 1947 when Indians' president Bill Veeck decided to replace manager Boudreau. Veeck changed his mind after the fans made it clear that they wanted Boudreau to be retained. And in 1948 Lou justified their faith, hitting .355 and leading the Indians to the worlds championship.

Milwaukee fans had two special favorites, shorstop-then outfielder Robin Yount and infielder-designated hitter Paul Molitor. Yount was an 18-year-old when he joined the Brewers in 1974 and, in his first four years, he was torn between playing baseball or golf, apparently his first love. But after he established himself as a first-class shortstop and fan favorite, the future Hall of Famer sparkled as one of the American League's best players even after a shoulder injury forced him to become a full-time outfielder. Molitor, beset by injuries throughout his career, was a workmanlike, line drive-hitting specialist who finished his career with 3,319 hits, eighth on the all-time list.

Only a few Pirates players have come close to approaching Honus Wagner's popularity. Fancy-fielding third baseman Pie Traynor was a favorite in the '20s along with Paul and Lloyd Waner, who hit for high averages and were among the best outfielders of the time. The heavy-drinking Paul was reputed to be occasionally under the influence during games with no apparent impact on his hitting effectiveness. More recently, outfielder-first baseman Willie Stargell was a long-ball hitter and an inspirational field leader who had an especially fine mutual rapport with the fans.

The most popular Phillies players over the years have been right-hander Robin Roberts, outfielder Richie Ashburn, and third baseman Mike Schmidt. Roberts was a durable, hard-throwing right-hander with excellent control who was the Phillies' stopper for many years. The fans appreciated his 286 career wins, his intelligence, and his ability to move games along quickly with his ability to throw strikes. Ashburn was another highly intelligent player, one of the best center fielders ever, and a well-spoken man who became a popular broadcaster. Schmidt was the most powerful hitter (548 home runs and eight-time home run leader) ever to play third base and one of the best fielding third basemen ever.

Right-hander Tom Seaver was the best and most popular New York Mets player in franchise history. After he carried the "Amazin' Mets" to the 1969 pennant with a 25–7 season, New York fans hailed him as the second coming of Christy Mathewson. And there is a strong resemblance — both handsome, extremely bright, with an effectively analytical approach to the pitching art — and both were idolized by the fans.

Third baseman George Brett is easily the most popular player in Kansas City history. Royals fans have admired Brett as much for his competitive spirit as for his tremendous hitting and fielding ability.

Similar to Brett, Tony Gwynn was the San Diego Padres icon during his 20-year career. He was not a power hitter but rather was a genuine hit machine, winning eight batting titles and with a lifetime .338 average and high ranking as a defensive right fielder. All fans held Gwynn in high esteem because of his pleasant demeanor in addition to the studious approach underlying his hitting mastery.

There are very few ballplayers in any generation who are truly beloved by the fans. This was the case in the pre-free agency era when players tended to remain with teams longer than they do today, when fans had more time to become attached to a player and he to the fans. But with today's freer movement of players resulting from free agency, true and lasting popularity is harder to attain because players change teams so frequently. Success in baseball, as in all professional sports, is usually measured in such absolute measurements as wins, statistical records, and monetary earnings. Popularity cannot be measured in such quantitative terms but, nevertheless, baseball fans still are gratified to see a favorite player do well; or to paraphrase Leo Durocher, to see a nice guy finish first.

10

Gambling

The leisurely pace of a baseball game is ideally suited to gambling for the bettor wishing to wager on the game while it is in progress. Football and basketball are fast-moving sports with little or no time to wager on what the next play will bring. But betting opportunities are boundless during a baseball game. There is ample time between a pitcher's deliveries to wager whether the next pitch will be a ball or strike, or whether the hitter will be retired or reach base safely. There also is an opportunity to bet whether the next hit will be a single or an extra base hit, or whether a runner on third base will score. From its earliest years, baseball has attracted all types of gambling, ranging from the fan interested in making a small wager to the professional gambler betting large amounts of money.

Small children used to engage in a harmless form of baseball "gambling." They used to collect baseball cards wrapped tightly with a red piece of virtually tasteless bubble gum in a small, flat, cellophane-covered package. Similar to today, the cards had a picture of a player on one side and his career statistics on the other side. The goal was to amass a complete collection of all of the baseball cards in that year's series, either by trading for a needed card or by buying new wrapped cards on the off chance that a desirable card was in the wrapped package.

The most prevalent game involved "tossing tickets." You held a card at your side and with a forward twist of your wrist, flipped the card end over end to the ground trying to match — head or tail — your opponent's already tossed card. If you matched the card, you won your opponent's card; if you did not match it, you lost your card. Another game involved pressing one or more cards against a wall with the palm and releasing the cards to fall randomly to the sidewalk. Your opponent followed by doing the same with his cards. He was the winner of any of your cards on the sidewalk covered by his cards, and you became the owner of all uncovered cards remaining on the sidewalk. These games are no longer in vogue as today's more efficient youngsters prefer to buy complete sets of mint baseball cards in the dubious hope that these virginal, mint cards will retain their value when sold in future years.

In high school, "gamblers" graduated to more advanced forms of wagering. Participation in these games involved placing a bet (in those days, a nickel) that any three players selected on a given day would accumulate a total of six hits. The bettor received a quarter for a total of six base hits, plus a graduated bonus for each base hit in excess of six hits. Of course, the odds were clearly against the bettor in this exercise.

Another popular high school betting game of the 1930s and 1940s was to wager for or against the proposition that the winning team would score more runs in one inning than the losing team would score during the entire game. It is unclear whether this run relationship remains valid given possible changes in scoring patterns over the last 65 years. Another betting game was to select and wager on the team scoring the highest total of runs over the last several days, usually a week. This running total was published every day in the sports section of most newspapers.

Gamblers were fascinating to watch in action. They tended to congregate in groups at a major league game. For example, in the Polo Grounds in the late 1930s, gamblers gathered in upper deck grandstand seats behind third base. The finer points of the game were of little concern to them: They were interested only in winning their bets. But watching them conduct their betting was an unforgettable experience. The scene was something straight out of a Damon Runyon story. It reminded the viewer of the song from *Guys and Dolls* that describes a gambling scene as "a floating crap game in New York." The gamblers were seated directed under a green "Betting Prohibited" sign, a prohibition ignored by the gamblers and usually unpoliced by the ball club. The group included about 20 men, most of them dressed in elaborately casual garb, presenting the sporty appearance of a Broadway dandy of that time. A few were dressed more tastefully and conservatively, apparently professional men slumming with a lower element while giving in to an uncontrollable compulsion to gamble.

The gamblers were in constant conversation with one another during the game. No one spoke loudly but the betting lingo was unmistakable: "Two to one the Cards score this inning" (with 1938 Cardinals sluggers Joe Medwick and Johnny Mize due to hit). "Twenty bucks says this stiff, weak-hitting St. Louis catcher Mickey Owen was the hitter *don't* bring in the man from third." When Giants outfielder Joe Moore (a notorious first-ball hitter) came up to hit, the offer went, "Two bucks say he swings at the first pitch." This series of off-the cuff bets went on continually.

No possible future occurrence was beyond the scope of the betting. This was illustrated by an event in a game at the Polo Grounds in the early 1930s. Giants infielder Fred Lindstrom broke a leg sliding into a base and the Giants rushed out of their dugout to assist their stricken teammate. With no stretcher available, big Giants pitcher "Fat Freddy" Fitzsimmons picked Lindstrom up bodily and started for the distant centerfield clubhouse. Halfway to the clubhouse, Fitzsimmons stumbled over the centerfielder's glove (this was the era when players left their gloves on the field between innings) and almost dropped Lindstrom. Immediately, one gambler rose to the occasion with the quick proposition, "Five bucks, even odds, says he drops Lindstrom on the stairway to the clubhouse."

The gamblers, of course, were primarily concerned with betting on the final score of the game. A pregame tip from anyone "in the know" as to whether either of the starting pitchers was not feeling well or perhaps had caroused the night before the game was valuable information to a professional gambler. They also were past masters at the art of hedging bets. Whenever they placed or accepted a bet on the final score of a game, they would try to at least break even if the team they wagered on was losing by midgame. To balance a potential loss, a gambler would seek out anyone offering him higher odds against his original bet. In effect, he was betting against his original choice. Very often a bettor would cancel out potential losses with such a reverse betting maneuver.

Means of large-scale betting have evolved over time. The original one-on-one wagers were largely supplanted by auction-style "pool betting," so called because the activity usually held took place in a poolroom. Another form of pool betting involved use of a lottery-style ticket. Eventually, pool betting was replaced by bookmaking. The bookmaker established odds Las Vegas style, handled the bettors' money, and served generally as an honest broker, all for a fee.

Society for Baseball Research member Phil Erwin explained the "odds system" by which most baseball betting is conducted:

> [Assume] the Mets are at home versus the Cardinals, favored by 6½ to 7½. This type of odds quote ... means that a player must risk $7.50 to win $5 if he backs the Mets, and will risk $5 to win $6.50 if he takes the Cardinals. In Las Vegas, the same proposition would be translated into a "money line," where the Mets would be –1.50 favorites, the Cards +1.30 underdogs. For every $1.50 risked on New York, a winner would profit by $1, or he

could risk $1 to win $1.30 on St. Louis.... The 20 cent difference of 1.50–1.30 is called a "20 cent line." ...The bookmaker's percentage [referred to as "vigorish' or "juice"] is derived from the varying payoffs. If a bookmaker has the same amount placed on both sides of the game, he is guaranteed a profit.

Baseball began as a game played by "gentlemen's clubs" to display sportsmanship and fellowship between sporting clubs. But extensive gambling was reported at games in Elysian Fields in Hoboken, New Jersey, as early as 1857. Most significant, wagers were made between players and sometimes with umpires in a game in which the umpire was officiating. By the 1860s, gambling at games increased even more as fans paid admissions to watch skilled players perform and to bet on their favorites.

Writing of the gambling scene in the early 1860s, Harold Seymour commented: "As the game started slipping ... into the more lusty embrace of the masses, its complexion began to change perceptibly. Rooting grew more vehement as spectators became noisy partisans. Betting began to creep in. At [an important all-star series], even women were exchanging small wagers."

Also in the 1860s, competition for coveted players increased and bribes from gamblers became an important source of funds to induce players to join a team. The involvement of gamblers led inevitably to the fixing of games as gamblers sought sure returns for their wagers. *Harper's Weekly*, a leading periodical in the 1860s, editorialized: "So common has betting become at baseball matches, that the most respectable clubs in the country indulge in it to a [high] ... degree, and so common the tricks by which games have been 'sold' for the benefit of gamblers that the most respectable of participants have been suspected of this baseness."

During the 1870s, the Brooklyn Atlantics were said to have fostered so much betting that one section of the grounds was known as the Gold Board, with activity that rivaled that of the stock exchange." The slang term "hippodroming" was used to describe a game fixed by gamblers which purported to be an honest, spontaneous contest in which the result was not predetermined. Rumors of fixed games during the period were so prevalent that a Buffalo writer suggested that any professional baseball club would throw a game for money. He wrote, "A horse race is a pretty safe thing to speculate on, in comparison with an average ball match."

Much concern about gambling was expressed by other moralists and early baseball journalists, notably the highly respected writer Henry Chadwick. Their special concern was directed at teams with unsavory gambling and political connections. After covering an annual meeting of the National Association of Professional Base Ball Players in 1870, Chadwick described some bitter reaction at the meeting to a report that New York's infamous politician William "Boss" Tweed had invested the then-considerable sum of $7,500 in the New York Mutuals, which, it was rumored, gave him a controlling interest in the team.

Tweed saw to it that Mutuals players were placed on the New York City payroll, many of them in the street-cleaning department, at an annual cost to the city of some $30,000. Other players were placed in well-paying jobs in such unexpected places as the coroner's office in New York and the U.S. Treasury Department in Washington. There were accusations that the notoriously corrupt Tweed probably got his money back, presumably from gambling interests. Similar charges were lodged against other suspected instigators of corrupt episodes, many of them involving gamblers.

Organized baseball faced its first gambling scandal in 1865. Boss Tweed's heavily favored New York Mutuals lost 28–11 to the Brooklyn Eckfords. It was learned later that two Mutuals players, Ed Duffy and William Wansley had offered a teammate, shortstop Thomas Devyr, money to help them throw the game. Duffy and Wansley were banished from match play by the Judicial Committee of the National Association. The Mutuals, undoubtedly with the help of the potent Tweed, worked successfully to have the charges against Devry dropped. Significantly, after a decent interval, all three players were reinstated.

Even the feats of the fabled, undefeated 1869 Cincinnati Red Stockings were tarnished by gambling charges. The only blemish in their record came as a result of a 17–17 tie with the Troy Haymakers. The Haymakers walked off the field in the sixth inning on a manufactured pretext to save gamblers from a heavy loss.

Chadwick, noting a number of rather questionable games in 1874, wrote that there had been collusion between gamblers and players. After the season he challenged teams to get rid of the guilty players. The situation worsened the following year when some teams adopted the practice of paying salaries to their best players and paying their other players on the more speculative basis of the gate receipts. Players feeling they were being cheated or otherwise underpaid were an easy mark for gamblers who paid them to fix games.

Chadwick wrote of the possibly devastating damage to the game presented by gamblers, the selling of games by players, team mismanagement to benefit owners, and the strongly negative reaction of the fans to these abuses. The crusading Chadwick demanded reform, calling for official action to deal with these abuses by punishing crooked team officials, and blacklisting corrupt players.

The National League, which began operations in 1876, survived in its earlier years largely because of its overall success in dealing with the bribing of players by gamblers. In 1877, the Louisville Grays expelled four players for throwing games. They were apprehended after they aroused suspicion by wearing diamond stickpins and rings and their guilt was proven by telegrams sent to the players by gamblers. Pitcher Jim "Terror" Devlin, the ringleader, offered the hollow alibi that he sold out to the gamblers because he needed money to support his family. Neither Devlin nor his fellow wrongdoers were ever reinstated despite their pleas for forgiveness. The Louisville club fared poorly, departing the National League before the 1878 season as local papers attributed the team's plight to the dishonesty of the players.

A dishonest umpire can change the course of a game. Fortunately, only one umpire has ever been removed from the major league scene because of documented dishonesty. Umpire Richard Higham handled many Detroit Wolverine games early in the 1882 season. Many fans, including Wolverines owner William Thompson, felt that an unusually high number of Higham's decisions on close plays went against the Detroit club. Thompson, who also was the Detroit mayor, hired a detective to investigate the umpire. The detective discovered that Higham telegrammed bets to a well-known gambler on games he was scheduled to umpire; then he made calls favoring the team he had bet on. Confronted with the evidence of his betting, Higham was immediately fired.

Gambling remained a continuing major league problem, becoming pervasive even among players, managers, and team owners, a positive sign of deterioration in the National League's standards. Bettors congregated in the stands with impunity. In New York and Boston, especially large groups of gamblers clustered behind third base as they would in many ballparks.

Harold Seymour described the gambling scene among baseball figures in the 1890s:

> Even worse [than gamblers in the stands] was the popularity of betting among the owners and managers themselves. In 1892 [Brooklyn manager] John Ward won twenty shares of [Giants] ... stock from Edward Talcott, a director of the Giants, as the result of a bet on where the Giants would finish in the standings. Magnates made numerous bets with each other, as high as $500, on the pennant races. According to Henry Chadwick, the players themselves purchased [baseball] pools openly before games, usually on their own club but sometimes, on the rival team.

The major league baseball establishment largely ignored gambling problems during the next three decades. Players associated freely with gamblers and some team owners were active gamblers. William "Big Bill" Devery and Frank Farrell were the original financial backers of the New York Highlanders when the American League began operations in 1901. Devery was recognized as the most corrupt New York City police commissioner up to that time. Farrell was a notorious player on the New York gambling scene with extensive contacts among the players.

Farrell was a close friend of "Prince Hal" Chase who became the Highlanders first baseman in 1905. Chase was admired by the fans as a graceful, supremely gifted fielder and competent hitter. He also was a heavy gambler who bet for and against his team and, as it developed, became a master at making subtle fielding misplays to improve chances of winning his wagers. Several of Chase's managers suspected him of throwing games but for many years organized baseball did nothing about these suspicions. Highlanders manager George Stallings, for one, made a public complaint about Chase's tactics but American League president Ban Johnson chose not to investigate the complaint but instead he expressed annoyance that the accomplished Chase's reputation was being besmirched.

It was learned after Chase left the major leagues that he had been involved in a series of gambling-related misdeeds involving other players. He had offered bribes to outfielders Benny Kauff and Lee Magee and to pitchers Fred Toney, Rube Benton, and Jean Dubuc to deliver substandard performances.

Without an accompanying public explanation at the time, Giants manager John McGraw later suggested that Chase and Giants third baseman Heinie Zimmerman's questionable play against Cincinnati helped the Reds win the 1919 pennant—lending, if true, an ugly but fitting symmetry to that year's corrupt World's Series. Chase's crowning achievement in this record of deceit was to bring gamblers and fixers together to throw the 1919 World's Series.

Chase's transgressions were only the most visible part of the game-fixing activities occurring before 1919. There was a reported attempt to bribe players in the first two World's Series, in 1903 and 1905. Boston catcher Lou Criger was offered a bribe before the first series. In the second series, the Philadelphia Athletics ace lefthander Rube Waddell did not pitch despite having led the American League with 27 wins and a 1.48 ERA. Although Waddell had ostensibly injured his shoulder, it was widely rumored that the gamblers had reached him to the tune of a $17,000 bribe. There was a widespread rumor that gamblers had tried to fix the 1908 season. And in 1916, the Giants were rumored to have aided the Dodgers to win the pennant with a lackluster performance in the final game of the season. John McGraw lent credence to the rumors by leaving the field in disgust in midgame

The 1919 World Series between the Chicago White Sox and the Cincinnati Reds surprised and shocked most fans when the heavily favored Sox lost to the Reds in seven games. During the series there were recurring rumors that several Sox players had deliberately permitted the Reds to score runs during games preceded by betting odds changes favoring those who had bet on the Reds. But these rumors were largely discounted or ignored by most baseball fans who would not hear of it, equating baseball with love of family and devotion to country. The strenuous efforts of the baseball establishment to convince fans of the game's integrity had been effective. As a result the general public, and certainly the majority of baseball fans, considered major league baseball to be on the up-and-up. But after the 1920 season, the vision had changed as the Black Sox scandal came to light.

Eight players from Charles Comiskey's White Sox were implicated in the 1919 World Series fix. They included such prime fan favorites as slugging outfielder Joe Jackson and pitchers Ed Cicotte and Claude "Lefty" Williams. The other players were infielders Swede Risberg, Fred McMullin, Buck Weaver, Chick Gandil, and outfielder Happy Felsch. The players were summarily barred from organized baseball by Commissioner Kenesaw Mountain Landis.

The disillusionment of the fans was exemplified by the probably apocryphal plea of a young fan said to have called plaintively to Sox slugger Joe Jackson, as he emerged from the courtroom, "Say it ain't so, Joe." The complete story of this profound insult to baseball's credibility and integrity has been told in many baseball writings, most notably in Eliot Asinof's classic *Eight Men Out*.

Despite the overpowering presence of Judge Landis, fans in the 1920s continued to have reason to lose their faith in the integrity of major league baseball. One unsettling occurrence involved journeyman Giants pitcher "Shufflin' Phil" Douglas. A curveballing right-hander, the lanky, heavy-drinking Douglas was picked up by John McGraw from the Cubs in midseason of 1919 after undistinguished tours of duty with the White Sox, Reds, Braves and Cubs. Furious with McGraw after being fined following a drunken binge, Douglas sent a crude, hand-written letter, on New York Giants stationery no less, to Cardinals outfielder Les Mann.

The Cards were pushing the Giants for the pennant and Douglas wrote that if Cardinals players "made it worth his while," he would help the Cardinals by "going fishing" for the rest of the season. Mann, an especially unfortunate choice because he was a clean-living teetotaler, turned the letter over to Commissioner Landis. Naturally, Douglas was banished from the game but the affair was another blow to the game's integrity because it impressed upon fans, coming on the heels of the Black Sox disaster, that games could be thrown by crooked, disgruntled, or naïve players.

Fans had to be further disenchanted two years later after learning of a matter some writers and fans feared could tear the game wide open. The near-disaster occurred late in the 1924 season. The Giants led Brooklyn by a game and a half with a few games left in the season. Young, inexperienced Giants outfielder Jimmy O'Connell offered Phillies shortstop Heinie Sand $500 "not to bear down" in a series against the Giants at the Polo Grounds. The guileless O'Connell freely admitted his guilt to Judge Landis and, to the further consternation of the fans, accused Giants players Frankie Frisch, George Kelly, Ross Youngs, and Coach Cozy Dolan of having induced him to make the offer to Sands.

Landis banished O'Connell, who admitted his guilt, and Dolan, who claimed unconvincingly that he could not remember the overture which had been made only two days before. The three Giants stalwarts (and future Hall of Famers)—Frisch, Kelly, and Youngs—denied any involvement and escaped any punitive action from Landis. But fans had to wonder what had really transpired. And the newspapers speculated about the sordid affair and kept rehashing the story for weeks.

Then there was the matter of Giants left-hander John "Rube" Benton. A more effective pitcher than Douglas, the veteran Benton joined the Giants in midseason of 1915 after five seasons with the Reds. A player with an unsavory reputation as a heavy gambler and drinker, the Alabama-born Benton was accused of perjury and prior knowledge of the 1919 World's Series fix. Benton had been offered an $800 bribe by Hal Chase and Giants third baseman Heinie Zimmerman to throw a game. The National League brass wanted to have him banned but Judge Landis decided to allow him to remain with the Giants. Still, the Benton matter resulted in adverse publicity and further disillusionment for baseball fans.

The last unpleasant episode in the scandal-ridden 1920s came to light after the 1926 season. It involved two of the game's player-managers and brightest stars, Ty Cobb and Tris Speaker. Both men resigned in November of that year in the wake of rumors that the two great players were involved in throwing a game in 1919 and betting on other games.

Judge Landis held a secret meeting with Cobb, Speaker, and former pitcher-outfielder "Smoky Joe" Wood. Former Tigers left-hander Dutch Leonard, who pitched for the Tigers under Cobb's managership, had written to Tigers outfielder Harry Heilmann that he (Leonard) had turned over to American League president Ban Johnson letters written to him by Cobb and Wood. The letters indicated that Cobb and Wood had bet on a Tigers-Indians game during the September 1919 pennant stretch drive, and that Cobb and Speaker conspired to assist the Tigers in their efforts to win third-place money. The Indians, with Speaker and Wood, had clinched second place but the Tigers finished half a game out of third place.

The American League's board of directors decided secretly to permit Cobb and Speaker to resign without any comments from the two stars or their clubs. The ensuing ugly rumors forced Landis to hold a hearing but Leonard refused to appear, claiming he would be killed by the "mob" if he testified. Cobb and Wood admitted writing the letters. Cobb claimed that Leonard had released the letters because he was angry with Cobb, who had sent him to the minors after a stormy relationship between the two men.

Speaker was not named in the correspondence and it was unclear why he felt it necessary to resign from the Indians. Similar to the supportive reaction of many fans when their Black Sox favorites were acquitted, the fans generally supported Cobb, Speaker, and Wood. Eventually, Landis issued a decision clearing Cobb and Speaker and ordering their reinstatement by their clubs. The aging stars became free agents and both men finished their playing careers with the Athletics in 1928. Unlike Pete Rose many years later, Speaker and Cobb had no problem in being voted into the Hall of Fame.

Since the Black Sox scandal, major league baseball has been extremely vigilant in dealing with the slightest hint of involvement by players and managers with professional gamblers. Commissioner A.B. "Happy" Chandler suspended Brooklyn manager Leo Durocher for one year in 1947 for conduct detrimental to baseball. Chandler had warned Durocher previously about associating with gamblers and other unsavory characters. Durocher, ignoring Chandler's warning, had been living with actor George Raft, who had connections with gamblers.

Pete Rose's gambling activities have been documented in detail. Other than the Durocher and Rose cases, there has been only one other instance where fans have had reason to suspect dishonest field performance. It involved righthander Denny McLain, on top of the baseball world after two great seasons in 1968–69 and out of the game three years later. In 1970, it became known that a Detroit grand jury was investigating McLain's rumored involvement with gamblers. He admitted to Commissioner Bowie Kuhn that he had invested $5,700 in a bookmaking operation.

When McLain failed to pay out a sizable betting amount in 1967, an organized crime enforcer allegedly injured McLain by stomping on the pitcher's foot. The injury forced McLain to miss two starts during the September 1967 pennant drive between the Tigers and the Red Sox. The brother of the enforcer had bet on the Red Sox to win the pennant and to win their last game of the season with Detroit. McLain started that game and lost it, his third consecutive loss. And the Red Sox won the pennant by one game over the Tigers and the Twins.

Kuhn suspended McLain for six months because of his bookie connection and the allegations of wrongdoing although the commissioner admitted later that there was no concrete evidence that McLain had bet on baseball games. That marked the end of McLain's tenure as an effective pitcher.

Major league baseball's antigambling efforts have otherwise concentrated on even the appearance of off-field gambling by people associated with major league baseball. In 1943, Landis permanently suspended Phillies owner William D. Cox for betting on his team's games. In 1969, Bowie Kuhn presented an ultimatum to four prominent baseball people, requiring them to sell their interests in a company owning casinos in Las Vegas. Some years later, Kuhn proclaimed that players or coaches could not engage in public relations work at casinos. This forced two of baseball's most illustrious batting instructors—Willie Mays and Mickey Mantle—to quit their baseball jobs to continue their far more lucrative work greeting patrons in Atlantic City casinos. Many fans resented this cavalier treatment of the two superstars and Kuhn's successor, Peter Uberroth, lifted the ban on the two superstars shortly after taking office.

Gambling has been part of baseball since the game has existed. To many baseball fans, a controlled level of friendly betting for small amounts enhances their enjoyment of the sport. Organized baseball's concern has always been restricted to gambling which could, in any way, compromise the honesty of the game.

Before World War II, player salaries were relatively low and there was always the possibility that some players might be susceptible to throwing games in return for a gambler's bribe. Current player salaries are so high as to reduce sharply the likelihood that a player would be susceptible to being bribed into attempting to throw a game. So there is a high probability that they are a thing of the past. And yet, player bribes for fixing games are always possible.

Major league baseball must continue to maintain its close vigilance to prevent significant potential or actual gambling activities which could be detrimental to the game. The baseball fan, along with everyone else connected to the game, is entitled to have complete confidence that such gambling activities are kept under control and that the game's integrity is maintained.

11

Attendance

Despite the inevitable ups and downs in attendance figures for individual years or individual teams, overall major league game attendance has risen steadily over the long haul. In large part, this is a function both of the continued population increase the United States has experienced since baseball became commercially important and the large increase in time and money available for recreation since the end of World War II.

In 1858, all-star teams in the New York–Brooklyn area were charging fans admission to cover the cost of preparing and maintaining playing fields. After the Civil War, baseball became the most important spectator sport in the United States. With peace restored, the game gained in popularity at an accelerating pace and record attendance figures were reached in 1868 when an estimated 200,000 people attended games played by the leading teams, with an estimated 10,000 fans attending the most important games. Prominent New York and Brooklyn teams were playing primarily for a share of the gate receipts and routinely charging a 10-cent admission charge. They were following the lead of New York promoter William H. Cammeyer who since 1862 had been charging the same admission price. He also took the canny step of enclosing his field to permit only paying fans in to watch games.

Even with large income from TV and radio broadcasting rights, adequate attendance remains the lifeblood of major league franchises. Although it is theoretically possible for small cities to aspire to have a major league team, as a practical matter cities with small populations have little chance of securing a franchise. (This occurred in the NFL in the case of the small-town Green Bay franchise but never has happened in major league baseball.) When the National League was being formed in the early 1870s, and for many years after when an opening in the eight-team circuit became available, prospective entrants had to represent a city of not less than 75,000 people in the absence of a special exemption by unanimous vote of league members.

Attendance figures at games were highly speculative for the years preceding the National League's first year of operation in 1876. Before that time, some games reportedly attracted as many as 40,000 fans. But these figures are approximations based largely upon unreliable head counts and rough estimates. Their accuracy was especially questionable when provided by team operators who had a financial interest in promoting baseball.

Recent research placed combined attendance during the 1870s for the two existing leagues, the National Association and the National League, combined at between 205,000 and 269,000 a year for most years throughout that decade. The ballparks of the time were mostly fields with small grandstands and ramshackle bleachers. Estimates of crowd sizes were probably thrown off by the differing sizes of the small seating areas in different ballparks. When all of the seats were occupied and the occupants were crowded into a small, compact seating area, it was difficult to accurately estimate crowd numbers. After all of the seats were filled, overflow crowds spilled out to the foul lines or watched games from an open center field sector, further distorting attendance estimates.

A self-registering turnstile, developed in 1876, increased the reliability of attendance figures. But the availability of the new turnstile did not completely ensure the accuracy of attendance counts. The National League made its use mandatory, but the National Association did not. Even National League figures were not completely reliable. Harold Seymour wrote:

> Despite turnstiles, some magnates still tried to cheat from each other. Before an exhibition game ... A.S. Stern, Cincinnati owner, ordered his business manager, Louis Hauck, not to use the turnstiles, and if questioned to say that they were out of order. By concealing ... ticket sales and cheating on the count at the gate, he could collect much more than his rightful 20 percent share.

Attendance at baseball games was held down severely in baseball's earliest years because games were not played on Sundays, the only day of the week when millions of six-days-a-week workers were free to attend games. Many teams did not play Sunday baseball during the 1870s because local laws forbade such amusements on the Sabbath. The free-and-easy National Association accommodated its fans by playing games on

Sundays where it was legal, or paying fines for playing in defiance of local laws.

The more conservative National League owners chose not to play Sunday games regardless of their legal status. Although pressure for Sunday games was growing in the 1880s, it was not until 1892, when the National League expanded from eight to 12 teams, that the league gave member teams the option of playing regular-season games on Sunday. Even then very few cities permitted Sunday games.

By 1902 the only major cities permitting Sunday baseball were Chicago, St. Louis, and Cincinnati. After considerable political pressure was exerted, Sunday baseball was legalized in 1918 in Detroit, Cleveland, and Washington although still banned in the major northeastern cities. By 1918 Sunday ball was permitted in the New York area. Boston and Philadelphia held out until the 1930s, and Pennsylvania clung to blue laws through the 1950s, requiring early completion of Sunday games. Many older baseball fans remember the frustration in seeing long Sunday games, especially double-headers, with the late game shortened because of the blue laws.

Total attendance at all major league National League games in 1880 was measured at about 256,400, quite similar to the number of fans attending games in the 1870s. Attendance during the 1880s peaked at 4.1 million in 1887. Official figures show that average attendance figures at major league games have increased steadily since the 1890s when average game attendance ranged from 2,000 to 3,000 fans.

In 1890 the new Players League outdrew the National League, a reported 981,000 fans to 814,000, with the total attendance for both leagues affected as both eight-team circuits competed head-to-head in seven cities. But the figures are suspect. It was understood that each league falsified attendance to suit its purposes. Al Spalding cleverly debunked the Players League's reported figures. He secretly positioned his agents at Players League entrance gates to keep count unobtrusively, and he triumphantly discredited the new league's attendance numbers by publicly listing them alongside his checkers' lower counts.

Bill James estimated total major league attendance during the 1890s at 24.8 million, including the National and Players League figures in 1890, and the expanded National League for the duration of the decade. The Philadelphia Phillies had the highest reported attendance during the decade and the Washington Senators the lowest. Major league gate receipts reported for competing teams were important to other teams in the league. Spalding claimed that teams with low attendance, and resultantly low gate receipts, were living off the prosperous clubs. Financially weak teams were able to continue in operation with the money they received as visiting teams playing in the more financially successful team's ballparks. Under today's rules, teams with lower player payrolls also benefit from equalization payments from teams with player payrolls totaling above a certain amount.

Attendance took off from 1900 to 1910, approaching a total of almost 50 million during the decade. The 1901 major league attendance figure of 3.6 million doubled by the end of the decade. More effective control of vulgar and unseemly conduct on the field was achieved, largely through the anti-umpire baiting influence of Ban Johnson's new American League. And there were a series of exciting pennant races, especially in the National League with John McGraw, Frank Chance, and Fred Clarke driving their highly competitive clubs. Other factors were the popular interest in the newly established World's Series as it was called then, construction of better-built stadiums, and more effective media coverage of games and players.

This was the period when ballpark concessions became recognized as an important attraction for the fans and a significant profit source. The distribution of food and drink at ball games on a modest scale dates to the early 1860s. But it was not until the 1880s that professional concessionaire Harry M. Stevens, a British immigrant, recognized the desire of fans to identify players. He saw the profit potential in selling scorecards, coining the famous slogan shouted by vendors since that time, "You can't tell the players without a scorecard." The enterprising Stevens expanded his profits by incorporating paid advertisements in the scorecards. In the 1890s, he increased his profits many times over by selling a variety of foods, including sandwiches, pies, and hard-boiled eggs. In a master stroke, Stevens obtained the Polo Grounds vending concession and exploited it to gain similar contracts with New York hotels and racetracks.

Paul D. Adomites wrote an article on ballpark concessions in the first edition of *Total Baseball*. He described Stevens, the innovator:

> On a cold day in the Polo Grounds in 1901, ice cream wasn't selling, but Harry had an idea. He sent an assistant for frankfurters [locally called "dachshund sausages"], which were sold in the neighborhood German groceries, heated the sausages in hot water, and put them in long buns so fans could hold them and eat them. The vendors shouted out what made these inventions so special: "Get 'em while they're hot! Get your red hots here!"... [As a result], sports cartoonist Tad Dorgan ... coined the term "hot dogs."

At present, hot dogs, soda pop, and beer remain the three biggest-selling food items in major league ballparks. Stevens, who apparently never missed a concession trick, enhanced sales of soda pop by including a straw with each bottle. He theorized that fans might not purchase soda pop because raising their heads to drink could cause them to miss some of the action. Distributing straws with the drink solved the problem.

Attendance increased slightly from 1910 to 1919, but the increase was much lower than might have been expected considering the increase in U.S. population over the period. Game attendance suffered largely because of international chaos, beginning with the war in Europe in 1914 and extending through the end of World War I. And then, shortly after the armistice, the Black Sox affair soured many fans on the game.

Attendance boomed during the Roaring '20s, up from 55.8 million in the previous decade to almost 93 million during the prosperous 1920s. The year 1920 featured a record-breaking major league attendance in excess of

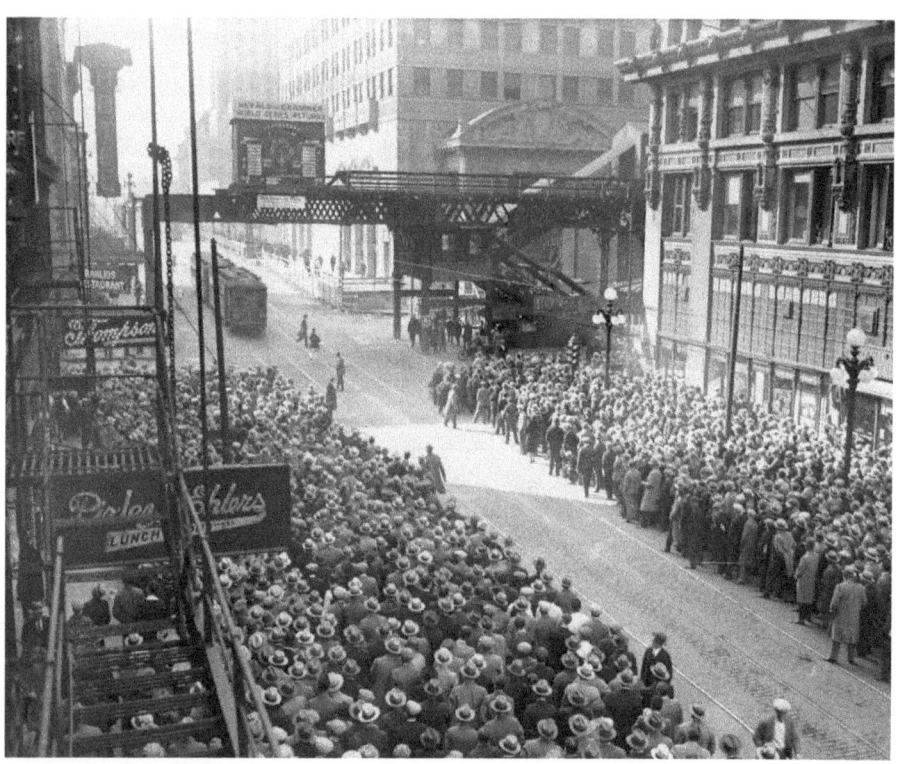

Fans watch World's Series game results on a temporary scoreboard mounted on a Los Angeles street. This was October 1929 when many fans soon would have an even-greater concern — the Wall Street crash signalling the start of the Great Depression (Transcendental Graphics, Boulder, CO).

9.1 million. After a Black Sox-related decrease over the next three years, a new record of 9.6 million was reached in 1924. That attendance level remained fairly constant through the remainder of the decade. The Yankees consistently drew more than a million fans during the '20s, and only the Cubs (1927–29) and Tigers (1924) attained that level during the decade.

Baseball attendance dropped during the Depression-ridden '30s with total attendance falling to 81 million from 1931 to1940. The full effect of the Great Depression was felt by the major leagues from 1932 through 1934, when yearly attendance fell below 7 million, the lowest since before World War I. Crowd levels improved after 1934, but they remained below the attendance totals of the 1920s.

World War II, and its accompanying prosperity, ended the attendance drought. Attendance figures from 1941 to 1950 skyrocketed to nearly 135 million. For the first five years of the period, fans turned out in numbers similar to those of the '20s but in 1946, the first full postwar year, attendance took a quantum leap to 18.5 million. Major league baseball attained this level for the next 15 years.

The flourishing post–World War II attendance was attributable in large part to the steadily expanding economy and increasing jobs and wages with resultant higher consumer spending. Baseball fans had more money to spend on baseball games. But there were other factors contributing to the increased attendance. Fans who had formally resided far from baseball cities moved into defense work in cities with teams during the war and they remained in these cities or nearby suburbs after the war. Better able to afford baseball tickets and living closer to ballparks, these fans attended games in much larger numbers than in the past. And the increasing number of night games after the war made it more feasible for a fan to see a game at night after working during the daytime.

The integration of baseball in 1947 by Jackie Robinson and Larry Doby had the effect of bringing more black fans into big league games and shifting their interest and rooting allegiance from the declining Negro League to major league teams. Many white fans were attracted by the ability and style of the black players, and they flocked to ballparks to see these players in action. And, of course, there was television. Many baseball executives felt that television, becoming more important in the late 1940s, would cause fans to stay at home rather than attend games. But they misjudged the desire of fans to see live action in the flesh rather than on a screen. TV had the effect of increasing interest in baseball and more people than anticipated elected to attend games rather than watch them at home.

Predictably, changes in a team's performance almost invariably trigger an attendance change. For example, the Anaheim Angels came from nowhere to win the worlds championship in 2002. By midseason in 2003, the Angels were averaging 36,6 fans per game, a remarkable increase of 11,000 fans per game over the previous season. The delayed reaction in fan attendance increase is a familiar pattern to baseball officials. By contrast, the 2003 Cleveland Indians, last in their division at midseason, suffered the largest attendance decline of all teams. They dropped from an average of 32,500 fans in 2002 to a depressing 21,600 during the first half of 2003.

Player strikes have had an immediate negative impact on fans as demonstrated by the disastrous players strike in 1994–95. The average attendance record number of 31,612 at games played in 1994 plummeted to 25,260 in 1995. It took five years for the fans' unhappiness to completely dissipate, as indicated by the average attendance in 2000.

Large attendance during the first year of any franchise's history may be expected because of the novelty and stimulated interest by a team's having attained major league status. That was the case with the Colorado Rockies in their first year of operation in 1993 when nearly 4.5 million fans streamed into brand-spanking-new Coors Field. No other team since has come close to equaling the Colorado attendance figure, including the Rockies who nevertheless attracted impressive yearly numbers of 3.3 to 3.9 million fans over the next five years. Contrast that with the dismal (20–134) 1899 Cleveland Spiders who drew a total of 6,088 lost souls in 1899. That was the season when the Spiders' ownership mistreated their fans. The club maximized receipts by shifting to opposing team's parks all of the hapless team's home games in the last two months of the season.

Baseball attendance was helped greatly by the changing status of women in the latter half of the 1800s. Women had displayed a growing interest in the game and teams encouraged their interest, not only for the added patronage but because the game's leaders felt womens' presence would add gentility to the baseball scene. A weekly magazine wrote as early as 1867 that women's attendance "purifies the moral atmosphere of a base ball gathering, repressing ... all outbursts of intemperate language which the excitement of a contest so frequently induces."

The Athletics and the Orioles designated each Thursday as Ladies Day in 1883 when women were admitted without charge when they were accompanied by a paying male. The plan was so successful that it was adopted by most of the leading clubs. The clubs also provided special facilities for women. In some ballparks, men were not permitted into the ladies' section unless they were accompanied by a woman, and smoking was strictly forbidden. Ladies Day subsequently became a key component in ball clubs' market expansion efforts.

11. Attendance

Ladies Day became an even more important attendance tool in the 1920s, particularly in Chicago. In 1930 women could obtain free tickets by showing up at the ballpark and requesting a ticket. Cubs owner William Wrigley talked of the financial benefit in cultivating attendance of women and thereby doubling the attendance from families (at non–Ladies Day games) where husbands and wives spent their holiday afternoons at the ballpark. Wrigley also described the wild scene on Ladies Days:

> A bargain-day rush at a big State Street store is a tame event alongside a ladies' day at Wrigley Field.... There is no such thing as controlling these crowds of women besieging the admission booths. The ladies listen to a speech urging them to take their time and assuring them that each applicant will be accommodated; then they storm [the booths], sweeping aside policemen and guards in a way to make men gasp and wonder how the phrase "the gentler sex" ever originated.... [Wrigley told of a little old woman who was swept into the park by a mob of women.] "I don't want a seat," she sobbed. "I want to get out. I came to visit my daughter, who lives near here."

Baseball team operators have always been aware that attendance is based largely upon team performance, and the converse is true. A 1952 U.S. House of Representatives report, *Organized Baseball,* showed the relationship between success on the field and percentage of a league's attendance. Weak teams almost never captured more than 8 percent of the league's annual attendance (when there were only eight teams in the league). Statistics showed that a team playing close to .600 ball would normally obtain at least 14 percent of the league's annual attendance, while a team playing at a .700 clip could make the pennant race unexciting and dampen interest and attendance even for that predominant team.

Of course, these observations have been contradicted in unusual cases. In the Depression year of 1934, the St. Louis Cardinals came from far behind to win a pennant, but the Gas House Gang drew only a measly 7 percent of total league attendance. And then there were the overpowering 1927 Yankees who drew 25 percent of all American League attending fans despite playing .714 ball and finishing 19 games over the second-place Philadelphia Athletics. Apparently, fans around the league were so fascinated by the powerful hitting of Babe Ruth, Lou Gehrig, et al. that the feats of these great players kept the fans coming to the ballpark even in the absence of competition for the pennant. So it is clear that baseball attendance is as difficult to predict as the pennant races.

Other than effective performance on the field, there have been many other activities designed to attract fans to the ballpark. Teams began advertising on streetcars, on signboards on street corners, and with banners carried in the street. As early as the 1880s, ball clubs could order colored scorecards and posters of teams and players. Some teams sold an early version of today's baseball cards aimed at adults and advertising products like cigars and patent medicines. And then there was room for outright showmanship, especially when team performance alone was not good enough to draw a satisfactory number of fans into the ballpark.

Chicago Colts player-manager Adrian "Cap" Anson was not only a truly great player but one of baseball's premier showmen in the 1880s. David Voigt described Anson:

> Gruff, tough, and outspoken, the mustachioed hero captivated fans with his proud swagger as he led his [Chicago White Stockings] onto the field in single file. A baseball Hercules ... but being a born showman, he celebrated Chicago's hosting the 1888 Republican convention by marching his men onto the field in black, swallow-tailed coats. Such antics titillated fans as much as his brawling, bullying tactics against umpires.... Over the years his frolicsome behavior inspired a sheaf of articles describing real and imaginary feats, which he rarely refuted.... [Late in his career and tiring of references to his "senility"], the forty-year-old manager showed up one day wearing whiskers and looking like Rip van Winkle.

Chris Von der Ahe was another baseball figure in that era whose off-field activities kept players and fans in constant turmoil but who stimulated fan interest and attendance. A German émigré turned saloon keeper (the Golden Lion) and boardinghouse owner in St. Louis, he noticed that after a baseball game fans enjoyed visiting his establishment for a beer. Long on bravado and chutzpah but short on knowledge of baseball, Von der Ahe sponsored the St. Louis Browns of the American Association for 10 years. In a certifiably clever move, he hired canny first baseman Charles Comiskey to manage his club and the Browns were off to four straight pennant wins and five flag wins in seven years. Comiskey accomplished this despite Von der Ahe's heavy-handed, Steinbrennerlike meddling with the players.

In those halcyon seasons, "der Poss Bresident," as Von der Ahe called himself, was said to have pulled down a yearly $75,000 profit. His self-glorification led him to the ostentatious practice of hauling cash receipts to the bank in a wheelbarrow after each home game. But the loud-mouthed braggart with the thick German accent looked after his fans' creature comforts, too. He maintained the ballpark in good condition and encouraged women's attendance by thoughtfully installing a ladies' toilet. Von der Ahe displayed over his Golden Lion saloon a golden ball inscribed "Game Today" or he flew a flag over it indicating "No Game Today."

One of Von der Ahe's master off-field strokes was to challenge Anson's supposedly superior White Stockings to a winner-take-all postseason series in 1886. The National Association Browns defeated the National League White Stockings, tying Anson's club in regulation time in the deciding game and winning in extra innings on a dramatic steal of home by Browns outfielder Curt Welch. The Browns won $13,000 of which the rotund Von der Ahe kept $6,900 and divided the remainder among his players. After this upset win, the thrilled Browns' fans carried Von der Ahe and his players on their shoulders in an emotional victory parade. This would prove to be Von der Ahe's apogee as a number of ensuing court suits and marital problems left him virtually penniless and alone when he died.

Hall of Famer Albert G. Spalding, a great pitcher and later a National League mover and shaker, pulled off a spectacular bit of showmanship when he promoted a six-month world tour in 1889. The 13-nation tour, covering every continent, featured Spalding's Chicago White Stockings playing against a group of all-star players drawn from other National League teams. As Harold Seymour summed up the tour: "The long excursion was hardly a great financial success, but it was hugely successful in other ways. Baseball and Spalding's sporting goods business were well publicized, and the enthusiastic reception given the players everywhere on their triumphal tour was evidence of the growing stature of baseball."

John McGraw was an extremely effective showman, well aware of its impact on the gate. He gloried in the role of troublemaker, stirring up the enmity of rival fans. Famed sportswriter Grantland Rice wrote of him: "His very walk across the field in a hostile town is a challenge to the multitude." McGraw's on- and off-the-field fights and his own rough play reflected his pugnacious and competitive nature and desire to win at all costs. But his attention-getting activities also were designed to call attention to his team and enhance gate receipts. Only McGraw would unexpectedly dress his club in the black flannels and white stockings his Giants wore in the 1905 World Series. He deliberately had his team driven to and from games in open carriages to incite their abuse by opposing team fans. He appeared on vaudeville stages in off-seasons and publicized baseball for handsome amounts of money.

McGraw and Charles Comiskey reenacted a portion of Spalding's world tour, took baseball teams to the Orient, the Middle East, and Europe after the 1913 season. And after a bitter loss in the 1924 World's Series, in cooperation with Comiskey, the stocky Irishman led another foreign tour, this time to Ireland, France, and England. The combative McGraw expressed his philosophy regarding attendance with the thought, "Sportsmanship and easygoing methods are all right, but it is the prospect of a hot fight that brings out the crowds."

Bill Veeck was baseball's most innovative promoter after World War II. He is remembered mostly for sending midget Eddie Gaedel up to bat as the leadoff hitter in a game between his St. Louis Browns and the Detroit Tigers in 1952. Beginning with his stewardship of the Milwaukee club of the American Association in 1941, he raffled off live pigs and food, and put on massive fireworks displays to keep fans entertained long after games ended.

Veeck gave away such large quantities of beer that the unmanageable antics of inebriated fans caused his team to lose games by forfeit. He staged weddings at home plate with all of the ceremonial touches. And during World War II, he had his club play morning games so that defense plant workers could attend. But, irritating as he was to his less-imaginative fellow team owners, no one could deny that the always casually attired Veeck knew his baseball and the fans.

Veeck was injured while in the Marines during World War II, forcing him to undergo a number of leg operations. But he continued in the game with undiminished vigor and enthusiasm. In 1946 he put together a group and bought the Cleveland Indians. He doubled attendance to 1.5 million in 1947 and his 1948 worlds champions drew an American League record 2.62 million. Always looking to hype attendance, the rugged, always upbeat, Veeck signed Larry Doby, the first black American Leaguer, and the great black right-hander Satchel Paige. He is remembered as a thorn in the side of his more stodgy colleagues, but as a true friend of the baseball fans of his era.

Charles Finley was a showman in the Veeck style although he was not as well-liked by the players and fans as Veeck. He was the most outrageous, controversial and yet most innovative club owner of his time. He entertained the fans with his off-the-wall practice of parading a mule, named "Charlie O" for the man himself, around the Oakland A's field. But he followed that with the completely zany, and socially unacceptable, gambit of having the mule walk through hotel lobbies and cocktail parties.

Always seeking a way to increase attendance, Finley introduced the employment of ball girls and two other innovations which never caught on — orange baseballs, and a mechanical rabbit to provide baseballs to the home plate umpire. He paid his players to grow mustaches and he dressed them in eye-catching yellow uniforms. Most significantly, he was an early advocate of night World Series games.

Finley shifted his club from Kansas City to Oakland for the 1968 season. The move was successful in that his clubs won five straight division titles from 1971–75 and world championships in three of those years. But the clubs he built did not draw the large attendance commensurate with the caliber of players he assembled — such stars as Reggie Jackson, Jim "Catfish" Hunter, Vida Blue, Rollie Fingers, Sal Bando, and Joe Rudi. And Finley's ability to obtain such players was tarnished by his manipulative treatment of his players and the dislike he engendered among baseball officials and fans.

Discussing the business of baseball, SABR member Steve Mann wrote:

> Where all this money [to support major league baseball] comes from, of course, is the fans. It is the fans who pay for the tickets, the fans who purchase the scorecards ... yearbooks, [pennants, caps, hot dogs, etc.] that supplement the gate receipts. Furthermore, it is the fans who ultimately pay for newspaper, radio, television ... it is they who absorb the built-in costs of advertising when they buy the sponsors' goods. And, for the moment ... the fans seem quite willing to pay the increasing costs of their spectatorship.... The external threat [to the baseball industry] comes from the fans, whose willingness to subsidize the excesses of the clubs and the players is being severely tested. Will the rising costs of attending games ... reduce the fan base? Will spectatorship become a privilege available only to those who can afford it?

Increases in ticket and concession prices always raise the ire of fans. Even with attendance estimated to be less costly for a baseball game than for a basketball or football contest, some baseball fans have expressed concern over their attendance costs. And Steve Mann has raised valid questions as to the continuing willingness of fans to support the game, at least at the gate, as admission prices continue to increase. However, if the past is any indicator of the future, it seems unlikely that baseball attendance will be significantly affected so long as prices for baseball tickets and concessions continue to remain below prices charged spectators of the other major sports.

12

Famous and Infamous Fans

Baseball fans cannot be categorized as to sex, occupation, religion, socioeconomic level, or nationality. There have been baseball aficionados among those who earn their livings as politicians, businessmen, housewives, students, and gangsters. But sadly there are many otherwise estimable people who cannot understand how a baseball fan can be concerned about a player whom he does not know personally and who has no background in the city he represents. And besides, they ask what material benefit (other than winning a bet) can there be to a fan just because his favorite team won while his most adored player went 3 for 5 and made a few sparkling plays in the field? This book is not only for the true believer but also for those not beyond redemption, who at present share the feeling of a member of the uninitiated who have been heard to proclaim dismissively that baseball is nothing more than "an opiate for the masses."

Love of baseball does not rank high as a qualification for the United States presidency. And the only presidential act directly involving baseball (other than throwing out a first ceremonial baseball) was that of President Franklin D. Roosevelt who gave baseball a green light to continue playing after Pearl Harbor when the game's continuance was in doubt. Yet, there are fans interested in learning whether a president genuinely cares about baseball or whether the apparent interest of the chief executive in baseball is merely a political gambit to send the voters a message that their leader truly is a man of the people.

Actually, most U.S. presidents have cared about baseball, at least as fans or, in a few instances, as players. Most recently, President George W. Bush was the managing partner of the Texas Rangers before he was elected to the presidency. In his new role, he welcomed to the White House baseball figures he knew and had dealt with in his baseball days. His role as the owner of a major league team was an extension of the involvement of earlier chief executives in various aspects of the game.

President Abraham Lincoln was the first certifiable baseball lover at the nation's helm. William B. Mead and Paul Dickson wrote of Lincoln:

> Baseball didn't need to mythologize Lincoln, because the Railsplitter really did play the game. Lincoln's interest in baseball is well documented. He even played while in the White House. An account of Lincoln playing baseball with youngsters was passed down by the grandson of [a Lincoln confidant]...." We boys hailed his coming with delight because he would always join us ... on the lawn. I remember vividly how he ran, how long were his strides, how far his coattails stuck out behind...." In addition to playing, Lincoln occasionally strolled out behind the White House to watch a few innings of baseball.

Lincoln's successor, President Andrew Johnson, watched games from a plush, straight-backed chair along the first base line. Johnson favored baseball enough to give federal government clerks and employees time off to watch games and he was the first president to host a team in the White House. His successors, Presidents Ulysses S. Grant and Chester A. Arthur, also were interested observers of games played by the brand-new National League.

President Grover Cleveland was a devoted fan and a friend of future Hall of Fame pitcher Jim "Pud" Galvin. Cleveland invited Cap Anson's Chicago White Stockings to the White House and shook hands with each player. But Cleveland declined Anson's invitation to attend a game, claiming that the electorate would be unhappy with him if "I wasted my time going to the ball game." As Mead and Dickson pointed out, staying away from the ballpark showed a commendable work ethic, but it proved to be a miscalculation as Cleveland lost the next election to Benjamin Harrison.

Harrison was not much of a baseball fan but he did participate in a baseball first — on June 6, 1892, he became the first president to attend a major league game. Harrison was succeeded by William McKinley, a man who apparently could take baseball or leave it alone. But McKinley left the scene tragically to be succeeded by Teddy Roosevelt, who apparently couldn't take baseball and who preferred to leave it alone.

The supermacho T.R. loved rugged outdoor activities. He considered baseball a "molleycoddle" game suitable for the middle-aged and he much preferred the rougher sports such as boxing, football, and lacrosse. But in 1908, the last year of T.R.'s presidency, he changed course and received at the White House the New York Highlanders (later renamed the Yankees) and the Cleveland club.

William Howard Taft loved the game. At the relentless urging of Washington Senators manager Clark Griffith, Taft attended his first game as president on April 19, 1909. Attired in formal tails and a top hat, he appeared to enjoy everything about the game — the game itself, the refreshments, and above all the fans who cheered him throughout the contest. A year later, on April 14, 1910, Taft set a precedent by throwing out the first ball at the Senators' opening game. Mead and Dickson wrote, "The effect of Taft's throw was indelible. Once and forever, it wrapped the flag and the president around the game." Since then, every president except Jimmy Carter has thrown out the first ball at least once.

Taft's genuine enthusiasm for baseball manifested itself a few weeks after his memorable first pitch toss when he became the first president to attend a game in each major league on the same day. He was in St. Louis at National League Park watching a game between his hometown Cincinnati Reds and the Cardinals but when the Cards took a 12–0 lead after two innings, Taft left the game and moved across town to Sportsman's Park to see Cleveland's great right-hander Cy Young pitch against the Browns.

President Woodrow Wilson had loved baseball as a youngster. He played freshman baseball at Davidson College and later with classmates at Princeton. Wilson carried his affection for the game with him for the rest of his life. He attended the opening game every year of his presidency except in 1917 with the start of World War I when his vice president filled in for him, throwing out the first ball. A youthful Franklin D. Roosevelt, then an assistant secretary of the navy, raised the flag before the game. At the urging of National League president John K. Tener, himself a former National League pitcher and governor of Pennsylvania, Wilson gave baseball a low-key endorsement to continue play during World War I.

Wilson never saw another major league game as president. He fell into a severe physical decline during and after the difficult post–World War I peace negotiations. Then he suffered a severe stroke after a grueling, unsuccessful campaign in support of the League of Nations. Deeply depressed by the public rejection of his public positions and his overwhelming defeat in the 1920 presidential election, Wilson retreated to a melancholy, embittered life. He became a professor of government at Princeton, but even at his alma mater he was not remembered fondly because, of all things, his unruly conduct as a sports fan. He had become an unusually obnoxious rooter, especially in protesting umpires' decisions loudly, so loudly that he had to be removed from the stadium. During his last years, the unhappy Wilson took solace from his continuing baseball interests, primarily in attending games and studying box scores and game accounts.

Warren Harding was a baseball team owner. He played ball as a young man with Bob Allen, who played shortstop for the Phillies in the 1890s, and he owned part of his hometown Marion, Ohio, minor league team in the early 1900s. Harding lost money on that investment but as president he boasted of having developed two major leaguers, right-hander Wilbur Cooper and first baseman Jake Daubert. Harding was an ardent fan, traveling to New York to see a game at spanking new Yankee Stadium in April 1923. A sportswriter wrote: "He was the sort that gloomed [sic] and did not enjoy his supper at the White House if he had seen the Washington team lose."

Calvin Coolidge, Harding's vice president, ascended to the presidency upon Harding's death in office in August 1923. A taciturn man with no discernible personal warmth, "Silent Cal" was completely oblivious to the charms of baseball. He dutifully threw out the first ball at the Senators' 1924 opener on the advice of his political advisers and even managed a well-received speech welcoming the team after it clinched the pennant. Coolidge became the first president to attend a World's Series game, gamely staying through a Senators' 12-inning loss to John McGraw's Giants. But Coolidge's ignorance of the game and its customs became apparent at the 1925 opener when he committed the unpardonable crime of taking his seventh inning stretch before the visiting Yankees came to bat.

The true baseball fan in the Coolidge family was the first lady. Grace Coolidge occasionally went to games without her husband and she even stayed through entire opening games after her disinterested husband left early. Clark Griffith confirmed that Mrs. Coolidge kept perfect score of the games on her scorecard, utilizing her earlier experience as the official scorer of her college's games.

Herbert Hoover loved baseball but the onset of the Depression and his resulting unpopularity with fans discouraged him from going to games. He was booed roundly by fans when he journeyed to Philadelphia to watch the third game of the 1931 World Series between the Cardinals and the Athletics. The fans' complete unhappiness with the deteriorating economy was exacerbated by the existing National Prohibition (prohibiting alcoholic beverage sales). In his memoirs, Hoover recalled, "I left the ball park with the chant of the crowd ringing in my ears: 'We want beer!'"

It was Franklin D. Roosevelt's favorable decision that kept baseball operating during World War II. Roosevelt had always been a baseball fan, appearing to enjoy the game as much as he seemed to enjoy everything else. New York reporter Harold C. Burr wrote, "Roosevelt enjoys himself at a ball game as much as a kid on Christmas morning. Once in his field

Franklin D. Roosevelt prepares to throw out the first ball of the 1934 opening day game in Washington, D.C., accompanied by Senators owner Clark Griffith and player-manager Joe Cronin and Red Sox manager Bucky Harris (Transcendental Graphics, Boulder, CO).

box ... he gets right in the spirit of the game, munches peanuts, applauds good plays and chuckles over bad ones."

Ever the consummate politician, FDR tended to take the most advantageous political position in his rooting interests. When he attended a game in Washington during the 1933 World Series between the Senators and the New York Giants, Senators owner Clark Griffith said to him before a game, "Mr. President, I assume you are rooting for our Senators." Roosevelt, the ebullient former New York governor, smiled and answered, "No, Clark, I wish both teams well but I don't have a favorite — remember, even though I live here now, I'm from New York."

Harry Truman was an avid baseball fan. In his 7½ years as president, Truman attended 16 games, all of them at Washington, D.C.'s Griffith Stadium, more than any president ever has seen while in office. And typically Truman, he ignored the fans' boos even when he attended the Senators opener in 1951, the day after his controversial dismissal of Gen. Douglas MacArthur. Truman and his staff built an annual routine around opening day. A luncheon was arranged, attended by Truman and his longtime friends from Congress, followed by the trip to Griffith Stadium. In 1948, a joint session of Congress was moved up an hour to permit Truman and his fellow fans to attend the session before heading for the opener.

In 1959, President Dwight D. Eisenhower missed the opening day game. In his place, Vice President Richard M. Nixon threw out the first ball. As reported by Mead and Dickson, the retired Truman's dislike of Nixon inspired him to send the following telegram to Clark Griffith before the opener:

BEST OF LUCK TO YOU ON OPENING DAY AND EVERY DAY. WATCH OUT FOR THAT NIXON. DON'T LET HIM THROW YOU A CURVE. YOUR FRIEND, HARRY TRUMAN

Eisenhower played a baseball role unlike any other president. Ike played the game professionally under the assumed name Wilson. Needing the money, the future president had "a cup of coffee" as a center fielder in the Kansas State League while he was a student at West Point. This was strictly forbidden under the NCAA regulation forbidding collegians from playing for money or for competing "for any prize against a professional."

Eisenhower downplayed his professional participation and for good reason. As a student athlete at West Point he undoubtedly had signed a required eligibility pledge to adhere to the NCAA provision. If his playing for money while a student had been found out by West Point officials, Ike very likely would have been expelled and his brilliant career in the military and his opportunity to throw ceremonial pitches as president would never have occurred. In June 1945, Ike, then a national hero, returned to a massive ticker-tape parade in New York City celebrating his victorious military leadership in Europe. His only stated wish was to see a major league game and the day after the parade he got his wish — another victory ride, this time around the Polo Grounds playing field before a Giants-Braves game.

John F. Kennedy, a devoted Red Sox fan, loved all sports, including baseball. He made himself at home at all three Washington Senators' openers during his short presidency, smoking cigars and rooting loudly. Stan Musial campaigned for Kennedy in 1960 and the two men became friends. When JFK attended the 1962 All-Star game in Washington the 45-year-old president called the 42-year-old Musial over and told the beaming Cardinals great, "A couple of years ago they told me I was too young to be president and you were too old to be playing baseball. But," he said, chuckling, "we fooled them."

Lyndon B. Johnson played sandlot ball as a teenager in his native Texas but he was not considered a baseball enthusiast even though he presided over three Washington openers. And he was in attendance when the Houston Astrodome opened in 1965, becoming the first president on hand when a major league stadium began its operations. But such profound problems in the 1960s as the Vietnam War and riots in the cities claimed his full attention.

Richard Nixon was a dyed-in-the wool baseball buff, a fan equipped with detailed knowledge of the game and the players and a willingness to express his thoughts as long there were no political hazards involved. He proudly compiled his list, with the assistance of his baseball fan son-in-law David Eisenhower, of his all-time baseball teams, broken down by eras. Nixon wrote a story about his selections, disseminated to newspapers by the Associated Press.

The *New York Times* published Nixon's article under his byline. The *Times's* own distinguished columnist Red Smith wrote slyly, "Allowing the cub [reporter] two or three times as much space as a staff member would get, the *New York Times* published his essay in full ... all 2,800 cliché-ridden words. Frankly, the new boy has a long ways to go if he's ever going to cut it in this department."

But to his credit, Nixon was an active fan who was willing to use his high office to express his views on baseball to constructive ends. He supported the Washington, D.C., area's desire for a major league team and when the players went on strike in 1972, he ordered the Federal Mediation and Conciliation Service to get the owners and players together to settle the strike.

Before resurrecting his political career by winning the presidency in 1968, Nixon was offered the position of director of the Major League Players Association and then offered the position of baseball commissioner when Ford Frick retired. But Nixon had his eye on the White House, and he declined both baseball positions.

Mead and Dickson described Nixon's minor misfortunes at his first opening day on April 7, 1969. They wrote:

> He entered the presidential box and found a misspelling on the presidential seal—"Presidnt [sic] of the United States." Then, with 60 players, managers, and coaches looking on, not to mention 45,000 fans ... he dropped the ball he was preparing to throw.

Gerald Ford attended two games as the nation's chief executive. He was recognized as more of a football fan than a baseball rooter. Jimmy Carter was a softball adherent rather than a major league baseball buff. In his White House years, he appeared interested more in playing softball than in watching a baseball game. Carter attended only one game as president, the final game of the 1979 World Series. But since leaving office, he frequently has been shown on cable station TBS, watching Atlanta Braves games and appearing engrossed in the proceedings.

Ronald Reagan was the first baseball announcer elected to the presidency. Well before Reagan's Hollywood career began, he was known throughout the Midwest as "Dutch" Reagan, a sportscaster for Des Moines radio station WHO. During his five-year broadcasting career, beginning in 1932, Reagan became friendly with many players, especially the Chicago Cubs of the Charlie Grimm, Gabby Hartnett, Billy Herman era. He had his first screen audition while covering the Cubs in spring training on Catalina Island, California. His association with baseball during his years in Hollywood is remembered best for his starring role as Hall of Fame right-hander Grover Cleveland Alexander in the 1952 movie *The Winning Team*.

During his two terms in office, Reagan participated in three season openers, and he hosted appearances of baseball stars at the White House. His last appearance in a baseball setting came after he left the presidency. On July 12, 1989, he joined Vin Scully in the broadcast booth at the All-Star game and, for old-times' sake, Reagan accepted Scully's invitation to "throw out the first adjective."

The first President George Bush was a celebrated "good field-no hit" first baseman on the Yale University team in 1947 and in 1948, when he captained the team. Bush had fleeting aspirations of a professional baseball career but he admitted receiving only one "nibble from the pros." Bush had impeccable baseball credentials as his father, Senator Prescott Bush, had batted cleanup on the 1917 Yale team. Never noted for his eloquence, the senior George Bush explained his love for baseball with the simple thought, "Baseball's just got everything." The senior Bush officiated at 10 games during his presidency. But his attachment to the game is best reflected by a not-completely-believable report; he was said to have kept his old first baseman's glove at the ready in his desk in the Oval Office.

Bill Clinton enjoyed following big league action when he was a youngster, a St. Louis Cardinals fan by virtue of the widespread coverage of Cards games throughout Arkansas. During the 1994 players strike, he took the characteristically bold step of setting a deadline for the owners and players to show progress in their negotiations, but the effort proved futile.

Clinton admitted defeat and his subsequent involvement in the baseball scene was limited to the usual ceremonial activities, attending openers and welcoming worlds championship teams to the White House. Clinton's attendance at season openers is best remembered for the time the new president threw out the first ball at the opening game in Baltimore in 1993—from the pitcher's mound.

Hillary Clinton is a devoted Cubs fans. The then-first lady gave a talk to a gathering of Cubs fans in Alexandria, Virginia, in 1993 when she was deeply involved in her abortive attempt to lead a congressional committee seeking a solution to the national health problem. She described the feeling of growing up in the Chicago area as a Cubs fan and impressed her listeners with her deep knowledge of the Cubs. She also impressed with her willingness to remain for the duration of the long luncheon despite the pressures her health committee responsibilities placed upon her.

Baseball players are entertainers and they always have attracted the special attention of other people in the entertainment field. In the early 1900s, the Giants were the team most entertainment figures followed, largely because of John McGraw's colorful personality and teams, and the intense coverage of the New York press. Frank Graham wrote:

> [By 1906] McGraw had become a familiar figure on the Gay White Way, as the stretch of Broadway between Thirty-fourth and Forty-fourth Streets was known in those days.... [During the off-season] ... he sought — or was sought by — the big bookmakers and trainers, the leading jockeys, the famous prize fighters and the great theatrical figures. He was seen almost nightly in the bars and dining rooms of the hotels or the more lavish Broadway restaurants.

The New York clubs had a close following among the Broadway and show-business crowd even before McGraw came on the scene. Giants shortstop great John Montgomery Ward was a Manhattan favorite in the 1880s, eventually marrying Helen Dauvray, a prominent Broadway actress. Giants outfielder "Turkey Mike" Donlin married Broadway singer Mabel Hite, and left-hander Rube Marquard married stage star Blossom Seeley. When he was on his good behavior, McGraw was a member of the prestigious entertainers' Lambs Club.

Babe Ruth changed Yankee fortunes in the 1920s and many show-business figures switched their rooting allegiance to the Yankees. Ruth married Claire Hodgson, a beautiful model who had appeared on stage in the Ziegfeld Follies and in silent movies. In the 1930s, Yankees catcher Bill Dickey married Violet Arnold, a Broadway show beauty, and pitcher Lefty

Gomez married stage actress June O'Dea. And the ultimate Yankees-show business matchup came when Joe DiMaggio met Marilyn Monroe.

During the late 1930s and early 1940s, Bernard "Toots" Shor's restaurant in midtown Manhattan was the Yankees' and the Giants' unofficial headquarters, as it was for many members of the New York show-business crowd. Joe DiMaggio had a table reserved for him at Shor's eatery whenever the Yankees were playing at home. And after Mel Ott hit his National-League-first 500th home run in June 1945, Shor threw a party to celebrate the feat. Before Mel arrived at the restaurant, Shor sat at a table with Sir Alexander Fleming, the Scottish bacteriologist who had been awarded the Nobel prize for discovering penicillin. When Ott walked in the door, Shor jumped to his feet and told Sir Alexander, "Excuse me, Alex, I've got to greet someone who just came in and who's *really* important."

Jack White's famous Club 21, also in midtown Manhattan, was another player and entertainer hangout before World War II, with proprietor White rooting for the Giants with unbridled enthusiasm. He had his own way of signaling his team's victories and defeats. A Giants win called for a large sign at the club entrance announcing the score with triumphant details. A Giants loss was reported with a terse "No Game Today" message.

Actress Tallulah Bankhead was an avid New York Giants fan. The Giants played only day games until lights were installed at the Polo Grounds in 1940. The colorful Bankhead attended many Giants games in the '30s before she went to the theater for her evening performances. Her favorite Giants players were second baseman Burgess Whitehead and Ott. She said of the agile, acrobatic Whitehead, "He's sweet and so graceful." But it was shy, Louisiana gentleman Ott who captured her Alabama-bred heart. She rhapsodized, as only she could, "He's so handsome, so *Southern!*"

Bankhead attended the 1939 All-Star game at Yankee Stadium. She was teased by friends who claimed she misidentified several players, including the Dodgers first baseman Dolph Camilli, who wore uniform 4, Ott's number. She retorted indignantly, "I have no desire to have my ashes cast in a silver urn at Cooperstown, but I can tell Ott from Camilli on a clear day, even if I am nearsighted and color-blind."

After Ott left the scene, the effervescent Bankhead idolized Willie Mays. The young Mays, as effervescent in his own way as Bankhead, was bound to become her favorite player and she lavished her affection on him. Her unforgettable tribute to Mays: "There are only two important Willies in my life — Shakespeare and Mays."

Bill "Bojangles" Robinson, the great black tap dancer, was an enthusiastic fan of both the Giants and the Yankees. Robinson was a happy man as the Giants defeated the Senators in Washington to win the 1933 World Series. The Giants went ahead in the top of the 10th inning of the final game on Ott's home run. The deliriously happy Robinson celebrated Ott's blow by jumping on the Giants' dugout and doing his famous buck and wing as the Senators came to bat for their last licks.

The Brooklyn Dodgers became entertainment figures' favorites after they became a winning team in the late 1930s. Durocher married Hollywood actress Laraine Day in a messy affair during which Day's husband accused Durocher of seeking Day's love while "posing as a family friend."

Television interviewer Larry King was a rabid Dodgers fan who was a budding interviewer even as a young fan growing up in Brooklyn. He told writer Peter Golenbock: "My friends and I weren't among the autograph hounds. We were questioners. We would wait around after the game for the players to come out.... Dumb questions, I suppose, but in general the players were responsive."

There were other, lesser known Ebbets Field fans who were more idiosyncratic than King. Dodgers third baseman Harry "Cookie" Lavagetto ate at a local Flatbush restaurant owned by a Jack Pierce and the two men got to know each other. Lavagetto recounted that Pierce, fortified by several generous gulps of scotch, used to bring to the ballpark gas-filled balloons with Lavagetto's name on them and release them while screaming incessantly, "Cookie! Cookie!" Pierce also had cards printed with the words "Cookie for President. Always good in the clutch." He continued the practice even when Lavagetto left the game for military service.

And then there was Hilda Chester. An Ebbets Field habitue for 30 years going back to the '20s, she originally gained entrance to Ebbets Field by working for a concessionaire, removing peanuts from large sacks and stuffing them into

Inimitable Brooklyn Dodgers fan Hilda Chester in an unusually mellow mood. She was a familiar sight at Ebbets Field, employing both her rasping voice and ever-present cowbell to noisy effect (Transcendental Graphics, Boulder, CO).

small bags. By the late '30s she was a regular paying customer at Dodgers games, screaming so loudly that the players could distinguish her voice regardless of the volume of crowd noise.

After she suffered a heart attack, Hilda's doctor forbade her from yelling or becoming overly excited. Undaunted, she returned to Ebbets Field banging a frying pan with an iron ladle to deafening effect. The Dodgers players replaced that with a slightly more sophisticated noisemaker, a brass cowbell. The constant racket produced by her cowbell became her identifying bleacher trademark. And disregarding her doctor's advice, Hilda took to hollering loudly again in a voice heard throughout Ebbets Field, shouting her exhortations loudly in a coarse, raspy bellow, and punctuating her shouts with her clanging cowbell throughout the entire game.

Brooklyn Dodgers rooters were entertained by a group of fans masquerading as musicians and calling themselves the Dodgers Symphony. Their most popular song was *Three Blind Mice*, played as the umpires came on the field before the game. The Dodgers management endorsed such fan activities, holding a fan appreciation night in August 1951, with free admission provided to fans who brought their musical instruments (Transcendental Graphics, Boulder, CO).

The bizarre scene at Ebbets Field in September 1940. A spectator attacked umpire George Magerkurth after his decision adversely affected the Dodgers (Transcendental Graphics, Boulder, CO).

There was a bizarre fan incident at Ebbets Field in 1940. During a Dodgers game, plate umpire George Magerkurth was attacked by a fan named Frank Germano, a dead ringer for then-popular boxer Tony Galento. Magerkurth was so taken by surprise that Germano remained on top of him punching away before he was pulled off the larger Magerkurth. Hustled off to jail and facing a stiff sentence, Germano proclaimed, "I don't care how long they send me away as long as I'm free by next season." In an attempt to understand the reason for Germano's unusual behavior, an unproven rumor circulated that the attack was made to distract the crowd while Germano's accomplices picked fans' pockets.

Dan Parker, sports editor of the New York tabloid *Daily Mirror* in the 1930s, was a masterful satirist. He wrote a wonderful poem describing mythical Brooklyn Dodgers fan Miss Murgatroyd Darcy's love for her team as expressed in a refrain to her equally mythical boyfriend Rodgers:

12. Famous and Infamous Fans   177

> Leave us go root for the Dodger, Rodgers,
> They're playing ball under lights.
> Leave us cut out all the juke jernts, Rodgers,
> Where we've been wastin' our nights.
> Dancin' the shag or the rhumba is silly
> When we can be rooting for Adolf Camilli,
> So leave us go root for the Dodgers, Rodgers,
> Them Dodgers is my gallant knights.

Writer Ernest Hemingway was an avid baseball fan. The Brooklyn Dodgers trained in Havana before the 1942 season. Hemingway, who lived in Havana, became friendly with several Dodgers and he invited them to his gun club. The group included pitchers Hugh Casey, Kirby Higbe and Larry French, second baseman Billy Herman, and outfielder Augie Galan. The players remained at the gun club for a couple of hours and then repaired to Hemingway's palatial home for numerous rounds of drinks. After the men were thoroughly drunk, Hemingway challenged Hugh Casey to a sparring match. Hemingway followed by sneak-punching Casey to the floor with the pitcher's arm knocking over trays of liquor, littering the floor with broken bottles and smashed ice.

Casey responded by climbing slowly to his feet and knocking the famed journalist to the floor repeatedly until the onlookers stopped the brawl. The next day, a sobered-up Hemingway came to the ballpark to apologize to the players, saying that he didn't know what had gotten into him. Billy Herman explained: "I knew exactly what got into him. About a quart, that's what."

While the Dodgers were still in Brooklyn, their show business devotees included song-and-dance man George M. Cohan, songwriter Harry Ruby, and singer Pearl Bailey. After the Dodgers moved to Los Angeles, manager Tommy Lasorda permitted his clubhouse to become a meeting place for a number of Hollywood types, including Frank Sinatra, Buddy Hackett, and Danny Kaye.

Singer Doris Day apparently was a passionate Dodgers fan, in the full sense of the word. Sports columnist Jim Murray wrote that Day "was smitten with [Dodgers shortstop Maury Wills] and began lavishing expensive gifts on him, like color TV sets. The official word was the friendship was platonic, but, of course, it wasn't."

A raucous St. Louis fan named Mary Ott had such a loud voice, bellowing a thunderous "Neigh," from her bleacher seat, that the Cardinals management offered her a free pass if she would keep her voice down to permit adjoining fans to enjoy the game. Not surprisingly, she turned down the offer. In the 1930s, Boston had Lollie Hopkins, who was a proper Bostonian to the core — she employed a megaphone to salute verbally good efforts by visiting players as well as the local heroes.

Harold Seymour wrote:

> Some of the more persistent ... [fans] had the satisfaction of getting publicized ... and becoming a part of the baseball scene. A Giant fan whose real name was Frank H. Wood became known far and wide simply as "Well! Well! Well!" because of his habit of jumping to his feet after every good or bad play and shouting this cry.... Zane Grey made him the hero of a boys' baseball book, *The Redheaded Outfield*.

Paul D. Adomites described loud fans in three major league stadiums. He wrote:

> Legendary lungs could be found in nearly every big league town. In the 1930s, the Kessler brothers, Bill and Eddie, of Philadelphia, would sit "on opposite sides of the grandstand and conduct what practically amounted to a private conversation across the diamond." In Pittsburgh, Bruce McAllister's screeching could be heard at every game and over the radio, too. Detroit's Patsy O'Toole was hailed as the "All-American earache."

Adomites discussed the old tradition of groups of fans who sat together, engaged in organized group cheers, and heckled players in unison. The original fan group was the Boston Royal Rooters, who became recognized as a cohesive group when they rooted for the Boston Pilgrims in the 1903 World's Series. In subsequent years, similarly organized fan groups appeared: the Ice Wagon Boys in St. Louis, the Stockyard Boys in Chicago, and the Steel Puddlers in Pittsburgh.

Organized fan rooters were less popular in the 1930s and 1940s but they reappeared in the 1990s as the Wrigley Field Bleacher Bums. The Bums developed their own special way of expressing disdain for opposing teams. They went against the usual fan's instinct to keep any baseball coming into his possession by throwing opposing teams' home run balls back onto the field.

Gangster Al Capone was an enthusiastic Chicago Cubs fan. He sat in his Wrigley Field box seat, protected by his personal army — a bodyguard on either side of him and three other bodyguards sitting behind him. One day Cubs catcher Gabby Hartnett stopped off at Capone's box and a photographer took a picture of the two men chatting. The next day a furious Commissioner Kenesaw M. Landis, fiercely protecting the game against any charges of gambler or gangster involvement, had bulletins posted in every major league clubhouse.

The bulletins proclaimed, "No more fraternizing in all ballparks. The umpires will be seated in the stands to watch all your movements. If any fraternizing occurs, a stiff penalty will be assessed." And Landis took Hartnett to task personally, forbidding him from talking to the gangster kingpin. The big catcher responded, "If you don't want anybody to talk to the Big Guy, Judge, why don't you tell that to Capone."

13

Fans' Impact on the Game

There have been occasions when the action of a baseball fan or fans has had a direct impact upon a game as it is being played. Baseball rules grant fans the right to go after any ball clearly hit into the stands, but umpires are expected to rule interference on a ball considered to be within a fielder's reach. This is among the toughest judgments umpires have to make.

A classic case of fan intervention occurred during the first game of the American League playoff in 1996. With the pennant going to the winner of the Yankees–Orioles series, the visiting Orioles opened the best-of-five-game set by taking a 4–3 lead after seven innings in the first game. Derek Jeter led off the Yankees home eighth by slicing a drive to deep right field. The Orioles' Tony Tarasco drifted back to the wall and appeared ready to make the catch.

But fate intervened in the form of 12-year-old Yankees fan Jeffrey Maier. The boy stretched out over the fence and deflected the drive into the stands. Right field umpire Rich Garcia ruled the ball a home run despite violent protests from the Orioles, especially O's manager Davey Johnson, who was thumbed out of the game. The Orioles retired the side without further damage and the game was tied at 4-all. The tie held until the bottom of the 11th when Bernie Williams homered to clinch a 5–4 Yankees win. American League president Gene Budig, after viewing a replay of Jeter's disputed home run, denied the Orioles' protest of the umpire's call. Orioles fans took no consolation when Garcia admitted subsequently that he had blown the call. The Yankees went on to win the series and pennant and jubilant Yankees fans treated juvenile fan Maier as one of their heroes.

And then there was Steve Bartman. He is the Chicago Cubs fan who was accused of doing in the 2003 Cubs in a complete reversal of Maier's role. It was the eighth inning of the sixth playoff game between the Cubs and the Florida Marlins at Wrigley Field with the Cubs only five outs from their first pennant in 58 years. The 26-year-old Bartman is a devoted Cubs fan, a mild-mannered financial analyst from a Chicago suburb who coaches a traveling team of 13- and 14-year-olds in a youth baseball league. The Cubs led 3–0 with one out and a runner on second base when the Marlins' Luis Castillo lofted a flyball down the line near the left field wall. Cubs left fielder Moises Alou leaped to attempt to make the catch by the wall, when Bartman, wearing headphones over his blue Cubs cap, knocked the ball back into the stands.

Alou was incredulous and furious, swatting at the air with his glove down and screaming loudly at the stunned Bartman. With that, the fortunes of the game changed dramatically as the Cubs imploded. After a few more pitches the Marlins had tied the game and they vaulted into a 7–3 lead before being retired.

After the Cubs lost the game, Alou manfully told writers in reference to Bartman, "Things like that happen. If you have a clean shot at a baseball, you go for it." But the Cubs fans were not so understanding and forgiving and Bartman had to be moved out of the stands for his own protection.

The mortified Bartman issued a public apology the next day from "the bottom of this Cubs fan's broken heart." Regardless, he was vilified by local fans and writers over the next few days, especially after the Cubs lost the seventh game and the pennant. The Illinois governor, Rod R. Blagojevich, had little sympathy for Bartman. He told reporters: "I hope he made it home. But I'm angry at the guy. Part of having home field advantage is that on every single pitch you do what you can to help the team win. In this case, that meant getting out of the way."

Washington Post writer Thomas Boswell defended the beleaguered fan. He wrote: "What I will remember about Bartman was his public statement the next day, which I consider the most sincere, pained and authentic apology by anyone involved in any controversy in this country in many years. Politicians, sports stars and other celebrities who get in trouble should show a fraction of the class and accountability that this fan showed for simply trying to catch a foul ball that, according to the umpire, he had every right to grab."

Over time, Cubs fans have mellowed and Bartman has been more or less restored to their good graces. The same cannot be said for the baseball Bartman deflected so disastrously. Grant DePorter, the managing partner of Harry Caray's Chicago area restaurants, outbid 37 bidders, paying $106,600 for the ball at an auction a month after the ball had ruined the

Cubs' season. His stated purpose was "to create closure to the way the season ended" by destroying the ball in a manner most Cubs fans desired. DePorter reported with unpardonable pride that his winning bid surpassed the amount paid for the ball that skipped through Bill Buckner's legs in the 1986 World Series. DePorter proclaimed proudly, "The Cubs fans' sorrow is worth more than the Red Sox fans' sorrow."

And then there are the fans who have found other ways to "participate" in a game. Over the last 30 years, there have been the streakers, exhibitionists who race out on the field sans clothing while the game was under way. And in recent years there have been people, usually overfortified with alcohol, who ran onto the field and without warning attacked a player or coach. On September 28, 1995, Cubs reliever Randy Myers was charged by a 27-year-old bond trader who jumped out of the stands at Wrigley Field. He charged the mound but Myers saw him coming, dropped his glove, and knocked him down with a well-placed forearm.

Four years later, almost to the day, a 23-year-old fan attacked Houston Astros rightfielder Bill Spiers in Milwaukee. Spiers ended up with facial injuries and a whiplash injury. On September 19, 2002, again four years later almost to the day, Kansas City Royals coach Tom Gamboa was in the first base coaching box at Comiskey Park when, completely unexpected, he was knocked to the ground and pummeled by a bare-chested father and his 15-year-old son. The 54-year-old Gamboa sustained several cuts and a large bruise on his forehead. The entire Royals' team and most of the White Sox players rushed to his aid and beat the attackers severely before they were handcuffed and removed from the field.

Players have always been fair game for those who take pleasure in throwing objects at players from the safety of the stands. Most fans, are aware of the Medwick-Owen affair during the final game of the 1934 World Series between the Cardinals and the Tigers. The Gas House Gang was in the final process of destroying the Tigers 11–0 when hot-tempered Cardinals left fielder Joe Medwick tripled and slid roughly into Tigers third baseman Marv Owen. After Owen responded with a retaliatory kick, the umpires calmed things down and Medwick moved to his left field position.

But the Detroit fans, in no mood to accept the impending loss of the series, had no interest in calming things down. They bombarded Medwick with a variety of fruits, vegetables, and bottles. Further incensed when the happy Cardinals played catch with the debris, the fury of the fans increased. Commissioner Landis summoned Medwick and Cardinals manager Frankie Frisch to his box before ordering Medwick out of the game. As J. Roy Stockton wrote: "It was the easiest way out. You can't eject all the cus-

13. Fans' Impact on the Game 183

The riotous scene as Detroit Tigers fans throw edible and inedible items at St. Louis Cardinals left fielder Joe Medwick (No. 7) as the Cards polish off the Tigers in the 1934 World Series. (Transcendental Graphics, Boulder, CO).

tomers in the left-field [sic] bleachers—and those vegetable and fruit volunteers certainly had made it plain that before they'd take any more of Medwick, there'd be a riot."

Fans have been near-participants in games since the game was in its earliest days. A dramatic example of the tension at games occurred at the deciding Brooklyn championship game in 1860 between the Excelsiors and the Atlantics. Feelings were running high as a result of the two earlier games between the teams. The Excelsiors won the first game 23–4, but the Atlantics evened the series with a 15–14 win in the second game. So the rubber match was played before an aroused crowd of Brooklynites, exhibiting the same enthusiasm and combativeness their descendants would show many years later in support of their beloved Dodgers.

In the sixth inning, the Excelsiors were leading 8–6 when the first riot in the game's history broke out. Vicious personal abuse by unruly Atlantics fans was followed by a barrage of edibles and nonedibles alike thrown at Excelsiors players. A free-for-all between fans and Excelsiors players ensued and the game was called when the Excelsiors captain understandably pulled his team off the field. After the game, both teams' captains harmoniously agreed to call the game a draw under the theory that the players had behaved properly and that the imbroglio had been the fault of the fans.

Harold Seymour wrote:

> The more brash tone of baseball was also evident at a game in Irvington, New Jersey, between the home team and the New York Mutuals. The field was surrounded by a dense crowd of some six or seven thousand people and hundreds of vehicles.... A disturbance started by pickpockets broke out.... The rioters surged onto the infield and, in the absence of police, had to be driven back by the players with their bats.... The new rowdy conduct was not restricted to the New York area. The Buffalo *Express* complained that the behavior of the Rochester Live Oaks in a game was "not exactly proper and creditable." When the umpire called a close play against ... [the Live Oaks], their captain heaved the ball in the air, and the team walked off the field.

There was another game between the Brooklyn Atlantics and the New York Mutuals in 1863 that was a forerunner of the tempestuous feuds which would enliven games between the New York Giants and the Brooklyn Dodgers during the next 95 years. It was a hot day and emotions boiled over as the Mutuals, down by eight runs in the bottom of the ninth inning, battled back to within striking distance of the Atlantics. Warren Goldstein wrote:

> By the time the Mutuals had come within one run of the Atlantics, the emotional equilibrium of the players and the spectators was long gone.... With a man on first, the Atlantics pitcher pitched more than fifty balls to William McKeever, hoping to induce him to swing at a bad pitch [this was the time when the batter had the right to call the pitch he wanted].... McKeever's patience wore thin and ... [after some time] the excited Atlantics players then tried to have the game called, citing the "poor excuse" of darkness.

The ensuing commotion, in which the fans took an active part, forced the game's suspension. Goldstein concluded his discussion of the controversy with the thought: "The principal villain of the afternoon was the excitement produced by the [hot] day, the crowd, the game, and the players." But, most significant, the fans had been instrumental in forcing the suspension of the game.

Abuse of umpires by fans was pervasive in the 1890s as "kranks" stopped at nothing in trying to intimidate umpires and thereby help their teams. Umpires were cursed loudly by fans and bombarded with beer bottles and rotten eggs, and even subjected to beatings dealt out by unrestrained fans. Of course, umpires were an endangered species well before the 1890s. In 1884, for example, the Baltimore club felt it necessary to intall a barbed wire fence around its playing field to protect umpires from being mobbed by aggrieved spectators. In that same year, angry fans assaulted umpire Tom Gunning after he called a game because of darkness. And a Philadelphia crowd turned on umpire Billy McLean, a former professional boxer. McLean retaliated by throwing a bat into a group of fans. He had to be rescued and escorted off the field by police. A year later, the combative McLean needed another police escort after being threatened physically by enraged fans.

Pittsburgh Pirates infielder Tommy Leach credited the Boston rooters, a group of loyal fans called the Boston Royal Rooters led by John F. Kennedy's grandfather John "Honey" Fitzgerald, with playing an important part in the Pirates' loss to the then-named Boston Puritans in 1903. Lawrence S. Ritter quoted Leach to that effect:

> That was probably the wildest World Series ever played. Arguing all the time between the teams, between the players and the umpires, and especially between the players and the fans.... The fans were *part* of the game in those days. They'd pour right out onto the field and argue with the players and the umpires.
>
> I think those Boston fans actually won the Series for the Red Sox. We beat them three out of the first four games, and then they started singing that damn *Tessie* song, the Red Sox fans did. They called themselves the Royal Rooters and their leader was some Boston character named Mike McGreevey. He was known as "Nuf Sed" McGreevey, because any time there was an argument about anything to do with baseball he was the ultimate authority. Once McGreevey gave his opinion that ended the argument: nuf sed!
>
> Anyway, in the fifth game of the Series, the Royal Rooters started singing *Tessie* for no particular reason at all, and the Red Sox won. They must have figured it was a good-luck charm, because from then on you could hardly play ball they were singing *Tessie* so damn loud.

There was a violent scene before the deciding seventh game when the Royal Rooters, who assumed mistakenly that their customary pavilion seats were being held for them, discovered that the seats were occupied by other fans who had bought them on a first come- first serve basis. Some 500 Royal Rooters stormed the stands and blocked the aisles, delaying the start of the game for half an hour until they were driven away by mounted police.

The fans had an impact on the 1922 World's Series, helped along by newly installed Commissioner Kenesaw M. Landis who carefully nurtured his persona as a man whose primary concern was to protect the rights of the fans. He proved this during the World's Series between New York City's rival Yankees and Giants, played at the Polo Grounds (Yankee Stadium opened the following April). This was almost 20 years before playing field lights were installed at the Polo Grounds.

The second game of the series was tied at three after 10 innings with almost an hour to go before sundown. The crowd watched anxiously to see whether the Babe Ruth–led Yankees would beat John McGraw's Giants. With score tied and the sun still high in the sky, the fans were stunned and then infuriated when the umpires called the game because of "darkness." The storm of seat cushions, pop bottles, and other hard objects cascading down from the stands testified to the profound anger of fans about the unexpected decision.

Landis was acutely aware of fans' suspicions that teams' financial benefits (by adding another game to the series) or possible gambler involvement might have prompted the abrupt suspension of the game. As a result, Landis checkmated any further fan demonstrations by ordering all gate receipts from the game to be turned over to a local charity. Fans and writers applauded the move.

The Yankees were playing an important game with the second- place Browns in September 1922 at Sportsmans Park in St. Louis. Yankees centerfielder Lawton "Whitey" Witt, racing back to catch a fly ball in a late inning of the close game, was skulled by a pop bottle thrown by a fan. He fell down stunned but managed to continue in the game, wearing a head bandage leading to a description by a New York writer as making "Little Whitey appear like a pirate as he patrolled his position for the rest of the game." The Yanks almost lost the game because of the fan's outrageous act.

Ban Johnson offered a $1,000 reward for the arrest of the rowdy and a number of other fans came forward with their differing versions. Johnson closed the incident by giving $100, railroad fare, and a ticket to the World's Series to a fan who provided a creative explanation. He offered the extraordinary thought that Witt had stepped on the neck of the bottle, causing it to fly up in the air and strike Witt in the head.

The constant availability to players of eager feminine fans anxious for relationships with idolized players always has the potential for affecting players and their teams. Before the development of drugs to deal with venereal diseases, an uncounted number of infected players have lost playing time because of these ailments. It is worth examining a few of these off-field relationships which became public knowledge.

In July 1932 Cubs shortstop Billy Jurges was living in a Chicago hotel.

He'd been dating Violet Valli, a local girl. He was asleep one morning when she knocked on his door. She came into his room, sat on his bed, and became furious when he told her he had no intention of marrying her. She threatened suicide and Jurges walked into the bathroom to get her a drink of water to calm her down. She followed him into the bathroom, and when he turned around, she pulled out a revolver and shot him in the hand and the ribs.

But the story had a happy ending. Jurges recovered in six weeks and played in the World Series as the Yankees devastated the Cubs in four straight games. He went on to a solid baseball career. Jurges refused to press charges against Valli and she, capitalizing on her sudden fame, obtained singing and dancing engagements in Chicago clubs.

Phillies first baseman Eddie Waitkus was shot in his Chicago hotel room in June 1949 by a local woman, Ruth Ann Steinhagen. A bachelor, Waitkus had never met Steinhagen before and she apparently was too shy to approach him. She had become obsessed with Waitkus after seeing him play with the Cubs for three years before the Cubs traded him to the Phillies earlier that season. She watched him play during weekends when he was with the Cubs and her mother told police that her mentally unbalanced daughter had told her, "I'm going to get a gun and shoot Eddie and myself."

Waitkus resumed his playing career in 1950 and had three decent years before losing his starting job with the Phillies. Steinhagen was committed to a mental facility. The episode attracted enough attention to be the basis for the successful movie *The Natural*.

While he was with the Red Sox, Wade Boggs, who was married, was involved in a relationship with Margo Adams, a woman from a Boston suburb. After she sued him, he admitted shamefully that she had accompanied him on road trips although it was never clear that he had promised to divorce his wife to marry her. The embarrassing furor reached its climax when the Red Sox played a night game in Kansas City before thousands of fans wearing cutout masks of Boggs's mistress. Boggs overcame his embarrassment sufficiently to lead all American League hitters with a .366 average. He continued to play in the majors for 10 more years, his indiscretion largely forgotten by the fans. Unlike Jurges and Waitkus, Boggs did not miss any playing time.

Some superstitious fans worry unduly about how their activities affect the fortunes of their teams. During the 1939 season, actress Tallullah Bankhead invited several New York Giants players to attend one of her hit shows after the Giants had a terrible home stand. She gamely took the rap for their misfortunes. Years later she told a *New York Times* reporter in characteristically breezy style:

Back in the summer of 1939 I thought I had voodoed the Giants. I invited the entire club to see a performance of "The Little Foxes." After the performance, I gave them a buffet supper—canapés and caviar and beverages. First, [Carl] Hubbell couldn't come because he was going to pitch the next day. Harry Danning couldn't show up because he had a poisoned foot. [Billy] Jurges had spit in an umpire's eye and had just escaped from Alcatraz. But Ott and Jo-Jo Moore and most of the rest of them came and said they had enjoyed the show. And what happened after that? The Giants lost eight in a row. Sure that I had hexed them, I stayed away from the ballpark. I even barred my maid from the Polo Grounds.

Baseball fans often have ideas not shared by the team's manager or general manager. The Brooklyn Dodgers picked up well-traveled outfielder Dixie Walker in July 1939 in what appeared to be an unimportant deal. But there was something about the blond, affable Walker that captured the fancy of the Dodgers fans. He became even more popular with Brooklyn fans when he led the Dodgers in hitting in 1940, and hit .436 against the hated Giants. But, for some reason, the Dodgers obtained 38-year-old Paul Waner after that season and manager Leo Durocher installed Waner in Walker's right field position during spring training and announced that Waner would start the 1941 season in right field.

A few days later, in West Palm Beach, Durocher received a remarkable telegram from Brooklyn. It read, "Put Walker back in right field or we will boycott the Dodgers." The telegram bore the duly attested signatures of 5,000 fans. Dodgers general manager Larry MacPhail ordered Durocher to ignore the telegram or he would be fired. But the Dodgers' hands were forced as Waner's performance showed his age shortly after the season opened. Walker took over his old position in a short time, and was one of the main reasons the Dodgers won their first pennant in 20 years. The fans' judgment had been vindicated.

There was one Brooklyn fan, 21-year-old John Christian, who almost cost Durocher his managerial job. In June 1945, after his medical discharge from the Army, Christian shouted epithets at Durocher from the Ebbets Field upper stands during a game, calling the Lippy One a crook, a bum, and worse. A few innings later, a beefy Ebbets Field policeman, Joseph Moore, told Christian that Durocher wanted to see him and insisted that the fan accompany him. According to Christian, he was led to an areaway between the Dodgers' clubhouse and dugout and Durocher shouted at him, "You've got a mother. How would you like somebody to call her names?"

With that, Moore knocked Christian down with a brass knuckles-enhanced fist, and after Christian regained his feet, Durocher grabbed the brass knuckles and knocked Christian down again. With his jaw broken, Christian managed to escape. Durocher and Moore were arrested, indicted by a grand jury, and released on bail.

Brooklyn fans were divided in their views on the matter. Some defended Durocher without reservation. But there was a general consensus that Durocher had no justification for sending Moore into the upper stands to collar Christian. Eventually, Durocher and Moore were acquitted, but significantly, Christian received a financial settlement. There was a general feeling that Durocher had been fortunate to avoid a felony charge.

Durocher's behavior problems continued. In 1946, he fell in love with his neighbor's wife. His neighbor, Ray Hendricks, was not known to the public. But Hendricks's wife was well-known movie actress Laraine Day. Hendricks charged that "Durocher clandestinely pursued the love" of Day while "posing as a family friend."

Durocher's well-publicized affair and eventual marriage to Day got him in deep trouble with the Catholic hierarchy in Brooklyn and the Dodgers, especially General Manager Branch Rickey, were well aware that many of their fans, especially Catholics, were very much concerned. Peter Golenbock wrote: "Durocher had been accused of outrageous acts before, including being a kleptomaniac, a deadbeat, a liar, a card cheat, and a brawler, but the public outcry against what it viewed as his adultery was the most violent." A few years later, some fans still had not forgiven Durocher for breaking up Laraine Day's marriage.

Durocher's continuing problems in adhering to acceptable levels of behavior led to a one-year suspension by Commissioner Happy Chandler in the spring of 1947, again because of the involvement of fans. Durocher had been warned repeatedly by Chandler of his associations with known and notorious gamblers and Durocher refused to take Chandler's warnings seriously. At the time, athletic figures in other sports had admitted receiving bribe offers, and Chandler was especially sensitive to any involvement of baseball figures with gamblers. Chandler had urged Rickey to correct the behavior of Durocher. Rickey had referred to Durocher as his "pet reclamation project," but Chandler felt that Rickey was incapable of improving Durocher's conduct.

The last straw occurred when the Dodgers were in Havana for an exhibition game with the Yankees in March 1947. Before the game, Durocher spied two fans with gambling backgrounds in Yankees general manager Larry MacPhail's box. One was Memphis Engleberg, a well-known bookmaker and gambler, and the other was Connie Immerman, a Havana casino operator. Durocher, chastised by Chandler for associating with gamblers, said caustically, "He [MacPhail] has gamblers as his guests. If I did that,

I'd get kicked out of baseball." After conducting a hearing on Durocher's complaint, Chandler responded by suspending Durocher for the 1947 season. This was a case where the presence of gambler-fans had been the specific reason for a serious action taken by the commissioner.

Before ballparks were fully enclosed, overflow crowds were allowed to stand in the deepest outfield sectors; after the parks were completely enclosed, teams constructed temporary outfield seats to accommodate larger-than-normal crowds attending World Series games. Early photos show that fans ringing the outfield were not restricted by temporary barriers such as fences or even ropes. On balls hit into distant outfield sectors, it was customary for home team fans to move out of the way of their team's player to increase his chance of making a play on balls near them. In contrast, visiting teams' outfielders were impeded by a solid, virtually impenetrable wall of spectators.

Mel Ott had two interesting experiences with overflow crowds. In the mid–1930s, when the St. Louis Cardinals played at small, antiquated Sportsmans Park, fans without seats were permitted to stand in front of the outfield walls as policemen on horseback maintained order. The New York Giants and the Cardinals played a crucial series in St. Louis in 1935 before an overpacked house. The Giants had three brave rooters among the largely hostile group ringing the outfield. Years later Ott talked of his experience as the Giants' right fielder in a game during that series:

> It took courage but those fellows always had something encouraging to shout to me. If I'd batted in a run, or even hit a loud foul, they would give me a little cheer. The rest of the mob squatted out there on the grass and gave 'em plenty of dirty looks and muttered threats. Late in the game, just as I backpedaled to catch a fly ball, I felt something tickle my ribs. I took my eye off the ball for a second and saw a pop bottle sail under my arm. It was the last out of the inning and naturally I turned around to see who tossed the bottle. "Come on, Mel," one of my buddies shouted indignantly. "Let's get him." The three of them went cruising around that mob, doing everything but step on faces, and I went along. But we couldn't spot anyone with a guilty look and had to give it up.

Ott's other experience came two years earlier in the 1933 World Series between the Giants and the Washington Senators at Griffith Stadium in Washington. Temporary bleacher seats were put in place for the series. The Giants, leading in the series three games to one, came to bat with the tense fifth game tied 3–3 in the top of the 10th. Ott, up with two out and none on, cocked his right leg and smoked a long drive toward the center field bleachers. Senators centerfielder Fred Schulte raced back and got his glove on the ball just as it was about to drop into the low, temporary seats in front of the permanent stands. But the ball bounced out of his glove as he disappeared from sight into the arms of a fan. At first, the drive was ruled a double by the second base umpire but he was overruled by the other two umpires. Ott crossed the plate with the go-ahead run and the Giants won the ballgame and series.

Many fans believe they can run a club more effectively than the manager can. St. Louis writer Bob Broeg told an amusing story of how manager Frankie Frisch dealt with a heckling fan who second-guessed him loudly from a box seat:

> Going back and forth from the coaching box, wearing a disarming smile, Frisch began soliciting suggestions. What would the patron prefer? The pleased customer asked for a bunt here, a hit-and-run there. Politely, the manager asked where the fan worked. The man gave him a downtown business address, but wondered why [Frisch] would want to know about ... him. "Because," blazed fire-eating ... Frisch, I'm going to be down at your office tomorrow morning, flannelmouth, and tell you how to run your blankety-blank business.

Fans exert pressure with varying degrees of success on front-office decisions regarding managers. A classic case of the fans having their say and making it stick came in 1948 when Cleveland Indians owner Bill Veeck gave in to the fans' clamor that Lou Boudreau be retained as the Indians' manager. When Veeck purchased the Indians, he planned to replace the popular shortstop-manager who had managed the club since 1942. When word leaked out of Veeck's plan after the 1947 season, there was a tremendous fan protest as Veeck was deluged with 4,000 letters from fans, the high majority of them in support of Boudreau's retention.

The fans' advice worked out beautifully as Boudreau produced one of the greatest individual seasons ever. He hit .355 as his club won the American League pennant in a one-game playoff when Boudreau led the attack with a four-for-four performance with two homers. To top it off, Boudreau's club won the World Series. It was a signal triumph for Boudreau and a good example of the participatory role baseball fans have played.

14

The Fan as a Participant

Over the last several decades, fans have become participants in baseball as well as observers of the game. These years have seen the formation of a very active, more focused, involvement by fans. The formation and growth of the Society for American Baseball Research has been the major vehicle through which fans have exchanged views and the results of their analytical research on the game. SABR (pronounced "saber") is an international organization headquartered in Cleveland. Its mission is to foster the study of baseball in every imaginable aspect — its history, statistics, the people who have run the game, the players, the managers, the media, etc. But more than that, it is the organization the true baseball fan has always wanted and needed.

SABR was organized in August 1971 at the Baseball Hall of Fame Library. Federal government official L. Robert Davids, assisted by 16 fellow baseball enthusiasts, founded SABR to provide a needed outlet for baseball publishing efforts. As the organization took form and matured, the variegated interests of its members led to expanded activities in addition to publication. These included improvement in the accuracy of baseball records, expanded private research not necessarily intended for publication on all manner of baseball subjects, and statistical research.

SABR's effectiveness has been enhanced by its publication of biographical books, and research, historical publications, and surveys producing authoritative results. There have been an increasing number of regional groups (some 49 by the year 2005), and committees concentrating on such obvious subjects as ballparks as well as more esoteric subjects like songs and poems. The dues-paying membership has grown steadily from the original 16 founding members in 1971 to 1,145 in 1980, to 7,000 members in 2004.

14. The Fan as a Participant

All SABR members are completely knowledgeable about the current baseball scene. But almost all of them also have a special interest in a specific aspect of the game. As might be expected, most members focus on a favorite team, player, or era. But other primary areas of interest include such less obvious subjects as baseball in Japan, Europe, and Latin America. And some members have a particular interest in even more unexpected areas, for example, the burial sites of baseball figures. A daily collection of member views, shown on a special Web site (SABR-L), includes a potpourri of baseball subjects ranging from the previous day's games to an obscure occurrence or player from the early days of the game.

Attendance at a SABR meting is an enjoyable experience. The meetings are long on lively, informal discussions and mercifully short on organizational business. More often than not, the meetings feature the appearance of a baseball official or player who usually recounts his experiences frankly and interestingly, confident that his listeners have the background and interest to understand and enjoy his remarks. Following the pattern set by founder Bob Davids, most SABR meetings include an oral trivia quiz during which members prove that no baseball matter or figure is beyond their powers of recognition, no matter how ancient or trivial. A special pleasure at the meetings is the congeniality between longstanding members and newer members, their only bond a mutual love of baseball

Similar to most athletes, baseball players have tended to be largely unaware of the history of their sport. Yet, the SABR membership has included many prominent players and major league executives. Well-known player-members have included, among others, Waite Hoyt, Hank Greenberg, Ken Keltner, Ralph Kiner, Joe Garagiola, Tim McCarver, Tony Kubek, Andy Pafko, Brooks Robinson, Terry Kennedy, and Ted Williams. Numbered among the influential executives who have been members are former Commissioner Peter Ueberroth and Commissioner Bud Selig, Peter O'Malley, and Calvin Griffith. Ted Williams, never one to hand out praise indiscriminately, always referred to SABR as "baseball's best-kept secret."

The computer is an invaluable tool for modern baseball fans. It is useful in systematically gathering and manipulating baseball records, and has made it possible to perform associated functions either impossible or impractical before the computer was developed to its present level of sophistication. And the increased speed of more advanced home computers has been remarkable. For example, one of the computer games available in 1985 permitted a player to schedule and simulate a complete, 162-game season and keep records of the developed statistics. "Playing" a full, simulated season at that time took several weeks, assuming each game took an hour to play. Remarkably, only 10 years later, a desk-size personal computer had the capability of replicating each play from a 162-game season in less than 15 minutes.

After marveling at the speeds computers exhibit in simulating baseball data, a fan has to ask how closely these simulations approach reality. A SABR researcher replayed a season on his computer 10 times to see how often the actual pennant winners duplicated their feat. He reported that the pennant winners averaged "winning" again six times out of 10, a reasonable result given the closeness of many pennant races and the random, unpredictable events which can determine the winner in a close race.

The first baseball statistics from 1845 to 1870 were concerned with an individual player's run production under the logical theory that runs and outs are the fundamental determinants of team victories and losses. But player statistics of that time showed only how many runs or outs the player accounted for. As the game became more professional and fans became interested in individual player achievements, baseball icon and writer Henry Chadwick began to record average runs and outs per game, and also home runs, total bases, and hits per game for individual players. By the 1870s, at-bats were shown and, in combination with hits, permitted the simple calculation of the batting average. Today's fans have come to recognize the limitations of the batting average which neither differentiates between singles and extra-base hits nor the effect of a hit on the scoring of a run.

The years between the mid–1870s and 1900 witnessed the development of several major stats for individual players— season totals of games played, at-bats, runs scored and runs scored per game, hits, and batting average. Pitching statistics included earned run average, hits allowed and hits per game, and opponents' batting average. Fielding statistics included averages based as today on putouts, assists, and errors. Since 1900, the major statistical measures developed (a few derived from earlier measures) were stolen bases, strikeouts, ERA, saves, RBI, on base percentages, and total bases. Most important to the baseball researcher, in 1951 A.S. Barnes published The *Official Encyclopedia of Baseball,* a compilation of career records of the nearly 9,000 players who appeared in a major league game from 1871 to 1949. That tome has been supplanted by today's updated, more comprehensive *Total Baseball.*

Baseball statistics have attracted the interest of baseball fans since the game's inception. A very thorough review of the development of baseball statistics, the *Numbers Game— Baseball's Lifelong Fascination with Statistics,* became available in 2004. The book traces the evolution of baseball statistics, discusses the people who have advanced and improved statistics, and the increasing ways in which fans and researchers have put this information to good use in improving fans' understanding of the game.

The term "sabremetrician," derived from SABR, refers to individuals dedicated to the analysis of baseball statistics. Henry Chadwick can be considered the first sabremetrician because of his original work in devising and publishing baseball statistics, rudimentary as they were. Branch Rickey, along with his profound overall impact upon baseball, was a more recent baseball maven who also deserves that designation. Rickey published a magazine article which set forth the need for a more sophisticated look at baseball statistics. The thrust of Rickey's article was the differentiation between widely used statistics which were not specifically related to a baseball team's success, such as batting average, and statistics which were directly related to winning games, such as runs and on base percentage. Rickey, in effect, was suggesting that the original baseball statistics devised by Chadwick were more appropriate for indicating the relative contribution individual players made to their team's wins and losses than statistics then in use.

Rickey, assisted by then–Dodgers team statistician Allan Roth, developed a formula to measure a team's ability to convert its offensive and defensive statistics into runs, and ultimately wins. Their theory, whose logic and validity have been confirmed many times, is that just as the team scoring the most runs wins the game, the team scoring more runs than it gives up over the course of the season will win more games than it loses. It follows then that the winning team with the largest difference between its wins and losses should finish higher than other competing, winning teams. From Rickey's day through to the present, sabremetricians have expended considerable research effort on developing methods for estimating run-scoring probability as a means of projecting team success.

The ever-increasing use of computers since the mid–1960s has produced the collection, dissemination, manipulation, and analysis of baseball statistics in forms not possible before the computer. Since that time, sabremetricians have utilized such supporting material as old scrapbooks and newspapers along with computers in updating old player records. Intensive efforts have been made to update player statistics for those who played in the era before such statistics as the RBI, slugging percentage, ERA, and saves were compiled.

Currently, and in the recent past, sabremetricians have concerned themselves with a myriad of baseball questions, such as: How do players of different eras compare? Is there such a thing as a clutch hitter? How significant is the effect of a player's home ballpark on his performance as measured by his hitting or pitching statistics? How can a player's performance be evaluated given such changes in conditions as the use of artificial turf and the liveliness of the baseball? Is the sacrifice bunt an effective strategy and the associated question as to the chances of a team scoring in a given inning when the first hitter gets on base? How effective have individual hitters been against specific pitchers and vice versa? How closely can a player's major league performance be predicted on the basis of his minor league statistics, and how closely can we project a player's total career statistics (and chances for Hall of Fame enshrinement) while he is still in midcareer?

Bill James has developed considerable material of use to today's fans in evaluating players. He has been a leader in measuring the impact of different ballparks on hitting and pitching performances. And he has developed methodology for projecting major league performance based upon a player's minor league statistics and has suggested objective criteria for electing players into the Hall of Fame.

Two types of methods are available to fans to compute a player's value and contribution to his teams over his career. One is the linear weights method created by Pete Palmer; the second is the win shares procedure, developed by Bill James. Palmer's calculation measures all events on a ballfield in terms of runs created and the individual player's contribution to his team's wins and losses. The linear weights system involves calculating a player's total player rating, based upon the seasonal and career totals of his offensive and defensive statistics compared to those of a comparable "average player."

James's procedure measures a team's superiority in runs scored or saved over the league average, and then determines the win shares the player has earned in that number of team wins in excess of the league average. A full explanation of the win shares system, as well as win shares for every player in every season, can be found in Bill James's *Win Shares*.

Both calculations yield a value ranking of the players' total contribution to his teams over his career, and a workable, objective comparison of the value of a player compared with that of other players. The 30 highest-ranking players, of whom Barry Bonds, Mike Piazza, Ken Griffey Jr., Jeff Bagwell, Rickey Henderson, Frank Thomas, and Edgar Martinez were active through the 2000 season, determined by each of the methods are as follows:

Win Shares Method	Linear Weights Method
1. Babe Ruth	Babe Ruth
2. Ty Cobb	Barry Bonds
3. Honus Wagner	Napoleon Lajoie
4. Willie Mays	Rogers Hornsby
5. Henry Aaron	Ted Williams

Win Shares Method	Linear Weights Method
6. Cy Young	Mike Schmidt
7. Tris Speaker	Mickey Mantle
8. Stan Musial	Mike Piazza
9. Eddie Collins	Willie Mays
10. Mickey Mantle	Lou Gehrig
11. Ted Williams	Tris Speaker
12. Walter Johnson	Ken Griffey Jr.
13. Pete Rose	Jeff Bagwell
14. Mel Ott	Ty Cobb
15. Frank Robinson	Joe Jackson
16. Rickey Henderson	Honus Wagner
17. Joe Morgan	Joe DiMaggio
18. Rogers Hornsby	Henry Aaron
19. Napoleon Lajoie	Rickey Henderson
20. Lou Gehrig	Frank Thomas
21. Carl Yastrzemski	Eddie Collins
22. Kid Nichols	Lou Boudreau
23. Grover Cleveland Alexander	Dan Brouthers
24. Mike Schmidt	Jimmy Foxx
25. Barry Bonds	Pete Browning
26. Sam Crawford	Frank Robinson
27. Christy Mathewson	Stan Musial
28. Eddie Mathews	Ed Delahanty
29. Reggie Jackson	Edgar Martinez
30. Al Kaline	Jackie Robinson

The more sophisticated player evaluation analyses currently available require today's knowledgeable fans to look at baseball statistics in a different light. This is done by normalizing data; that is, by making adjustments to accommodate changes in factors—ballparks, the liveliness of the baseball in use, rule changes, etc.—affecting player performance to increase the true comparability of statistics from one player era to another. For example, Bill Terry's National League-leading .401 batting average in 1930 is one of the benchmark offensive performances of the modern era. By comparison, Carl Yastrzemski's American League-leading .301 average in 1968 is often derided as a mediocre performance by the league's leading hitter. But sabremetricians see a different picture, one in which they have determined that the two Hall of Famers were almost equally effective in their two league-leading seasons. The researchers observed that Terry hit .401 in 1930 when National League players (exclusive of pitchers) hit for an average of .312. In contrast, Yaz's American League competitors hit for a meager league average of .238 when he hit .301.

Sabremetricians calculated that in 1930 Terry was a better hitter than the National League's average hitter by 28.5 percent in 1930 (if you ignore the limitations of the batting average measurement), and Yastrzemski exceeded the average American League hitter by a very similar 26.5 percent. The following calculation puts the mere 2 percent separation between Terry and Yastrzemski in perspective. Let us assume that both men played in the National League in 1983 when the league's hitters averaged .255. The Terry of 1930 might have hit the equivalent of .328 in 1983 and the Yastrzemski of 1968 might have hit .323 in 1983. The same kind of adjustment should be made in the case of pitchers' ERAs where an unusually high or low league-leading ERA needs to be evaluated in terms of the average league ERA.

Advances in statistical analysis have led to the invention of Rotisserie Baseball, an ingenious (you could say addictive) game played by millions of fans since its first appearance in the early 1980s. Rotisserie Baseball, so-named because it was conceived by Daniel Okrent (an estimable baseball author and fan who since has found greener pastures as the ombudsman for the *New York Times*) and several co-midwives over lunch in the La Rotisserie Francaise, a French restaurant on Manhattan's East Side.

Rotisserie Baseball is a game in which baseball fans assume the role of a club owner or general manager in running a mythical major league team. There are many variations in Rotisserie Baseball as played by different groups but the general format is as follows: Before the actual baseball season starts, a fan takes control of a major team and competes with other devotees who control the operation of competing teams in the same league. Each "owner" or "general manager" pays an agreed-upon amount of money to select a team of pitchers and position players from the actual rosters of all of the clubs in the league. Maneuvering within agreed-upon, equal financial constraints, the operator(s) engineer a series of player trades with other "team owners." The idea is to "buy" players who will produce the best statistics at the lowest "cost" to the team operator. At the end of the season, the operator whose "players" have produced the best total team statistics is the pennant winner.

The trick in winning at Rotisserie Baseball is to rely less upon the blue-chip players who "cost" a lot of the fan's limited, available funds but rather to trade for lower-cost, unsung players who hopefully will outdo themselves and deliver better-than-expected statistics. Winning at Rotisserie Baseball depends upon the statistical production of selected individual players rather than the many player intangibles also contributing to actual team victories. Game players have commented on the way Rotisserie Baseball has changed the way they watch a real game. Many of them used to concentrate on rooting for their favorite team; now they root for the players they "own" to the possible detriment of their long time favorites. A Rotisserie player told of going to Wrigley Field to watch his favorite Cubs. But with one of his mythical relief pitchers coming in the game attempting to stop a last-minute Cubs rally, he was conflicted. He struggled to decide whether he could afford to "let" the Cubs lose so that his relief pitcher could improve his precious statistics.

Peter Golenbock has described the compulsive fan behavior engendered by the Rotisserie game:

> You develop a junkielike need for baseball minutia. It's like overstudying for an exam. You don't have to do it, and it won't improve your grade, but you do it anyway because your need to know becomes magnified. One Rotisserie owner said to me, "If I miss the sports report at the end of the night, I could use a straitjacket. I constantly wake up, pace, look at the clock, waiting for 2:30 A.M. when ESPN comes back on — and then I'll get out of bed to watch it. Even if I tape the 2:30 show, I *still* get up to watch it live."

Sabremetrics has taken the first steps toward moving from the theoretical to the practical. The more progressive major league officials have started evaluating player talent in terms of more sophisticated measurements of accomplishments, many of which have been developed by SABR members, most notably Bill James. The theory is that baseball statistics can be manipulated usefully to predict future performance of players and also identify players whose potential may not be apparent when evaluated by long-standing performance measurements like batting average, RBI, fielding percentage, and pitchers' wins and losses.

At this writing, several bright young general managers are confirmed sabremetrics devotees. Oakland's general manager Billy Beane is the best known of the group because of the crisp account of his high-energy operation of the Athletics' front office, as described by Michael Lewis. Beane, a former major league player, has maintained a highly successful level of team performance with the Athletics despite operating with one of the lowest major league player payrolls and losing such stars as Jason Giambi and Miguel Tejada to wealthier clubs.

The Red Sox hired 30-year-old Yale graduate Theo Epstein as their general manager in 2002 in their annual attempt to overtake George Steinbrenner's well-heeled Yankees. The Dodgers, after finding their vast treasury unequal to the task of buying a pennant, hired 31-year-old Harvard graduate Paul DePodesta, a Beane protégé, to be their cost-conscious front-office leader. Toronto Blue Jays general manager J.P. Ricciardi is another Beane disciple. Phillies GM Ed Wade is a former SABR member who is another believer. These young men have been the first general managers to publicly downgrade use of such traditional measurements as batting average, home runs, RBI, and ERA. They now concentrate more on newer sophisticated computer analyses of baseball statistics to evaluate players and to uncover unrecognized gems playing elsewhere in the major and minor leagues.

Actually, it would be overstating the case to claim that these Beane/SABR-developed concepts can by themselves replace the time-honored need for player procurement decisions based upon the subjective views of scouts and other experienced player evaluators. Most clubs utilizing these concepts consider them as only one resource in a systematic player evaluation process. And Tampa Bay GM Chuck Lamar represented the other end of the spectrum, expressing the view, "If I had to choose one tool to use, it would be a scout and not statistical data. People have been using statistical data to analyze baseball players since there were stats. But I'll never let it be the ultimate tool and I believe that scouting instincts win."

The most promising of the new offensive measurements is the hitter's OPS, the combination of his on base percentage (the ability to get on base via hits and walks) with his power (as measured by extra-base hits). Greater emphasis is placed on a player's patience and ability to draw base on balls, both as a means of getting on base and as a method of forcing the opposing pitcher to tire himself out through higher pitch counts. This fact has long been recognized intuitively by managers and players but it has taken the efforts of current researchers to produce convincing evidence that a walk is a very useful offensive factor. So apparently a walk may be at least as good as a hit.

For all the confidence sabremetricians have in the modern offensive statistics, very little confidence is placed on fielding statistics. A fielder's job is to make as many plays as possible. But errors (the number of times he fails) and fielding percentage (the rate at which he makes the play successfully) often obscure the achievements of the talented fielder in making a play that a mediocre gloveman cannot even attempt. As far back as 1868, Henry Chadwick said, "It is in the record of [a fielder's] good plays that we are to look for the most correct data for an estimate of skill." Branch Rickey also despaired of developing good fielding stats with the thought, "There is nothing on earth anybody can do with fielding."

There are a number of variables the researcher has to consider in evaluating fielding proficiency. They include: How many balls were hit into the fielder's area? Where was the fielder positioned when the ball was hit?

How skillful is the fielder in positioning himself for the hitter? How fast was the runner? Was the fielder distracted by a runner or, so common in today's game, a splintered bat fragment? Did the fielder's teammates play a supportive role if appropriate? Was crowd noise a factor? And so on.

Technological relief may be in sight. All major league stadiums are being equipped with a three-dimensional camera system that will measure everything that happens on the field, from the exact trajectory of fly balls to the precise speed of the fielders who chase them. The data would instantly allow grading of plays as to their degree of difficulty, and which fielders converted them into outs when other players were unable to make the play. If the system proves effective, fielding evaluation will have moved from suspect statistics and the subjectivity of the human eye to a very objective camera.

A ball club's general manager has the responsibility of measuring player performance against the cost of obtaining the player and paying him. (This function does not apply completely to the Yankees who, with the club's tremendous revenues, are in a position to buy players more speculatively). Theo Epstein feels that computer analysis can produce a bottom line relating player performance to player value. As an example, in the winter following the 2002 season, the Red Sox resisted conventional wisdom in refusing to trade unproven pitcher Casey Fossum for Cleveland ace Bartolo Colon. In 2002, Colon won four times as many games as Fossum but his salary was 24 times higher. At the same time, Epstein was criticized for acquiring Jeremy Giambi, Jason's younger brother, who in 2002 hit a mediocre .255 with 20 homers and 45 RBIs. Jeremy also was considered a poor outfielder and slow baserunner. But he had a commendable .414 on base average and .919 OPS, not too far below his superstar brother's .434 on base average and 1.034 OPS. And so the deal was made.

After the 2002 season, sabremetrics guru Bill James was hired by the Red Sox as a consultant. He commented at the time, "The real question is why did it take baseball this long to wake up to it [the importance of the fan as a baseball analyst]." He added, "But it's scary being at the table. For years I've expressed opinions and the only consequence of a bad call was that people made fun of me. Now I have a lot more at stake." Whether James can help the Red Sox capture that elusive pennant, his employment by the club confirms a virtually unrecognized fact — the baseball fan has become a participant in the game without wearing a baseball glove, swinging a bat, or operating a ball club.

15

Summing Up

It has been a century and a half since baseball began depending upon its kranks or fans to support the game financially. First there was the casual, nonpaying onlooker at games before 1860, when the game was still by and large an amateur pastime of the leisure class. Then there were the avid and sometimes rowdy fans attending games before the existing dual major league system became established in 1901. Next came the generations whose ties to the game were arguably stronger and closer out of necessity, as baseball became a reliable distraction from economic depression and two world wars. Then the fans of the postwar era financed the sport's expansion supporting baseball directly at the turnstile and indirectly by purchasing radio and TV sponsors' products. And finally today's fans, still supporting the game financially while becoming participants of a sort in the game through the activities described in the preceding chapter.

The enjoyment a major league team provides a fan most often is related to the team's performance on the field or to the exploits of favorite players. But many fans also have learned that there is more involved than mere wins and losses or the heroics of player favorites. For example, veteran New York Giants fans bonded with fellow Polo Grounds bleacher companions, people with whom they had nothing else in common except an affinity for the Giants. SABR has made many of today's fans feel some of that old camaraderie.

Today's fans have so much more to contemplate in following baseball than the fans of the past. Baseball buffs in the 1930s followed the game during the season by attending games, listening to radio broadcasts, and reading the daily newspapers and periodicals like the weekly the *Sporting News* or the monthly *Baseball Magazine*. During the off season, after a respite for the NFL season, fans became preoccupied with player trades and rumors of trades. There were occasional winter stories of baseball contract signings and players holding out. Then came the welcome days of late February when all the players were signed and the spring training camps opened. The regular season was just around the corner.

Today's baseball fans experience continuing coverage of baseball happenings throughout the entire year. Each game is covered in detail in multiple editions of a day's newspaper and described and dissected on radio and television. Fans can watch each pitch of every game on TV if they are so inclined and have the necessary television hookup. Off season news is largely consumed with the financial aspects of the game and tales of player misdeeds (drugs, assaults, etc.). But most important are the newer participatory roles fans play today, described in the preceding chapter.

There are a number of baseball issues of concern to fans. The most troublesome problems involve off-field matters. Substance abuse by players became a matter of concern in the two decades before they emerged as the game's most serious problem in the first years of the new century. Originally, use of hard drugs was an earlier matter of much concern until significant steroid use became apparent in 2003 when 6 percent of the players failed their tests for steroids, incredibly after being warned in advance that the tests would be conducted.

Fans could not help noticing that many players appeared bigger and more heavily muscled, especially a matter of concern as long-existing home run records fell during the previous decade. This has led some pundits, fans, and even players to speculate about the widespread use of steroids, especially among the game's most dominant hitters. The growing concern about possible steroid abuse has been shared, apparently, even by politicians who threatened to deal with drug abuses if the baseball establishment is unable to do so. Possibly injurious health effects from steroids are a matter of concern to the player alone. But to fans, there are other deep concerns. There are questions of competitive fairness and the game's basic integrity. Competitive equality between players is altered when players taking steroids compete against others who abstain. And the validity of baseball records also is of utmost importance. Some fans, only partially in jest, have suggested that it may be appropriate to place an asterisk opposite a steroid-enhanced record if it can be shown that the record is so tainted.

Competitive balance obviously is reduced with large differences in financial strength between and among teams. Michael Lewis, in his *Moneyball,* described the illuminating story of how Oakland Athletics general manager Billy Beane has led his team to consistently high finishes despite having at his disposal one of the lowest payrolls in the major leagues. And yet it remains a fact that inequality in teams' payrolls is one of the fundamental baseball problems. It is of profound concern to fans, especially to adherents of major league teams with little or no realistic chance of competing for a pennant.

There has been one ineffectual attempt to level the financial playing field among major league clubs by requiring teams with payrolls above a certain level to pay into a league fund to assist teams with lower payrolls. But this system is more a palliative than a real solution. Thinking fans have suggested that baseball seek to develop some variation of the effective system used by NFL teams in which television revenues are divided equally among the teams. But try selling that idea to the likes of George Steinbrenner!

Fans are divided as to the use of the designated hitter. It is recognized that the DH has relieved American League managers of some decision making. But there is wide disagreement among fans as to whether the added offensive strength provided by the use of the DH is worth the loss of strategic moves required of a manager. In addition, regardless of the pros and cons of the DH, many fans would prefer to have both major leagues operate on the same basis regarding use of the DH. This concern apparently is not matched by the owners and especially the players union, more concerned with keeping player-members gainfully employed than with uniformity between the two major leagues.

Interleague games as part of the regular season are another new feature of the game with which many fans disagree. Some fans feel that having teams from one league play teams representing the same area in the other league stimulates interest as teams play for bragging rights with intercity rivals. But many others feel that inter-league games cheapen the World Series and dilute the traditional league rivalries baseball fans treasure. Unlike the DH, the continuance of interleague play is still subject to change.

Some fans are in favor of using instant television replay procedures, especially in games of special importance such as league championship and World's Series games. Instant replay would not be used to replace the irreplaceable human element involved in umpires calling balls and strikes. Rather, it would be available to umpires, at their request, in calling plays on the bases, in judging whether a ball has been caught or trapped, whether a drive is fair or foul, or where possible fan interference may have occurred.

Entrance into the Hall of Fame is a frequent conversational topic among fans. Many fans would like to see objective criteria in use. Such qualifications for selecting a player for the Hall of Fame were developed by Bill James. With regard to the character of players considered for selection, the Pete Rose gambling case and "Shoeless Joe" Jackson's disqualification decades earlier raised the question as to whether off-field transgressions should prevent the selection of a player whose playing achievements would otherwise clearly qualify him for election to the hall At this writing, Rose's chances of selection remain highly problematical and a hotly debated issue among fans and writers.

Transfer of a failing team to another area has been a bone of contention among all baseball followers and a heartsick experience to many. *Washington Post* sportswriter Thomas Boswell has often written of his affection for the inept, long-gone Washington Senators, even during their last 16 years when they averaged 93 losses a season. Writing as an unabashed fan rather than an esteemed baseball scribe, Boswell wrote, "Yet, they [the Senators] are still my team because baseball is about people and place, not pennants." Boswell wrote fondly of his recollections of such old Washington favorites as shortstop Eddie Brinkman and outfielders Frank Howard and Roy Sievers. Not quite of Hall of Fame quality but Boswell, like many other fans, cherishes the memories they left behind. And the same sentiments apply to fans in every other city which has had a baseball team, whether in the majors or the minor leagues.

Delay in the anticipated transfer of a team rose to ridiculous heights after 2000 when major league baseball resorted to maintaining ownership of the failing Montreal Expos for several seasons rather than transferring the team to an obviously more favorable site. Baseball's reluctance to move the club has led to extreme fan frustration, disillusionment and disgust. *Washington Post* writer Bob Thompson wrote of an annual charade, the long- hoped-for possibility of Washington, D.C.'s obtaining another major league team (which became a reality in 2005):

> Though it feels like heresy to say this, I'm not entirely sure that importing 21st century baseball to the District [of Columbia] or Northern Virginia would be a good thing. The game that poet and Red Sox fan Donald Hall once described as "small, exact, formal, whole, pleasing and separate from ordinary reality: a green island in a sea of change," is reality-proof no more. Like so much of the American psychic landscape, it's been disfigured by the forces of greed, "entertainment value" and marketing hype.

There is no way of predicting how baseball's institutions or its rules and playing styles may change in the years ahead. The only safe prediction is that millions of baseball fans will continue to pay the freight, to continue to support the game as they have for the last 150 years.

Chapter Notes

References are to page numbers

There were no scholarly histories of baseball until Harold Seymour published the first of his three *Baseball* volumes in 1959, titled *Baseball — The Early Years*. That work was followed by *Baseball — The Golden Age* in 1971 and by *Baseball — The People's Game* in 1990.

David Q. Voigt published a complementary three-volume baseball history series beginning with his *American Baseball — From the Gentleman's Sport to the Commissioner System*, in 1966. Next came his *American Baseball — Volume II, From the Commissioners to Continental Expansion* in 1970. In 1983, Voigt published *American Baseball — Volume III, From Postwar Expansion to the Electronic Age*.

These two histories provide much of the historical information utilized in this book.

Introduction

2 "an enthusiastic devotee..." *Webster's College Dictionary*.

2 "Thomas Lawson wrote an informal publication" *The Krank: His Language and What It Means* (Boston: Rand Avery, 1888). To many other "more normal" fans, the kranks were considered a nuisance. They harassed and argued obnoxiously with other fans, nagged the baseball writers, and continually shouted at players and umpires throughout games.

3 "Albert G. Spalding described..." *America's National Game* (New York: America Sports, 1911). Spalding parlayed his excellence as a pitcher, baseball leader, and entrepreneur into one of the most successful careers the game has produced. A man of unshakable faith in his own views, Spalding was the leading proponent of the questionable theory that baseball was a pure American invention rather than an adaptation of cricket, as many other baseball historians believe.

4 "[Wrigley Field] is like..." William Freedman, *More Than a Pastime* (Jefferson, NC: McFarland, 1998, p. 21).

4 "William Freedman discussed..." *ibid.*, p. 10.

4 "The reality of baseball..." George Will, *Men at Work* (New York: Macmillan, 1990), p. 2. Will rates as one of the most effective analysts of baseball, and a man whose occasional cynicism about the game cannot hide his love for it. His sophisticated writings on the game are a joy.

5 "Television is conditioning..." Leonard Koppett, *The New Thinking Man's Guide to Baseball* (New York: Simon & Schuster/Fireside, 1991), p. 378. Koppett was one of the most distinguished of his contemporaneous writers. He was considered a leading intellectual in his field, lighthearted enough to write about the humorous aspects of the game but opinionated enough to be thought-provoking and quoted by other writers.

6 "What draws intellectual...?" *Time Magazine*, May 19, 2003.

7 "My youthful recognition..." *Birth of a Fan* (New York: Macmillan, 1993); *Wait Till Next Year* (New York: Simon & Schuster, 1997); *The Red Smith Reader* (New York: Random House, 1982). Roger Angell and Doris Kearns Goodwin are distinguished writers on general political and historical subjects whose love of baseball is reflected in their baseball writing. Both of them are native New Yorkers who grew up following New York teams closely, Angell, both the Yankees and Giants, and Goodwin, the Dodgers. Red Smith, a Pulitzer Prize winner, covered all sports with distinction for major newspapers in St. Louis, Philadelphia, and New York from 1928 until his death in 1982.

7 "I am sometimes asked..." George Will, *Bunts* (New York: Simon & Schuster/Touchstone 1999).

8 *Sporting News*, 1980.

9 "The things I liked best..." Roger Angell, *The Summer Game* (New York: Popular Library, 1972), p. 70.

11 "Baseball ... is meant..." William Freedman, *More Than a Pastime* (Jefferson, NC: McFarland 1998), p. 21.

11 "A ball team used to be a family..." *ibid.*, pp. 58–59.

13 "We know everything about [baseball today]..." Ron Fimrite, ed., *Birth of a Fan* (New York: Macmillan 1993), p. 24.

13 "I wish I could explain..." Art Hill, *I Don't Care If I Never Come Back* (New York: Simon & Schuster, 1980), back flap of jacket.

13 "I had a bartender friend..." Freedman, p. 13.

Chapter 1

15 "The first organized..." Harold Seymour, *Baseball — The Early Years* (New York: Oxford University Press, 1959), p. 15.

15 "The game spread rapidly..." *ibid.*, p. 25.

17 "Some other factors..." John Thorn, et al., eds., *Total Baseball*, 6th ed. (New York: Penguin Books, 1999), p. 587.

17 "Baseball of that era..." Seymour, pp. 38–39.

17 "The hardships of the Civil War..." David Q. Voigt, *American Baseball — From the Gentleman's Sport to the Commissioner System* (University Park: Pennsylvania State University Press, 1966), p. 11.

18 "The game continued to grow..." Seymour, pp. 41–42.

18 "After the Civil War..." *ibid.*, pp. 48–49.

18 "Harold Seymour described a practice..." *ibid.*, p. 51.

19 "By 1868, many teams comprised..." *ibid.*, p. 56.

20 "It is well worth..." *ibid.*, p. 67.

22 "Serious problems with the 50-cent..." *ibid.*, p. 90, 91.

23 "In making him [Kelly] their superhero..." Voigt, p. 179.

23 "The newly named New York Giants..." *ibid.*, p. 117.

24 "A Sporting Life writer..." *ibid.*, pp. 27, 28.

Chapter 2

26 "During the late 1880s..." Seymour, *Baseball— The Early Years*, p. 221.
26 "Concerned about fan opinion..." *ibid.*, p. 231.
28 "But there is little doubt that..." Voigt, p. 187.
28 "Before the 1890s..." *New York Clipper*, September 17, 1887; *Washington Post*, July 26, September 13, 1897.
28 "Bill James commented..." Bill James, *The New Bill James Historical Baseball Abstract* (New York: Free Press, 2001), p. 53.
29 "Opposing teams' players also..." Norman Macht and Jack Kavanagh, *Uncle Robby* (Cleveland: Society for Baseball Research 1999), p. 28.
29 "Cleveland attendance fell off..." Voigt, p. 265.
30 "The 1890s witnessed one..." Seymour, p. 199.
30 Growing up in South Philadelphia..." Fred Lieb, *Baseball as I Have Known It* (New York: Coward, McCann & Geoghegan, 1977), p. 13.
32 "Major league baseball became..." Harold Seymour, *Baseball— The Golden Age* (New York: Oxford University Press, 1971), p. 3.
33 "Owner John T. Brush..." *ibid.*, p. 5.
35 "Although fans were more mellow..." *ibid.*, p. 112.
35 "Ty Cobb was involved..." *Ty Cobb— My Life in Baseball* (Lincoln: University of Nebraska Press/Bison Books), 1993), pp. 131–132.
35 "Writer Fred Lieb claimed that..." Lieb, pp. 59, 61.
35 "Players and managers develop..." Frank Graham, *McGraw of the Giants* (New York: G.P. Putnam's Sons, 1944), p. 84.
37 "By midseason of 1914..." Seymour, *Baseball— The Golden Age*, p. 219.
37 "The Cardinals inaugurated..." *ibid.*, p. 61.
39 "Attendance at major league games..." John Thorn, et al., eds., *Total Baseball*, 6th ed. (New York: Total Sports, 1999), pp. 104–109.

Chapter 3

40 "Major league baseball..." Eliot Asinof, *Eight Men Out* (New York: Holt, Rinehart and Winston, 1963).
42 "Since World War..." Fred Stein, *And the Skipper Bats Cleanup* (Jefferson, NC: McFarland, 2002), p. 185.
47 "(A St. Louis writer's...")" Bob Broeg, "Super Stars of Baseball," *Sporting News*, St. Louis, 1971, p. 128.
48 "The doughty little manager..." Graham, *McGraw of the Giants*, pp. 136–139.
49 "Robbie's warmth and simplicity..." Seymour, *Baseball— The Golden Age*, pp. 454, 457.
51 "The Cardinals' hellbent playing style..." J. Roy Stockton, *The Gas House Gang* (New York: A.S. Barnes, 1945), pp. 69, 70.
52 "Fans remember the '30s..." Peter Golenbock, *Wrigleyville* (New York: St. Martin's Press, 1996), pp. 238, 239.
53 "Even at ballgames, important war news..." Fred Stein, *Under Coogan's Bluff* (Glenshaw, PA: Chapter and Cask, 1979), p. 80.
56 "Often gaiety was mingled with..." David Q. Voigt, *American Baseball— From the Commissioners to Continental Expansion* (Norman: University of Oklahoma Press, 1970), p. 268.
57 "The 4-F–laden Cubs and Tigers..." Stein, *Under Coogan's Bluff*, p. 114.

Chapter 4

59 "Subject to regulations..." Voigt, *American Baseball — From the Commissioners to Continental Expansion*, p. 301.
60 "The postwar changes in baseball..." *ibid.*, p. 299.
60 "With working hours in 1950..." *ibid.*, pp. xvi, xvii.
61 "People were afraid to go..." James, p. 241.
62 "Casey introduced a radical departure..." John Thorn, et al., eds., *Total Baseball*, 6th ed., p. 114.
66 "In response to the explosive..." James, *The New Bill James*, p. 249.
68 "Three things happened to make baseball..." *ibid.*, p. 252.
71 "The increase in minority group players..." *ibid.*, p. 277.

Chapter 5

74 "A *New York Times*/ CBS poll indicated that..." David Q. Voigt, *American Baseball — From Postwar Expansion to the Electronic Age* (University Park: Pennsylvania Sate University Press, 1983), p. 348.
74 "As fans, we were presented..." John Thorn, et al., eds., *Total Baseball*, 6th ed., p. 11.
75 "Sportswriter Red Smith summed up..." Voigt, *American Baseball — From Postwar Expansion to the Electronic Age*, p. 349.
78 "No less an authority..." James, *The New Bill James*, p. 308.
79 "The number of relievers..." *ibid.*, pp. 309, 310.
81 "As Bill James pungently put it..." *ibid.*, p. 304.
83 "Bob Costas has suggested..." Bob Costas, *Fair Ball — A Fan's Case for Baseball* (New York: Broadway Books, 2000), pp. 91–104.

Chapter 6

The National Baseball Hall of Fame is the primary source of information on the backgrounds and achievements of outstanding baseball writers who have been the recipients of the J.G. Taylor Spink award.
84 "The baseball fan..." John Thorn, et al., eds., *Total Baseball*, 6th ed., p. 586.
84 "Chadwick was born..." *ibid.*, pp. 586, 587.
85 "Timothy Murnane..." *ibid.*, p. 587.
85 "Baseball writing..." *ibid.*, 587.
85 "Ring Lardner..." National Baseball Hall of Fame release, 1970.
85 "Hugh Fullerton..." *ibid.*, 1964; Thorn, *Total Baseball*, 6th ed., pp. 588, 589.
86 "Fans in the late 1890s..." *ibid.*, 1965.
86 "Dryden's slightly off-color wit..." Fred Lieb, *Baseball as I Have Known It*, p. 20.
86 "John McGraw had..." Graham, *McGraw of the Giants*, pp. 103–106.
88 "Grantland Rice..." National Baseball Hall of Fame release, 1966.
89 "Broun's lead comment..." Stein, *Under Coogan's Bluff*, p. 22.
89 "Broun was the founder..." *ibid.*, p. 1970.
89 "Fred Lieb..." *ibid.*, p. 1972.
89 "Frank Graham began..." *ibid.*, p. 1971.
90 "Dan Daniel was..." *ibid.*, p. 1972.
90 "In a way, the..." Jerome Holtzman, *No Cheering in the Press Box* (New York: Holt, Rinehart and Winston, 1973), p. 1.
91 "Tom Meany's..." National Baseball Hall of Fame release, 1975.

92 "Sid Mercer..." *ibid.*, 1969.
92 "John Kieran..." *ibid.*, p. 1973.
92 "Jimmy Cannon..." Holtzman, pp. 276–277.
93 "Walter "Red" Smith..." National Baseball Hall of Fame release, 1976.
94 "Baseball coverage changed..." Lang, pp. 589, 590.
96 "Fans received little or no information..." Lieb, *Baseball as I Have Known It*, p. 159.

Chapter 7

Curt Smith's updated "Voices of the Game," published in 1987, is the indispensable information source on radio (Chapter 7) and television (Chapter 8) baseball announcers. As such, it provides the bases for much of the material in these chapters. Several books by Red Barber also provided informative background on radio and TV announcers.

101 "Baseball announcing on the radio..." Curt Smith, *Voices of the Game*, updated edition (New York: Simon & Schuster, 1992), p. 10.
102 "Red Barber, eminently..." Red Barber, *The Broadcasters* (New York: Da Capo Press, 1985), p. 29.
102 "By the mid–'30s..." Stein, *Under Coogan's Bluff*, p. 43.
102 "The Yankees, Giants, and Dodgers..." Curt Smith, p. 39.
103 "For economic reasons..." *ibid.*, pp. 29, 30.
104 "I never tried..." *ibid.*, pp. 27, 29.
105 "Curt Smith compared..." *ibid.*, pp. 45–47.
106 "Curt Smith wrote that..." *ibid.*, p. 14.
106 "Laux was a quiet..." *ibid.*, p. 97.
107 "New York sportswriter Til Ferdenzi..." *ibid.*, p. 23.
108 "Ty was so vivid..." *ibid.*, p. 34, 35.
108 "Any announcer who broadcasts..." *ibid.*, p. 88.
110 "Hoyt was hired..." *ibid.*, p. 71.
110 "He'd be [talking about]..." *ibid.*, 76.
112 "Veteran Baltimore writer John Steadman..." *ibid.*, p. 31.
112 "Radio is the best medium..." *ibid.*, p. 242.

Chapter 8

114 "But Barber, a no-nonsense..." Curt Smith, *Voices of the Game*, p. 109.
115 "Scully took over as..." *ibid.*, p. 488.
116 "In Los Angeles..." Ernie Harwell, *Tuned to Baseball* (South Bend, IN: Diamond Communications, 1985), p. 104.
116 "Gowdy was called..." Curt Smith, p. 287.
118 "He shouldn't have been..." *ibid.*, p. 188.
118 "Wolff, a handsome..." *ibid.*, p. 207.
119 "My whole philosophy..." *ibid.*, p. 459, 460.
120 "Harry Caray also is remembered..." *ibid.* p. 462.
121 "Garagiola has a virtually..." *ibid.*, p. 428.
122 "Michaels became a prime..." Wells Twombly, *San Francisco Chronicle*, 1975.
123 "Costas has won many..." Bob Costas, *Fair Ball* (New York: Broadway Books, 2000).
123 "Jon Miller is considered..." Curt Smith, p. 447.

Chapter 9

129 "In the first month of the season..." Charles C. Alexander, *John McGraw* (New York: Viking Penguin, 1988), pp. 283, 284.

129 "Sandy Koufax was a special favorite..." Jane Leavy, *Sandy Koufax — A Lefty's Legacy* (New York: HarperCollins, 2002).

130 "The public perceptions of some players..." personal communication to the author from Leonard Koppett, 1994.

130 "Ted Williams was not a fan favorite..." James, *The New Bill James Historical Baseball Abstract*, pp. 652, 653.

132 "If his stories were incredible..." John Thorn, et al., eds., *Total Baseball*, 6th ed., p. 205.

132 "There have been other great players..." James, *The New Bill James*, p. 136.

132 "One of Anson's best-known..." Voigt, *American Baseball — From the Gentleman's Sport to the Commissioner System*, p. 101.

133 "Mike 'King' Kelly was Anson's..." Harold Seymour, *Baseball — The Early Years* (New York: Oxford University Press, 1959), p. 175.

133 "Giants right-hander Christy Mathewson..." James, *The New Bill James*, p. 851.

134 "It is doubtful..." Henry W. Thomas, *Walter Johnson — Baseball's Big Train* (Lincoln: University of Nebraska Press, 1995), *Baseball Magazine*, August 1912.

134 "Dodgers fans were drawn..." Thorn, *Total Baseball*, p. 159; Frank Graham, *The Brooklyn Dodgers* (New York: G.P. Putnam's Sons, 1945), p. 113.

137 "In 1938, a cereal company..." Fred Stein, *Mel Ott — The Little Giant of Baseball* (Jefferson, NC: McFarland, 1999), p. 95.

Chapter 10

143 "[Assume] the Mets are at home..." Phil Erwin, John Thorn, et al., eds., *Baseball Betting* (New York: Professional Ink, 1989), p. 674.

144 "Writing of the gambling scene..." Seymour, *Baseball — The Early Years*, p. 29.

144 "Also in the 1860s..." Voigt, *American Baseball — From the Gentleman's Sport to the Commissioner System*, p. 16.

145 "After covering an annual meeting of the National..." *ibid.*, p. 12.

145 "Even the feats..." *ibid.*, p. 13.

146 "The National League, which began..." Seymour, *Baseball — The Early Years*, pp. 87, 88.

146 "A dishonest umpire can change..." *ibid.*, p. 343.

146 "Even worse [than gamblers] in the stands] was..." *ibid.*, p. 295, 296.

147 "And in 1916, the Giants were rumored..." Fred Stein and Nick Peters, *Giants Diary — A Century of Giants Baseball in New York and San Francisco* (Berkeley, CA: North Atlantic Books, 1987), p. 36.

148 "Despite the overpowering presence..." Graham, *McGraw of the Giants*, pp. 182–185.

149 "The last unpleasant episode..." Seymour, *Baseball — The Golden Age*, p. 382–384.

150 "Since the Black Sox scandal..." Peter Golenbock, *Bums — An Oral History of the Brooklyn Dodgers* (New York: G.P. Putnam's Sons, 1984), pp. 109–114.

Chapter 11

152 "They were following the lead..." Seymour, *Baseball — The Early Years*, pp. 48, 49.

152 "To ensure gate receipts..." *ibid.*, p. 81.
153 "Recent research placed combined attendance..." John Thorn, et al., eds., *Total Baseball*, 6th ed., pp. 104, 105.
153 "A self-registering turnstile..." Seymour, *Baseball — The Early Years*, pp. 210, 211.
153 "Attendance at baseball games..." *ibid.*, p. 91.
154 "Total attendance..." Thorn, *Total Baseball*, 6th ed., p. 105.
154 "Al Spalding cleverly debunked..." Seymour, *Baseball — The Early Years*, pp. 237, 238.
154 "Spalding claimed that teams with low attendance..." *ibid.*, p. 209.
155 "This was the period..." Thorn, *Total Baseball*, 1st ed. (New York: Professional Ink, 1989), pp. 669, 670.
156 "Attendance increased slightly..." *Total Baseball*, 6th ed., pp. 104–109.
159 "A bargain-day rush..." Golenbock, p. 214.
159 "Baseball team operators..." Organized Baseball, U.S. House of Representative Report No. 2002, 82nd Congress, Second Session, 1952.
159 "Other than effective performance..." Seymour, *Baseball — The Early Years*, pp. 196, 199.
160 "Chicago Colts player-manager..." David Q. Voigt, *American Baseball — From the Gentleman's Sport to the Commissioner System* (University Park: Pennsylvania State University Press, 1966), pp. 100–105.
160 "Chris Von der Ahe..." *ibid.*, pp. 138–144.
163 "Steve Mann wrote..." Thorn, *Total Baseball*, 1st ed., p. 628.

Chapter 12

The primary source of information on each U.S. president's interest and involvement in baseball is from *Baseball — The Presidents' Game* by William B. Mead and Paul Dickson, published in 1993. This is the most thorough (and entertaining) book on this subject.
164 "Love of baseball does not rank..." William B. Mead and Paul Dickson, *Baseball — The Presidents' Game* (New York: Walker, 1993), p. 79.
165 "President Grover Cleveland..." *ibid.*, p. 12.
166 "William Howard Taft..." *ibid.*, p. 12.
166 "President Woodrow Wilson..." *ibid.*, pp. 31–40.
167 Warren Harding..." *ibid.*, pp. 41–44.
167 "Herbert Hoover..." *ibid.*, p. 60.
167 "It was..." Harold C. Burr, *Baseball Magazine*, June 1939.
168 "Ever the consummate politician, FDR..." Stein, *Under Coogan's Bluff*, p. 29.
169 "BEST OF LUCK..." Mead and Dickson, p. 14.
169 "Eisenhower..." *ibid.*, p. 95.
169 "John F. Kennedy..." Bob Broeg, *Super Stars of Baseball* (St. Louis: Sporting News, 1971), pp. 180, 181.
170 "The *New York Times* published..." Mead and Dickson, p. 139.
170 "Mead and Dickson described..." *ibid.*, p. 137.
172 "[By 1906] McGraw had become..." Graham, *McGraw of the Giants*, pp. 35, 36.
173 "During the late 1930s..." Stein, *Mel Ott*, p. 152.
173 "Bankhead attended the 1939 All-Star..." *ibid.*, pp. 100–101.
174 "Television interviewer Larry King..." Golenbock, *Bums*, p. 58.
177 "Writer Ernest Hemingway was..." *ibid.*, pp. 48, 49, 51.

177 "Singer Doris Day..." Jim Murray, *Jim Murray — The Autobiography of the Pulitzer Prize Winning Sports Columnist* (New York: Macmillan, 1993), p. 47.
178 "Some of the more persistent..." Seymour, *Baseball — The Early Years*, pp. 330.
178 "Legendary lungs could be found..." *ibid.*, p. 665.
179 "The bulletins proclaimed..." Bob Broeg, "Super Stars of Baseball," *Sporting News*, St. Louis, 1971, p. 126.

Chapter 13

181 "After the Cubs lost the game..." Monica Davey, *New York Times* game report, October 15, 2003, p. 1.
181 "The mortified Bartman..." Thomas Boswell, *Washington Post* column, October 27, 2003.
181 "Over time, Cubs fans..." AOL News, December 19, 2003.
182 "And then there are..." AOL News, September 20, 2002.
182 "Commissioner Landis summoned..." Stockton, p. 130.
183 "In the sixth inning..." Seymour *Baseball — The Early Years*, pp. 29, 30.
184 "The more brash tone..." *ibid.*, pp. 9, 10.
184 "There was another game..." Warren Goldstein, *Playing for Keeps* (Ithaca, NY: Cornell University Press, 1989), p. 34.
184 "Abuse of umpires..." Seymour, *Baseball — The Early Years*, pp. 340, 341.
185 "Pittsburgh Pirates infielder..." Lawrence S. Ritter, *The Glory of Their Times* (New York: Macmillian, 1966), pp. 26, 27.
185 "The fans had an impact..." Seymour, *Baseball — The Golden Age*, pp. 446, 447.
186 "The Yankees were playing..." *ibid.*, p. 113.
187 "Some superstitious fans worry..." Stein, *Mel Ott*, pp. 100, 101.
188 "Baseball fans often have ideas..." Graham, *Brooklyn Dodgers*, pp. 197–199.
190 "Before ballparks were fully enclosed..." Stein, *Under Coogan's Bluff*, p. 42.
190 "temporary outfield seats..." Broeg, p. 194.
191 "Many fans believe..." *ibid.*, p. 94.
191 "Fans exert pressure..." Lou Boudreau and Russell Schneider, *Lou Boudreau* (Champaign, IL: Sagamore Publishing, 1993), pp. 100–103.

Chapter 14

192 "Over the last..." Information obtained from the Society for American Baseball Research, Cleveland, OH.
193 "The computer is an invaluable..." John Thorn, et al., eds., *Total Baseball*, 6th ed., p. 595.
194 "After marveling at the speeds..." *ibid.*, p. 597.
194 "Baseball statistics have attracted the interest of fans..." Alan Schwarz, *The Numbers Game* (New York: St. Martin's, 2004).
195 "The term 'sabremetrician,' derived..." Branch Rickey, "Goodbye to Some Old Baseball Ideas," *Life Magazine*, August, 1954.
196 "Two types of methods..." *ibid.*, pp. 631–635; Bill James and Jim Henzler, *Win Shares* (New York: Stats Publishing, March 2002).
197 "The more sophisticated player evaluation..." Thorn, *Total Baseball*, 6th ed., p. 636.

199 "Peter Golenbock has described…" Peter Golenbock, *How to Win at Rotisserie* (New York: Vintage Books, 1986), p. 5.
199 "At this writing…" Michael Lewis, *Moneyball* (New York: W.W. Norton, 2003).
200 "For all the confidence sabremetricians…" Thorn, *Total Baseball*, 6th ed., p. 634.

Chapter 15

203 "Competitive balance…" Lewis.
204 "Entrance into the Hall of Fame…" Bill James, *Whatever Happened to the Hall of Fame* (New York: Free Press, 1995).
205 "Delay in the anticipated transfer…" Bob Thompson "Diamond Dilemma," *Washington Post*, August 31, 2003.

Bibliography

Newpapers, Periodicals, Biographical Releases

AOL News
Baseball Magazine
Life Magazine
National Baseball Hall of Fame releases
New York Clipper
New York Daily Mirror
New York Daily News
New York Herald-Tribune
New York Sun
New York Times
New York World-Telegram
The Sporting News
San Francisco Chronicle
Time
USA Today Baseball Weekly
Washington Post (DC)

Interview

Leonard Koppett, by telephone

Books

Adomites, Paul D. *Baseball on the Air* (New York: Professional Ink, 1989)
Alexander, Charles C. *John McGraw* (New York: Viking, 1988)
Angell, Roger. *The Summer Game* (New York: Popular Library, 1972)
Asinof, Eliot. *Eight Men Out* (New York: Holt, Rinehart and Winston, 1963)
Barber, Red. *The Broadcasters* (New York: Da Capo Press, 1985)
_____. *1947— When All Hell Broke Loose* (New York: Doubleday, 1982)
Bjarkman, Peter C., ed. *Encyclopedia of Major League Team Histories* (Westport, CT: Meckler, 1991)
Boudreau, Lou, and Russell Schneider. *Lou Boudreau* (Champaign, IL: Sagamore Publishing, 1993)

Broeg, Bob. *Super Stars of Baseball* (St. Louis: Sporting News, 1971)
Cobb, Ty. *Ty Cobb — My Life in Baseball* (Lincoln: University of Nebraska Press, 1993)
Costas, Bob. *Fair Ball — A Fan's Case for Baseball* (New York: Broadway Books, 2000)
Durocher, Leo. *Nice Guys Finish Last* (New York: Simon and Schuster, 1975)
Erwin, Phil. *Baseball Betting* (New York: Professional Ink, 1989)
Fimrite, Ron, ed. *Birth of a Fan* (New York: Macmillan, 1993)
Freedman, William. *More Than a Pastime* (Jefferson, NC: McFarland, 1998)
Goldstein, Warren. *Playing for Keeps* (Ithaca, NY: Cornell University Press, 1989)
Golenbock, Peter. *Bums — An Oral History of the Brooklyn Dodgers* (New York: G.P. Putnam, 1984)
_____. *How to Win at Rotisserie* (New York: Vintage Books, 1986)
_____. *Wrigleyville* (New York: St. Martin's Press, 1996)
Goodwin, Doris Kearns. *Wait Till Next Year* (New York: Simon and Schuster, 1997)
Graham, Frank. *The Brooklyn Dodgers* (New York: G.P. Putnam, 1945)
_____. *McGraw of the Giants* (New York: G.P. Putnam, 1944)
Harwell, Ernie. *Tuned to Baseball* (South Bend, IN: Diamond Communications, 1985)
Hill, Art. *I Don't Care If I Never Come Back* (New York: Simon and Schuster, 1980)
Holway, John, and Bob Carroll. *The 400 Greatest* (New York: Total Baseball, 1999)
Holtzman, Jerome. *No Cheering in the Press Box* (New York: Holt, Rinehart and Winston, 1973)
James, Bill. *The New Bill James Historical Abstract* (New York: Free Press, 2001)
_____. *Whatever Happened to the Hall of Fame* (New York: Free Press, 1995)
_____, and Jim Henzler. *Win Shares* (New York: Stats Publishing, 2002)
Lawson, Thomas. *The Krank: His Language and What It Means* (Boston: Rand Avery, 1888)
Leavy, Jane. *A Lefty's Legacy* (New York: HarperCollins, 2002)
Lewis, Michael. *Moneyball* (New York: W.W. Norton, 2003)
Lieb, Fred. *Baseball as I Have Known It* (New York: Coward, McCann and Geoghegan, 1977)
Macht, Norman, and Jack Kavanagh. *Uncle Robby* (Cleveland: Society for American Baseball Research, 1999)
Mead, William B., and Paul Dickson. *Baseball — The Presidents' Game* (New York: Walker, 1993)
Murray, Jim. *Jim Murray — An Autobiography* (New York: Macmillan, 1993)
Porter, Daniel, ed. *Biographical Dictionary of American Sports* (Westport, CT: Greenwood, 1987)
Ritter, Lawrence S. *The Glory of Their Times* (New York: Macmillan, 1966)
Schwarz, Alan. *The Numbers Game* (New York: St. Martin's Press, 2004).
Seymour, Harold. *Baseball: The Early Years* (New York: Oxford University Press, 1959)
_____. *Baseball — The Golden Age* (New York: Oxford University Prees, 1971)
_____. *Baseball — The People's Game* (New York: Oxford University Press, 1990)
Shatzkin, Mike, ed. *The Ballplayers* (New York: William Morrow, 1990)
Smith, Curt. *Voices of the Game* (New York: Simon and Schuster, 1987)
Smith, Red. *The Red Smith Reader* (New York: Random House, 1982)
Spalding, Albert G. *America's National Game* (New York: American Sports Pub. 1911)
Stein, Fred. *And the Skipper Bats Cleanup* (Jefferson, NC: McFarland, 2001)
_____. *Mel Ott — The Little Giant of Baseball* (Jefferson, NC: McFarland, 1999)
_____. *Under Coogan's Bluff* (Glenshaw, PA: Chapter and Cask, 1981)
_____, and Nick Peters. *Giants Diary — A Century of Giants Baseball in New York and San Francisco* (Berkeley, CA: North Atlantic Books, 1987)
Stockton, J. Roy. *The Gas House Gang* (New York: A.S. Barnes, 1945)

Thomas, Henry W. *Walter Johnson — Baseball's Big Train* (Lincoln: University of Nebraska Press, 1995)
Thorn, John, et al., eds., *Total Baseball*, 1st ed. (New York: Total Baseball, Warner, 1989). Subsequent editions cited also.
Tiemann, Robert L., and Pete Palmer. *Major League Attendance* (New York: Total Sports, 1999)
Voigt, David Q. *American Baseball — From the Commissioners to Continental Expansion* (Norman: University of Oklahoma Press, 1970)
_____. *American Baseball — From the Gentleman's Sport to the Commissioner System* (University Park: Pennsylvania State University Press, 1966)
_____. *American Baseball — From the Postwar Expansion to the Electronic Age* (University Park: The Pennsylvania State University Press, 1983)
Will, George F. *Bunts* (New York: Simon and Schuster, 1999)
Williams, Peter. *When the Giants Were Giants* (Chapel Hill, NC: Algonquin, 1994)

Index

Aaron, Henry 137, 138
Adams, Ace 59
Adams, Franklin P. "F.P.A." 88
Adams, Margo 186
Adomites, Paul D. 155, 178
Alda, Alan 122
Alexander, Charles C. 47, 99
Alexander, Grover Cleveland 171
Allen, Mel 105, 112
Alou, Felipe 66
Alou, Moises 76, 181
Alston, Walt 66
American Association (of Base Ball Clubs) 24, 26, 30, 31, 32, 36, 37, 160
American League 49, 50, 150, 155, 197
Amoros, Sandy 64
Angell, Roger 7, 9, 13, 98
Anson, Adrian "Cap" or "Pop" 23, 24, 28, 30, 132, 160, 161, 165
Appling, Luke 138
Arizona Diamondbacks 81
Arlin, Harold 101
Arnold, Violet (Mrs. Bill Dickey) 172
Arnovich, Morrie 57
Arthur, Chester A. 165
Ashburn, Richie 139
Asinof, Eliot 40, 98, 148
Atlanta Braves 64, 76
Averill, Earl 139

Bagwell, Jeff 198
Bailey, Pearl 177
Baltimore Orioles 28, 29, 66, 68, 75, 180
Bando, Sal 163
Bankhead, Tallulah 173, 186, 187
Banks, Ernie 138

Barber, Red 102, 104, 105, 107, 112, 113
Barrow, Ed 131
Bartell, Dick 8
Bartman, Steve 180, 181
Barzun, Jacques 6
Baseball magazine 202
Baseball Writers Association 86
Beane, Billy 199
Bell, Bob 80
Bell, David 80
Bell, Gus 80
Belle, Albert 127
Bench, Johnny 68, 77, 138
Benton, John "Rube" 147, 149
Berman, Chris 124
Berra, Yogi 67, 136
Bevens, Bill 62
Black Sox 34, 40, 41, 42
Blagojevich, Rod R. 181
Blattner, Buddy 111
Blount, Roy, Jr. 7
Blue, Vida 163
Bock, Hal 100
Boggs, Wade 186
Bonds, Barry 77, 81, 82, 132, 196
Bonilla, Bobby 76
Boone, Bob 80
Boone, Brett 80
Boone, Ray 80
Boston Beaneaters 29
Boston Braves 53, 62
Boston Pilgrims 178
Boston Puritans 31
Boston Red Sox 42, 49, 61, 66, 151, 182, 201
Boston Royal Rooters 31, 32, 178

Index

Boswell, Thomas 11, 99, 100, 181, 205
Boudreau, Lou 139, 190
Bradlee, Ben 94
Branca, Ralph 117
Brett, George 74, 140
Brickhouse, Jack 115
Bridwell, Al 34
Brinkman, Eddie 205
Britt, Jim 113
Brock, Lou 67
Broeg, Bob 91, 94, 100, 106, 190
Brooklyn Atlantics 18–20, 144, 183
Brooklyn Dodgers 7, 11, 29, 49, 60, 61, 102, 134, 174, 175, 177, 183, 184, 187
Brooklyn Excelsiors 183
Brosnan, Jim 99
Brotherhood of Professional Base Ball Players (Players League) 26, 27, 30, 60
Broun, Heywood 88, 89
Brouthers, Dan 23
Brown, Mordecai "Three Finger" 34
Brown, Warren 57, 94
Brush, John T. 33
Buck, Jack 122
Buck, Joe 122
Buckner, Bill 75, 182
Budig, Gene 180
Buffalo Express 154
Bulger, Bozeman 87
Burdette, Lou 64
Burick, Si 94
Burns, Ken 6
Burns, Ric 6
Burr, Harold C. 167
Bush, Prescott 171

Camilli, Dolph 7, 173
Cammeyer, William H. 152
Campanella, Roy 135, 136
Cannon, Jimmy 89, 92, 93
Capone, Al 178, 179
Caray, Harry 110, 113, 119–121, 181
Caray, Harry, Jr. "Skip" 120
Caray, Harry, III "Chip" 120
Carbo, Bernie 70
Carlton, Steve 74
Carmichael, John 94
Carter, Jimmy 171
Cartwright, Alexander Joy 13
Casey, Hugh 53, 177
Castillo, Luis 181
Cauldwell, William 84

Cavaretta, Phil 51
Cedeno, Cesar 81
Cepeda, Orlando 66, 137
Chadwick, Henry 16, 19, 22, 84, 85, 90, 144–146, 195, 200
Chance, Frank 33, 35, 88, 155
Chandler, A.B. "Happy" 150, 188, 189
Chapman, Ray 42
Chase, Hal 133, 147, 149
Chass, Murray 100
Chester, Hilda 174, 175
Chicago Cubs 4, 8, 33, 38, 50, 51, 57, 172, 182, 186
Chicago White Sox 86, 148
Chicago White Stockings 19, 23, 160, 161, 165
Christian, John 187
Cicotte, Ed 148
Cincinnati Red Stockings 19, 20, 145
Cincinnati Reds 40, 52, 70, 71, 110, 148, 166
Clarke, Fred 33, 155
Clemens, Roger 77
Clemente, Roberto 68, 69
Cleveland, Grover 165
Cleveland Indians 55, 133, 162, 190
Cleveland Spiders 29
Clinton, Bill 171, 172
Clinton, Hillary 172
Cobb, Ty 34, 35, 40, 44, 46, 75, 99, 132, 149, 150
Cobbledick, Gordon 94
Cochrane, Mickey 47, 48, 138
Cohan, George M. 177
Cohen, Andy 129
Collins, Eddie 34
Collins, Jimmy 34
Colon, Bartolo 201
Colorado Rockies 158
Comiskey, Charles 24, 28, 86, 160
Comiskey Park 182
Concessions 155, 156
Connor, Roger 23, 26
Coolidge, Calvin 167
Coolidge, Grace 167
Cooper, Wilbur 167
Coors Field 158
Costas, Bob 83
Cox, William D. 151
Crane, Sam 87
Cravath, Cactus 43
Crawford, Sam 34, 35

Creamer, Robert W. 62, 99
Criger, Lou 147
Cronin Joe 52, 168
Crosetti, Frank 129

Daniel, Dan 89, 90
Danning, Harry 8, 187
Daubert, Jake 167
Dauvray, Helen 36, 172
Davids, L. Robert 192, 193
Davis, Tommy 66
Day, Doris 177
Day, Laraine 174
Dean, Dizzy 23, 50, 51, 103, 111, 136
Dean, Paul 50
Delahanty, Ed 34, 35
Dent, Bucky 71
DePodesta, Paul 199
DePorter, Grant 181, 182
Derringer, Paul 50, 52
Designated hitter 69, 204
Detroit Tigers 35, 57, 59, 66, 113, 151, 162, 182
Devery, William "Big Bill" 147
Devlin, Jim "Terror" 146
Devyr, Thomas 145
Dickey, Bill 47, 105, 136, 172
Dickson, Paul 165, 166, 169, 170
DiMaggio, Joe 50, 52, 53, 59, 62, 79, 105, 129–131, 136, 173
DiMaggio, Vince 90
Doby, Larry 60, 162
Doerr, Bobby 117, 139
Dolan, Patrick "Cozy" 149
Donlin, Mike "Turkey Mike" 36, 172
Dorgan, Tad 155
Douglas, Phil "Shufflin' Phil" 148
Doyle, Ed "Dutch" 11
Dreyfuss, Barney 87
Drugs 75
Dryden, Charles 85, 86, 94
Drysdale, Don 65, 66, 67
Dubuc, Jean 147
Dudley, Jimmy 106
Duffy, Ed 145
Durocher, Leo "Lippy Leo" 50, 62, 63, 92, 140, 150, 174, 187-189

Ebbets, Charles 30
Ebbets Field 49, 62, 174–176, 187
Eisenhower, Dwight D. 169
Elson, Bob 113

Engleberg, Memphis 189
Epstein, Theo 199, 201
Erwin, Phil 143
Evers, Johnny 34, 88
Ewing, Buck 24, 26

Falls, Joe 100
Farrell, Frank 147
Federal League 36, 37, 39
Feller, Bob 52, 59, 139
Feller, Sherm 124
Felsch, Happy 148
Fenway Park 9
Ferdenzi, Til 107
Fewster, Chuck 135
Fingers, Rollie 69, 163
Finley, Charles 162, 163
Fisk, Carlton 70
Fitzgerald, John "Honey" 31
Fitzsimmons, Fred "Fat Freddy" 143
Fleming, Sir Alexander 173
Florida Marlins 76
Ford, Edward "Whitey" 136
Ford, Gerald 171
Fossum, Casey 201
Fox, Charley 123
Fox, Nellie 138
Foxx, Jimmie 47, 48, 50, 52, 139
Frazee, Harry 42
Freedman, William 4, 11
French, Larry, 51, 177
Frick, Ford 66
Frisch, Frankie 47, 50, 111, 136, 149, 182, 190
Frost, Robert 6
Fullerton, Hugh 85, 86, 94

Galan, Augie 51
Galento, Tony 176
Gallery, Tom 118
Galvin, Jim "Pud" 165
Gamboa, Tom 182
Gammons, Peter 100
Gandil, Chick 148
Garagiola, Joe 121, 122, 193
Garcia, Rich 180
Garciaparra, Nomar 77
Gehrig, Lou 47, 50, 52, 53, 80, 90, 105, 136
Gehringer, Charley 138
Germano, Frank 176
Giamatti, Bart 74, 76

Giambi, Jason 201
Giambi, Jeremy 201
Gibson, Bob 67
Gillespie, Earl 113
Gionfriddo, Al 62
Glavine, Tom 138
Goldstein, Warren 184
Golenbock, Peter 11, 98, 174, 199
Gomez, Vernon "Lefty" 105, 136, 172, 173
Goodwin, Doris Kearns 7
Gould, Stephen Jay 6
Gowdy, Curt 115–117
Graham, Frank 36, 48, 87, 89, 90, 172
Graney, Jack 109
Grant, Ulysses S. 165
Green, Shawn 130
Green Bay 152
Greenberg, Hank 53, 57, 129, 193
Grey, Zane 178
Griffey, Ken, Jr. 80, 196
Griffey, Ken, Sr. 80
Griffith, Calvin 64, 193
Griffith, Clark 166–169
Griffith Stadium 169, 190
Grimm, Charlie 171
Grossman, Lev 6
Grove, Lefty 47, 48
Gunning, Tom 29
Gwynn, Tony 140

Hack, Stan 51
Hackett, Buddy 177
Halberstam, David 99
Hall, Donald 205
Hanlon, Ned 28
Harder, Mel 139
Harding, Warren 167
Hargrove, Mike 79
Harper's Weekly 144
Harris, Bucky 62, 168
Harrison, Benjamin 165
Hartmann, Harry 113
Hartnett, Leo "Gabby" 51, 138, 171, 178, 179
Harwell, Ernie 104, 107, 112, 113
Hauck, Louis 153
Heilmann, Harry 113, 149
Hemingway, Ernest 177
Henderson, Rickey 74, 75, 196
Herman, Billy 51, 171, 177
Herman, Floyd "Babe" 134, 135
Hershiser, Orel 75

Higbe, Kirby 177
Higham, Richard 146
Hill, Art 13
Hite, Mabel 36, 172
Hodges, Gil 135
Hodges, Russ 112
Hodgson, Claire (Mrs. Babe Ruth) 172
Hoey, Fred 107
Holden, John 16
Holmes, Tommy 94
Holtzman, Jerome 90, 93, 100
Holway, John 98
Honig, Donald 98
Hoover, Herbert 167
Hornsby, Rogers 39, 46, 47, 129
Houk, Ralph 65
Houston Astrodome 170
Houston Colts (Astros) 64, 182
Howard, Frank 205
Hoyt, Waite 109, 110, 193
Hubbell, Carl 47, 50, 51, 52, 54, 89, 106, 137, 187
Hunter, Jim "Catfish" 69, 163
Husing, Ted 101

Immerman, Connie 189
Isaminger, James 94

Jackson, Joe "Shoeless Joe" 34, 39, 40, 148, 205
Jackson, Reggie 71, 163
Jackson, Travis 137
James, Bill 28, 42, 61, 68, 79, 81, 99, 100, 130, 133, 196, 199, 201, 204
Jennings, Hughie 34
Jeter, Derek 137, 180
Johnson, Andrew 165
Johnson, Byron Bancroft "Ban" 31, 87, 147, 150, 185
Johnson, Davey 180
Johnson, Lyndon B. 170
Johnson, Randy 81
Johnson, Walter 47, 134
Jones, Chipper 138
Jones, Fielder 34
Jurges, Billy 51, 186, 187

Kaese, Harold 94
Kahn, Roger 98
Kaline, Al 138
Kansas City Athletics 61
Kansas City Royals 74, 182

Index 225

Kauff, Benny 147
Kavanagh, Jack 29
Kaye, Danny 177
Keane, Johnny 67
Keefe, Tim 24
Kelly, George 149
Kelly, Mike "King" 23, 132, 133
Keltner, Ken 193
Kennedy, John F. 6, 31, 169, 170
Kennedy, Terry 193
Kent, Jeff 132
Kessler, Bill 178
Kessler, Eddie 178
Kieran, John 89, 92
Kiner, Ralph 77, 193
King, Larry 174
Kloppett, Louie 8
Knickerbocker Base Ball Club 15
Knothole Gang 37
Koppett, Leonard 5, 98
Koufax, Sandy 65–67, 129, 130
Kubek, Tony 193
Kuenn, Harvey 66
Kuhn, Bowie 8, 74, 150, 151

Ladies Day 30, 33, 37
LaGuardia, Fiorello 89
Lajoie, Napoleon, "Nap" 34, 135
Lamar, Chuck 200
Landis, Kenesaw M. 40, 42, 54, 109, 111, 148–151, 178, 179, 182, 185 186
Lang, Jack 85, 100
Lanier, Max 59
Lardner, Ring 85, 94, 102
Larsen, Don 64
Lasorda, Tommy 177
Laux, France 106
Lavagetto, Harry "Cookie" 62, 174
Lawson, Earl 94
Lawson, Thomas 2
Lazzeri, Tony 47, 129
Leach, Tommy 31
Leavy, Jane 129
Lee, Bill 51
LeFlore, Ron 74
Lemon, Bob 71
Leonard, Dutch 149
Lewis, Michael 199, 203
Leyland, Jim 76
Lieb, Fred 30, 35, 86, 89, 97, 98
Lincoln, Abraham 165
Lindsay, Vachel 132

Lindstrom, Fred 143
Lolich, Mickey 67
Lomax, Stan 104
Lombardi, Ernie "Schnozz" 138
Lonborg, Jim 67
Lopez, Al 63
Los Angeles Dodgers 61, 62, 66, 75
Louisville Grays 146
Lyons, Ted 138

MacArthur, Douglas 169
Macht, Norman 29
Mack, Connie 34, 47, 48, 61, 131
MacPhail, Larry 52, 102, 187, 189
Maddux, Greg 78, 138
Magee, Lee 147
Maier, Jeffrey 180
Majerkurth, George 176
Mann, Les 148, 149
Mann, Louis 86
Mann, Steve 163
Manning, Tom 106
Mantle, Mickey 23, 62, 63, 90, 105, 136, 151
Maranville, Rabbit 137
Marichal, Juan 137
Maris, Roger 82
Marquard, Richard "Rube" 36, 172
Martin, Billy 71
Martin, Pepper 50, 51
Martinez, Edgar 196
Mathews, Eddie 137
Mathewson, Christy 34, 97, 99, 133, 134, 140
Mattingly, Don 136
Mauch, Gene 66
Mays, Carl 42
Mays, Willie 63, 66, 80, 137.151, 173
Mazeroski, Bill 65
McCarthy, Joe 51
McCarver, Tim 193
McCormick, Harry 34
McCovey, Willie 65, 137
McGinnity, Joe "Iron Man" 34
McGraw, John 28, 33, 34, 36, 47, 48, 51, 52, 86, 87, 90, 91, 97, 99, 129, 131, 137, 147, 148, 155, 161, 162, 167, 172, 185
McGreevey, Mike "'Nuf Sed" 31, 32
McGwire, Mark 80-82, 136
McKechnie, Bill 52
McKeever, William 184
McKinley, William 165

McLain, Dennis "Denny" 150, 151
McLean, Billy 29
McMullin, Fred 148
McNamee, Graham 101, 102, 105
Mead, William B. 165, 166, 169, 170
Meany, Tom 89, 91, 92
Medwick, Joe 50, 142, 182, 183
Mercer, Sid 87, 89, 91
Merkle, Fred 34
Messersmith, Andy 70
Mexican League 59
Michaels, Al 122, 123
Miller, Jon 123, 124
Miller, Marvin 70
Milman, Steve 57
Milwaukee Braves 61
Minnesota Twins 66, 80
Minoso, Minnie 138
Mize, Johnny 7, 51, 142
Molitor, Paul 139
Monaghan, Tom 113
Monroe, Marilyn 131, 173
Montreal Expos 64, 205
Moore, Joe "Jo-Jo" 142, 187
Moore, Joseph 187
Moore, Terry 51, 90, 136
Moreno, Omar 74
Morgan, Joe 68, 124, 138
Mulcahy, Hugh 53
Munzel, Edgar 94
Murnane, Timothy 85
Murphy, Dale 138
Murray, Eddie 80, 128, 129
Musial, Stan 59, 62, 131, 169
Myers, Randy 182

National Association of Professional Base Ball Players 18, 20
National League 21, 23, 27, 30–32, 36, 37, 47, 49, 50, 146, 153, 154, 165, 197
Nelson, Lindsey 117–119
New York Clipper 17, 28
New York Daily News 88
New York Evening Mail 88
New York Giants 26, 33, 42, 49, 50, 51, 53, 54, 61, 102, 184, 186, 189, 190, 202
New York Herald-Tribune 88
New York Highlanders 165
New York Mets 12, 64, 76, 143
New York Mercury 84
New York Mutuals 19, 145, 184
New York Times 170, 187

New York World-Telegram 90
New York Yankees 12, 49, 52, 55, 63, 75, 76, 81, 102, 180, 186, 199
Nichols, Kid 75
Nixon, Richard M. 169, 170

Oakland Athletics 64, 69, 70, 162, 199
O'Connell, Jimmy 149
O'Dea, June (Mrs. Lefty Gomez) 173
Okrent, Daniel 198
O'Malley, Peter 193
O'Neill, Paul 137
Ott, Mary 177
Ott, Mel 7, 47, 51, 54, 92, 136, 137, 173, 187, 189, 190
Owen, Marv 182
Owen, Mickey 53, 59, 142

Pafko, Andy 193
Paige, Satchel 162
Palmer, Pete 196
Parker, Dan 89, 91, 176, 177
Parnell, Mel 17
Pasquel, Bernardo 59
Pasquel, Jorge 59
Pepe, Phil 100
Perez, Tony 68, 138
Perry, Gaylord 75
Philadelphia Athletics 18, 19, 109
Philadelphia Phillies 59, 66, 74, 109
Piazza, Mike 77, 196
Pierce, Jack 174
Pittsburgh Pirates 31, 33, 71
Player rankings 196, 197
Players League 154
Players strike 73, 171
Plimpton, George 6
Podres, Johnny 65
Polo Grounds 8, 9, 23, 32, 43, 44, 53, 63, 86, 102, 143, 169, 185, 202
Povich, Shirley 94
Powell, Boog 68
Powers, Jimmy 89, 91
Prince, Bob 110
Providence Grays 23
Puckett, Kirby 131

Radbourn, Charles "Ol' Hoss" 23
Raft, George 150
Reagan, Ronald 103, 171
Reese, Pee Wee 7, 135
Ricciardi, J.P. 200

Rice, Grantland 33, 88, 101, 161
Richardson, Bobby 65
Richman, Milton 100
Rickey, Branch 91, 188, 195, 200
Ripken, Cal 77, 80, 127, 128
Risberg, "Swede" 148
Ritter, Lawrence 31, 98
Rizzuto, Phil 136
Roberts, Robin 139
Robinson, Bill "Bojangles" 173, 174
Robinson, Brooks 68, 127, 193
Robinson, Frank 68
Robinson, Jackie 59, 60, 62, 98, 129, 135, 157
Robinson, Wilbert 49, 98, 134
Rodriguez, Alex 77
Roosevelt, Franklin D. "F.D.R." 54, 55, 165-168
Roosevelt, Theodore "T.R." 165
Root, Charley 51, 52
Rose, Pete 68, 70, 74, 75, 76, 80, 138, 150, 205
Roth, Allan 195
Rotisserie Baseball 198, 199
Roush, Edd 87
Rowswell, Rosey 110
Ruby, Harry 177
Rudi, Joe 163
Ruffing, Red 105
Runyon, Damon 88, 89, 142
Ruth, George Herman "Babe" 24, 39, 42–46, 50, 52, 81, 82, 90, 91, 97, 99, 109, 130, 132, 172, 185

Saam, Byrum 108, 109
SABR (Society for American Baseball Research) 192, 193, 195, 199, 202
St. Louis Browns 24, 61, 160, 162, 186
St. Louis Cardinals 37, 42, 50, 51, 55, 57, 61, 66, 143, 166, 171, 182, 189
Salsinger, Harry G. 94
San Diego Padres 12, 64
San Francisco Giants 61
Sand, Heinie 149
Sandberg, Ryne 138
Sandburg, Carl 32
Sanford, Jack 66
Schilling, Curt 81
Schmelz, Gus 28
Schmidt, Mike 74, 139
Schoendienst, Red 136
Schulte, Fred 190

Schumacher, Hal 50
Scully, Vince 107, 115, 116, 171
Seattle Mariners 71
Seaver, Tom 75, 140
Seeley, Blossom 36, 172, 178
Seitz, Peter 70
Selig, Bud 193
Seymour, Harold 15, 18, 22, 32, 33, 49, 98, 144, 146, 153, 184
Shakespeare, William 173
Shepard, Bob 124
Shor, Bernard "Toots" 173
Sievers, Roy 205
Simmons, Al 47, 48, 52
Sinatra, Frank 177
Sisler, George 46
Slaughter, Enos "Country" 51
Slavin, John C. 48
Smith, Curt 102–106
Smith, Ken 43, 89, 91
Smith, Ozzie 10
Smith, Walter "Red" 7, 13, 75, 89, 93, 170
Sosa, Sammy 80–81, 138, 139
Spahn, Warren 137
Spalding, Albert G. 3, 16, 28, 97, 154, 161
Speaker, Tris 46, 149, 150
Spiers, Bill 182
Sporting News 8, 85, 90
Sportsmans Park 166, 185
Stallings, George 147
Stargell, Willie 71, 139
Statistics (history) 194
Stein, Bill 2
Stein, Fred 2
Steinbrenner, George 65, 71, 81, 160, 199
Steinhagen, Ruth Ann 186
Stengel, Casey 62, 63, 65, 97, 98
Stern, A.S. 153
Steroids 82
Stevens, Harry M. 30, 155
Stockton, J. Roy 94, 183
Stone, Steve 74
Sullivan, Ted 2
Summers, Bill 55
Sunday baseball 153, 154
Sutton, Don 75

Taft, William Howard 165
Talcott, Edward 146
Tampa Bay Devil Rays 12, 200
Tanner, Chuck 71
Tarasco, Tony 180

228   Index

Tejada, Miguel 199
Tenace, Gene 69
Tener, John K. 87, 166
Terry, Bill 42, 43, 47, 50, 51, 91, 92, 197, 198
Terry, Ralph 65
Tesreau, Jeff 39
Thomas, Frank 196
Thomas, Henry W. 134
Thompson, Bob 205
Thompson, William 146
Thomson, Bobby 6, 49, 63, 112
Thorn, John 74, 99
Thorpe, Jim 34
Tinker, Joe 88
Toney, Fred 147
Torre, Joe 76, 81
Totten, Hal 105, 106
Trammell, Alan 138
Troy (New York) Haymakers 19, 145
Truman, Harry 168, 169
Turley, Bob 64
Tweed, William "Boss" 145
Twombly, Wells 123
Tyson, Ty 108

Uberroth, Peter 151, 193
Updike 6

Valli, June 121
Valli, Violet 186
Vance, Dazzy 135
Vander Meer, Johnny 90
Veeck, Bill 162, 190
Vizquel, Omar 10
Voigt, David Q. 17, 23, 27, 29, 34, 60, 98, 160
Von der Ahe, Chris 24, 28, 160, 161

Waddell, Rube 147
Wade, Ed 200
Wagner, Honus 34, 131, 139
Waitkus, Eddie 186
Walker, Dixie 135, 187
Walters, Bucky 50, 52
Waner, Lloyd 47, 139
Waner, Paul 47, 139, 187
Wansley, William 145

Ward, John Montgomery 23, 26, 36, 97, 146, 172
Warneke, Lon 50, 51
Washington Post 28
Washington Senators 166, 205
Weaver, Buck 148
Weaver, Earl 71
Weiss, George 62, 65
Welch, Curt 161
Welch, Mickey 24
Wertz, Vic 63
Wheat, Zackary (Zach) 134
White, Jack 173
Whitehead, Burgess 173
Whitman, Walt 6
Will, George F. 4, 99
Williams, Bernie 137
Williams, Claude "Lefty" 148
Williams, Edward Bennett 128
Williams, Joe 52, 89, 91
Williams, Pete 91
Williams, Ted 50, 52, 53, 59, 62, 79, 130, 131, 139, 193
Wills, Maury 66, 177
Wilson, Bert 113
Wilson, Hack 50, 51, 138
Wilson, Woodrow 166
Witt, Lawton "Whitey" 185
Wolff, Bob 118
Wood, Frank H. 178
Wood, Joe "Smoky Joe" 149, 150
World Series 31, 40, 43, 52, 56, 57, 61, 75, 76, 101, 102, 105, 147, 167, 168, 184, 186
Wright, Harry 16, 20, 21
Wrigley Field 4, 38, 56, 178, 181, 199

Yankee Stadium 38, 43, 186
Yardley, Jonathan 99
Yastrzemski, Carl 67, 197
Young, Cy 166
Young, Dick 89, 93, 94, 100
Youngs, Ross "Pep" 149
Yount, Robin 139

Zimmerman, Heinie 147, 149

www.ingramcontent.com/pod-product-compliance
Ingram Content Group UK Ltd.
Pitfield, Milton Keynes, MK11 3LW, UK
UKHW041946140426
5217IPUK00014B/676